The Shurangama Sutra

Volume One

The Shurangama Sutra

Volume One

with commentary by the

Venerable Master Hsuan Hua

A nine book series

First Edition, 2003
Sutra Text and Supplements, Volumes 1 to 8

English translation by the
Buddhist Text Translation Society
ISBN 0-88139-949-3

The Shurangama Sutra - Volume One

Published and translated by:

Buddhist Text Translation Society
1777 Murchison Drive, Burlingame, CA 94010-4504

© 2003   **Buddhist Text Translation Society**
Dharma Realm Buddhist University
Dharma Realm Buddhist Association

First edition 2003

12 11 10 09 08 07 06 05 04 03   10 9 8 7 6 5 4 3 2 1

ISBN 0-88139-941-8

Printed in Malaysia.

Addresses of the Dharma Realm Buddhist Association branches are listed at the back of this book.

Library of Congress Cataloging-in-Publication Data

Hsüan Hua, 1908-
   The Shurangama sutra with commentary / by Hsuan Hua ; English translation by the Buddhist Text Translation Society.-- 1st ed.
      p. cm.
Sutra translated from Chinese, originally written in Sanskrit. "The Shurangama sutra/ Sutra & suppliments" (ISBN 0-88139-940-X) issued together.
   ISBN 0-88139-949-3 (set : alk. paper) -- ISBN 0-88139-941-8 (v. 1 : alk. paper) -- ISBN 0-88139-942-6 (v. 2 : alk. paper) -- ISBN 0-88139-943-4 (v. 3 : alk. paper) -- ISBN 0-88139-944-2 (v. 4 : alk. paper) -- ISBN 0-88139-945-0 (v. 5 : alk. paper) -- ISBN 0-88139-946-9 (v. 6 : alk. paper) -- ISBN 0-88139-947-7 (v. 7 : alk. paper) -- ISBN 0-88139-948-5 (v. 8 : alk. paper)
   1. Tripiṭaka. Sūtrapiṭaka. Sūraṅgamasūtra--Commentaries. I. Buddhist Text Translation Society. II. Tripiṭaka. Sūtrapiṭaka. Sūraṅgamasūtra. English. III. Title.

BQ2127.H7813 2003
294.3'85--dc21

2002151845

Contents

Introduction vi
User's Guide viii
Exhortation to Protect and Propagate ix
The Eight Guidelines xii
Outline xiii

Chapter 1. The Ten Doors of Discrimination 1
    The General Explanation of the Title 4
    Causes and Conditions for the Arising of the Teaching 30
    The Division and The Vehicle 51
    The Depth of the Meaning and Principle 53
    The Teaching Substance 61
    Individuals Able to Receive the Teaching 63
    Similarities, Differences and Determination of Time 65

Chapter 2. The History of the Transmission and Translation .. 67
    The Translator 69
    The Reviewer, Certifier and Editor 75

Chapter 3. The Testimony of Faith 78

Chapter 4. Ananda's Fall 119

Chapter 5. The Way to Shamatha 152
    The False Consciousness is Without a Location 164
    The False Consciousness is Not the Mind 211
    The False Consciousness is Without a Substance 249

Chapter 6. Ananda Repents and Seeks the Truth 263

General Index 273

Introduction

This is Volume One of the *Shurangama Sutra* series, with commentaries by the Venerable Master Hsuan Hua.

In "The Ten Doors of Discrimination," the Venerable Master uses the traditional Xian Shou School's method of expounding the Sutra's deep contents. Here the Master discusses the complete title of the Sutra, its causes and conditions, division, depth and meaning, teaching substance, individuals able to receive the teaching, similarities and differences, and the determination of time.

In "The History of the Transmission and Translation," the Master introduces Shramana Paramiti, Shramana Meghashikara, Shramana Huai Di and disciple Fang Yong, who were the translator, the reviewer, the certifier and the editor respectively.

In "The Testimony of Faith," Shakyamuni Buddha's great disciples are mentioned as testification to the awesome faith in the Buddha. Shariputra, Mahamaudgalyayana, Mahakaushthila, Purnamaitreyaniputra, Subhuti, Upanishad, and other great bodhisattvas and arhats were among those who were present.

Then, the causes and conditions for the Sutra is revealed in "Ananda's Fall," where the Venerable Ananda, the Buddha's youngest cousin, was tempted by Matangi's daughter, the prostitute. Fortunately, the Buddha, knowing this in advance, instructed the greatly-wise Manjushri Bodhisattva to rescue

E1	The circumstances leading to his fall. 125
E2	The incident of the actual fall. 132
D4	The Tathagata compassionately rescues him. 135
E1	He quickly returns and speaks the mantra. 135
E2	The messenger is sent and Ananda is rescued. 139
B2	Text proper. 142
C1	A complete explanation of the wonderful samadhi for accomplishing Buddhahood. 142
D1	Ananda requests samadhi. 142
E1	He regrets excessive learning and requests samadhi. 142
D2	The Tathagata replies about Shamatha. 152
E1	He explains the wonderful samadhi from beginning to end. 152
F1	He explains the general name of the Buddha's samadhi causing Ananda to know the causes cultivated and the fruition obtained by all Buddhas. 152
F2	He explains the path of Shamatha, causing Ananda to awaken to the secret cause and have a great blossoming forth of complete understanding. 156
G1	He destroys upside-down thinking by speaking of the empty Tathagata store. ... 156
H1	The Tathagata smashes the false and reveals the true. 156
I1	He casts out and destroys the false mind to which Ananda attaches by opening the way to Shamatha. 156
J1	He establishes that Ananda grasps at the mind. 156
K1	He asks him about his resolve based on grasping at the appearance he saw. ... 156
K2	He points out that all living beings have a misconception. 162
J2	He actually destroys the false mind. 164
K1	The Tathagata thoroughly refutes three points of confusion. 164
L1	His refutation that the false consciousness is without a location. 164
M1	He instructs that Ananda should reply to the teaching with a straightforward mind. 164
M2	He asks Ananda about his ability to see and his ability to love. 166
M3	He asks Ananda where his mind and eyes are. 168
M4	The seven places which are attached to are all non-existent. 169
N1	Ananda attaches to the mind as being in the body. 169
O1	Ananda brings up the ten kinds of beings as all alike reckoning the mind as inside. 169

Outline of Shurangama Sutra – Volume One

- O2 The Tathagata uses not seeing inside the body to refute this. 171
  - P1 The Tathagata brings up an example. 171
  - P2 The place where the text originally was. 173
  - P3 The Tathagata questions him about the example. 173
  - P4 From that example comes the refutation. 174
  - P5 The concluding refutation. 176
- N2 Ananda attaches to the mind as being outside the body. 176
  - O1 Ananda presents the analogy of the lamp and determines it is the same as the Buddha's meaning. 176
  - O2 The Tathagata refutes by using the mutual awareness of body and mind. 178
    - P1 The analogy makes clear there would be no connection. 178
    - P2 Investigation shows there is a connection. 180
    - P3 Concluding refutation. 181
- N3 Ananda attaches to the mind's being hidden in the eyes. 182
  - O1 Ananda uses the analogy of crystals covering the eyes. 182
  - O2 The Buddha uses a method show the analogy is not apt. 185
    - P1 He discusses its aptness. 185
    - P2 Both possibilities explored and refuted. 186
    - P3 The concluding refutation. 187
- N4 Ananda attaches to the mind as being divided between light and dark. 187
  - O1 Ananda takes seeing light and dark as divisions of inside and outside. 187
  - O2 The Tathagata uses the fact that seeing inside is not possible as his refutation. 189
    - P1 His refutation: that which is seen is not inside. 189
    - P2 His refutation: the ability to see is not actual. 190
    - P3 Concluding refutation. 193
- N5 Ananda attaches to the mind as being that which exists in response. 193
  - O1 Ananda reckons the mind exists in response to whatever it joins with. 193
  - O2 The Tathagata uses the refutation that it lacks a substance or a fixed place. 195
    - P1 His refutation that it lacks a substance. 195
    - P2 His refutation that a substance exists. 196

Ananda from the indecent artifact which nearly caused Ananda to break his precept substance.

Realizing his great error and his lack of samadhi, Ananda then reverently requested instruction. In "The Way to Shamatha," Shakyamuni Buddha attempts to reveal the true reason for Ananda's fall; it was because Ananda did not realize the falseness of his own mind. Even with all his years of learning, Ananda still had not yet recognized his true mind and so had not attained sagehood.

Finally, in "Ananda Repents and Seeks the Truth," Ananda realizes that the Buddha cannot bestow salvation upon him. He has to actually walk the path and cultivate the Way. Again, Ananda requests the Buddha's compassionate instruction.

The Buddha then prepares to erect the great dharma banner for all living beings so that they can obtain the wondrous subtle secret, the pure nature, the bright mind, and attain the pure eye.

The wondrous journey into the *Shurangama Sutra*'s deep, profound teachings begins.

User's Guide

to the Shurangama Sutra series

Because of the length of the *Shurangama Sutra*, and the need to provide aid to various readers, the sutra has been compiled into a series of 9 books: the "Sutra Text and Supplements," and the remaining volumes one to eight.

The "Sutra Text and Supplements" contains:

1. the entire sutra text, consisting of over 2700 paragraphs;
2. the entire outline, consisting of over 1670 entries; and
3. a master index for the eight commentarial volumes.

Volumes one to eight contain:

1. sutra text, with commentaries by Venerable Master Hua;
2. local outline entries; and
3. a local index.

Readers who wish to read, study or recite the sutra in its entirety will find the "Sutra Text and Supplements" very useful.

Those who wish to deeply delve into the sutra will find the commentaries in volumes one to eight indispensable.

Exhortation to Protect and Propagate

by Tripitaka Master Hsuan Hua

Within Buddhism, there are very many important sutras. However, the most important sutra is the *Shurangama Sutra*. If there are places which have the *Shurangama Sutra*, then the proper dharma dwells in the world. If there is no *Shurangama Sutra*, then the dharma ending age appears. Therefore, we Buddhist disciples, each and every one, must bring our strength, must bring our blood, and must bring our sweat to protect the *Shurangama Sutra*. In the *Sutra of the Ultimate Extinction of the Dharma*, it says very, very clearly that in the dharma ending age, the *Shurangama Sutra* is the first to disappear, and the rest of the sutras disappear after it. If the *Shurangama Sutra* does not disappear, then the proper dharma age is present. Because of that, we Buddhist disciples must use our lives to protect the *Shurangama Sutra*. We must use vows and resolution to protect the *Shurangama Sutra*, and cause the *Shurangama Sutra* to be known far and wide, reaching every nook and cranny, reaching into each and every dust-mote, reaching out to the exhaustion of empty space and of the dharma realm. If we can do that, then there will be a time of proper dharma radiating great light.

Why would the *Shurangama Sutra* be destroyed? It is because it is too true. The *Shurangama Sutra* is the Buddha's true body. The *Shurangama Sutra* is the Buddha's sharira. The *Shurangama Sutra* is the Buddha's true and actual stupa and shrine. Therefore, because the *Shurangama Sutra* is so true, all the demon kings use all kinds of methods to destroy the *Shurangama Sutra*. They begin by starting rumors, saying that the *Shurangama Sutra* is phony. Why do they say the *Shurangama Sutra* is phony? It is because the *Shurangama Sutra* speaks too truly, especially in the sections on the Four Decisive Deeds, the Twenty-five Sages Describing Perfect Penetration, and the States of the Fifty Skandha Demons. Those of off-center persuasions and externally-oriented ways, weird demons and strange freaks, are unable to stand it. Consequently, there are a good many senseless people who claim that the *Shurangama Sutra* is a forgery.

Now, the principles set forth in the *Shurangama Sutra* are on the one hand proper, and on the other in accord with principle, and the weird demons and strange freaks, those in various cults and sects, all cannot hide away their forms. Most senseless people, in particular the unwise scholars and garbage-collecting professors, "tread upon the holy writ." With their extremely scant and partial understanding, they are confused and unclear, lacking real erudition and true and actual wisdom. That is why they falsely criticize. We who study the Buddhadharma should very deeply be aware of these circumstances. Therefore, wherever we go, we should bring up the *Shurangama Sutra*. Wherever we go, we should propagate the *Shurangama Sutra*. Wherever we go, we should introduce the *Shurangama Sutra* to people. Why is that? It is because we wish to cause the proper dharma to dwell long in the world.

If the *Shurangama Sutra* is regarded as true, then there is no problem. To verify its truth, let me say that if the *Shurangama Sutra* were phony, then I would willingly fall into the hells forever through all eternity – for being unable to recognize the Buddhadharma – for mistaking the false for true. If the *Shurangama Sutra* is true, then life after life in every time I make the vow to propagate the great dharma of the Shurangama, that I shall in every time and every place propagate the true principles of the Shurangama.

Everyone should pay attention to the following point. How could the *Shurangama Sutra* not have been spoken by the Buddha?

No one else could have spoken the *Shurangama Sutra*. And so I hope that all those people who make senseless accusations will wake up fast and stop creating the causes for suffering in the Hell of Pulling Out Tongues. No matter who the scholar is, no matter what country students of the Buddhadharma are from, all should quickly mend their ways, admit their mistakes, and manage to change. There is no greater good than that. I can then say that all who look at the *Shurangama Sutra*, all who listen to the *Shurangama Sutra*, and all who investigate the *Shurangama Sutra*, will very quickly accomplish Buddhahood.

composed by,
Gold Mountain Shramana Tripitaka Master Hua

The Eight Guidelines

of the Buddhist Text Translation Society

1. A volunteer must free him/herself from the motives of personal fame and profit.
2. A volunteer must cultivate a respectful and sincere attitude free from arrogance and conceit.
3. A volunteer must refrain from aggrandizing his/her work and denigrating that of others.
4. A volunteer must not establish him/herself as the standard of correctness and suppress the work of others with his or her fault-finding.
5. A volunteer must take the Buddha-mind as his/her own mind.
6. A volunteer must use the wisdom of Dharma-selecting Vision to determine true principles.
7. A volunteer must request Virtuous Elders in the ten directions to certify his/her translations.
8. A volunteer must endeavour to propagate the teachings by printing Sutras, Shastra texts, and Vinaya texts when the translations are certified as being correct.

Outline

of the Shurangama Sutra

The outline for the *Shurangama Sutra*, compiled by Dharma Master Yuan Ying, categorizes the various parts of the sutra text of over 2,700 paragraphs to over 1,670 entries.

These entries are presented in the form of a tree-like structure which divides the various parts of the sutra text into sections and sub-sections.

Though the outline is not a prerequisite to reading the sutra text and the accompanying commentaries, it serves as a useful tool for students of the Way who wish to systematically study the sutra. Without this outline, students may find it difficult to refer to specific parts of the text.

Only outline entries which pertain to the sutra text contained within this volume is included.

For the outline of the entire sutra, please refer to the "Sutra Text and Supplements."

Outline of Shurangama Sutra – Volume One

- A1 The general explanation of the title. ... 4
- A2 The causes and conditions for the arising of the teaching. ... 30
- A3 The division in which the sutra is included and the vehicle to which it belongs. ... 51
- A4 The examination of the depth of the meaning and the principle. ... 53
- A5 The expression of the teaching-substance. ... 61
- A6 The identification of the appropriate individuals able to receive the teaching. ... 63
- A7 The similarities and differences between the principle and its implications. ... 65
- A8 The determination of the time. ... 66
- A9 The history of the transmission and translation. ... 67
  - B1 The translator. ... 69
  - B2 The reviewer. ... 75
  - B3 The certifier. ... 75
  - B4 The editor. ... 76
- A10 The specific explanation of the meaning of the text. ... 78
  - B1 The preface. ... 78
    - C1 The testimony of faith. ... 78
      - D1 An explanation of the six fulfillments. ... 78
      - D2 A broad explanation of the fulfillment of an audience. ... 92
        - E1 Sound-hearers. ... 92
          - F1 Listing their number. ... 92
          - F2 Praising their virtues. ... 97
          - F3 Listing the names of the leaders. ... 106
        - E2 Those enlightened to conditions. ... 109
        - E3 Bodhisattvas. ... 112
          - F1 First, the pravarana assembly gathers. ... 112
          - F2 The assembly that arrived later after hearing the Buddha's voice. ... 116
    - C2 The prologue. ... 119
      - D1 The king and officials prepare offerings. ... 119
      - D2 The Buddha and Sangha go to accept the invitation. ... 125
      - D3 Ananda's fall is revealed. ... 125

P3 Concluding refutation.	200
N6 Ananda attaches to the mind as being in the middle.	200
O10 Ananda attaches to the mind as being in the middle of the organ and the defiling object.	200
P1 Ananda brings up the teachings and recklessly reckons the mind is in the middle.	200
P2 The Tathagata says the location of the middle must be fixed.	202
P3 Ananda brings up an alternative view.	204
O2 The Tathagata uses combining the two or not combining the two to refute his argument.	205
P1 He brings up two possibilities.	205
P2 He shows that both possibilities are impossible.	205
P3 Concluding refutation.	206
N7 Ananda attaches to the mind as being non-attachment.	207
O1 Ananda presents the idea of non-attachment as being the mind.	207
O2 The Tathagata uses the existence or non-existence of the appearance of the mind as refutation.	208
P1 He asks if it exists or not.	208
P2 He shows that neither are possible.	209
P3 Concluding refutation.	210
L2 The Tathagata admonishes that the false consciousness is not the mind.	211
M1 Ananda reproves himself and asks for instruction.	211
M2 The Tathagata reveals it is not the mind.	217
N1 The display of light destroys the manifestation of all appearances.	217
N2 The two roots of true and false are revealed.	221
O1 The Tathagata brings up former reasons and illustrates them with an analogy.	221
O2 The Tathagata explains what the two roots are.	230
N3 The Tathagata tells him directly that the false consciousness is not the mind.	241
O1 The Tathagata firmly admonishes him with a straight, "hey!"	241
O2 Ananda is alarmed and asks what it is called.	246

Outline of Shurangama Sutra – Volume One

```
            O3  The Tathagata reveals its name and clears up the mistake. .............. 246
        L3  Determining that the false consciousness is without a substance. .......... 249
            M1  Ananda expresses his fear and asks for instruction. .................. 249
            M2  Tathagata comforts him. ............................................. 252
                N1  He bestows the profound meaning of the teaching. ................ 252
                N2  He often speaks of the wonderful mind. .......................... 254
                N3  He confirms that the true mind has substance. ................... 255
                N4  He shows that the false consciousness has no substance. ......... 255
        J3  Conclusion: the Tathagata reiterates the reason. .......................... 260
    I2  He reveals the true nature that is inherent and causes him to see the substance of the Tathagata's treasury. 263
        J1  Ananda renounces the false and seeks the true. ............................ 263
            K1  He is sorrowful and repentant. ...................................... 263
            K2  He reveals his confusion and seeks instruction. ..................... 267
        J2  The Tathagata manifests the ultimate true substance. ...................... 268
            K1  He displays light and promises to explain. .......................... 268
```

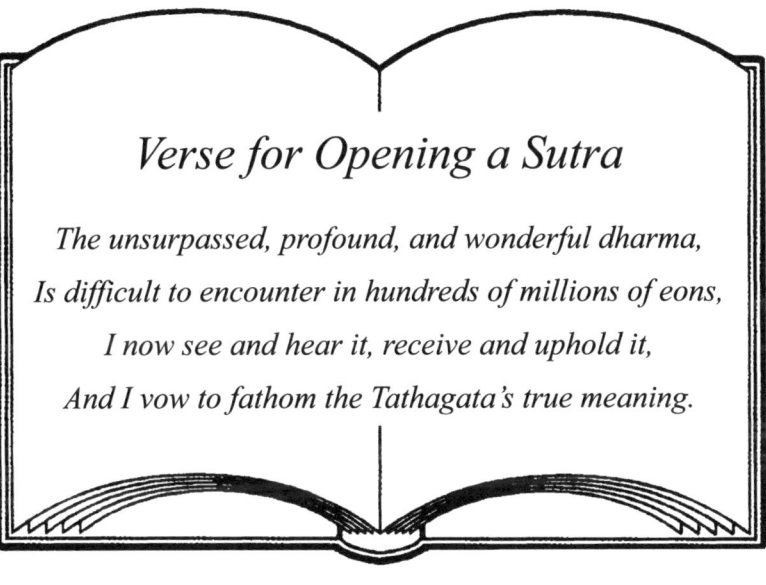

Verse for Opening a Sutra

The unsurpassed, profound, and wonderful dharma,
Is difficult to encounter in hundreds of millions of eons,
I now see and hear it, receive and uphold it,
And I vow to fathom the Tathagata's true meaning.

CHAPTER 1

The Ten Doors of Discrimination

Sutra:

The Sutra of the Foremost Shurangama at the Great Buddha's Summit Concerning the Tathagata's Secret Cause of Cultivation, His Certification to the Complete Meaning and All Bodhisattvas' Myriad Practices.

Commentary:

These words are the complete title of the sutra. All but the word "sutra" are the specific designation which differentiates this sutra from others. The word "sutra" is the general designation for all the discourses of the Buddha.

The sutra titles in the *tripitaka*[1] are divided into seven classes, which are more broadly divided into three kinds of single titles, three kinds of double titles, and complete titles.

The three kinds of single titles are:

1. Sutra titles that refer only to people. The *Buddha Speaks the Amitabha Sutra* is an example of this kind. The "Buddha" and "Amitabha" are both people; only people are named in this title.

---

[1]. The "three treasuries" of the Buddhist canon

2. Sutra titles that refer only to a phenomena. The *Maha-Parinirvana Sutra* is an example. "Nirvana" is the phenomena of non-production and non-extinction.

3. Sutra titles that contain only an analogy. The title *Brahma Net Sutra* refers to the analogy, discussed in that sutra, of the circular curtain of netting of the Great Brahma King.

The three kinds of double titles are:

4. Sutra titles that refer both to a person and to a phenomenon. The title *Sutra of Manjushri's Questions on Prajna* indicates that Manjushri, a person, requests prajna, a phenomenon.

5. Sutra titles that refer both to people and to analogies. In the title *Sutra of the Tathagata's Lion's Roar*, the "Tathagata" is a person, and the "Lion's Roar" is an analogy for the Buddha's speaking of dharma.

6. Sutra titles that refer both to a phenomenon and an analogy. An example is the *Wonderful Dharma Lotus Flower Sutra*. "Wonderful Dharma" is the phenomenon, and "Lotus Flower" is the analogy.

The complete titles are:

7. Sutra titles that refer to a person, to a phenomenon, and to an analogy. The *Buddha's Universal Great Means Expansive Flower Adornment Sutra* is an example. "Great" and "Universal" refer to phenomena, the "Buddha" is a person, and "Flower Adornment" is an analogy, in which the myriad practices that lead to enlightenment are said to be flowers that adorn the unsurpassed and virtuous attainment of enlightenment.

Every sutra title belongs to one of these seven classes, and everyone who lectures sutras should be able to explain them. If you do not understand these seven, how can you explain sutras for others? How can you teach others to become enlightened when you yourself have not awakened? You should not be like people who decide to call themselves dharma masters after reading a book or two, despite the fact that they can't explain even one of the seven types of sutra titles or the fivefold mysterious meanings or a single door of the ten doors of discrimination. That is truly a case of premature exuberance. By speaking sutras and lecturing dharma without having reached a true understanding of them, these people send most of their listeners to the hells, and they themselves fall, too. Once in the hells, neither they nor their followers know how they got there. How pitiful! Only after reaching a genuine understanding and gaining genuine wisdom in the study of the Buddhadharma can one teach and transform living beings without making mistakes.

To explain the inexhaustible principles contained in the *Shurangama Sutra*, I will use the ten doors of discrimination of the Xian Shou ("Worthy Leader") school rather than the fivefold mysterious meanings of the Tian Tai ("Heavenly Vista") school. The Xian Shou and the Tian Tai are two great schools of Buddhism in China. Some dharma masters who lecture sutras have studied only one of the two schools, and so their explanations do not always reach the level of "perfect penetration without obstruction."

The ten doors of discrimination of the Xian Shou school are:

1. The general explanation of the title;
2. The causes and conditions for the arising of the teaching;
3. The division in which the sutra is included and the vehicle to which it belongs;
4. The examination of the depth of the meaning and the principle;
5. The expression of the teaching-substance;
6. The identification of the appropriate individuals able to receive the teaching;
7. The similarities and differences between the principle and its implications;
8. The determination of the time;
9. The history of the transmission and translation;
10. The specific explanation of the meaning of the text.

The General Explanation of the Title

<u>A1</u> The general explanation of the title.

The *Sutra of the Foremost Shurangama at the Great Buddha's Summit Concerning the Tathagata's Secret Cause of Cultivation, His Certification to the Complete Meaning and All Bodhisattvas' Myriad Practices* is the complete name of this sutra.

The word **Great** has four aspects and refers to a great cause, a great meaning, a great practice, and a great fruition.

The great cause is a **Secret Cause**. It differs from other causes in that ordinary people do not know of it; adherents of externalist religions do not understand it; and those of the two vehicles, sound-hearers and pratyekabuddhas[2], have not awakened to it. Thus it is great.

The great meaning is the **Complete Meaning**: the culmination of one's **Cultivation** of the Way leading to **Certification**.

The great practice includes all the **Bodhisattvas' Myriad Practices**.

The great result is the **Foremost Shurangama**. Because of these four kinds of greatness, the specific title begins with the word *da* (大) "great."

[2.] Those enlightened by conditions.

Buddha comes from a Sanskrit word that was transliterated into Chinese as *fo tuo ye* (佛陀耶) and subsequently abbreviated to *fo* (佛). Although many people think the word *fo* is Chinese for Buddha, it is in fact only the first syllable of the full transliteration of the Sanskrit for Buddha. Buddha means "enlightened," "awakened." There are three kinds of enlightenment: enlightenment of self, enlightenment of others, and the perfection of enlightened practice.

The Buddha is enlightened. His state of being is different from that known to ordinary, unenlightened people. To be enlightened oneself is not enough, however. One must also enlighten others. The enlightenment of others involves thinking of ways to cause everyone else to become enlightened.

Within the enlightenment of self and the enlightenment of others there are various stages and myriad distinctions. There are, for instance, small enlightenments, which are not complete, and there is great enlightenment, which is total. The Buddha has by himself realized great enlightenment, and he also causes others to obtain great enlightenment.

When one has perfected both the enlightenment of self and the enlightenment of others, one attains the perfection of enlightenment and practice.

The Buddha has perfected the three kinds of enlightenment and so is adorned with myriad kinds of virtuous practices.

> The three enlightenments perfected,
> The myriad virtues complete:
> Thus is he called the Buddha.

Someone may wonder why people believe in the Buddha. It is because we ourselves are Buddhas. That is, fundamentally we are Buddhas, but at present we are confused and unable to attain certification as Buddhas. The reason I say we are basically Buddhas is that the Buddha himself said: "All living beings have the Buddha-nature; all can become Buddhas. It is only because of polluted thinking and attachments that they are unable to attain certification." The polluted thoughts of living beings shift to the north, south, east, and west, above, and below. They suddenly pierce the heavens, suddenly drill into the earth. They reach to every conceivable place and their number is incalculable. Do you know how many polluted thoughts you have in a single day? If you do, you are a bodhisattva. If not, you are still an ordinary person.

People become attached to possessions and constantly make distinctions of "me" and "mine." They are unable to put aside material objects or physical pleasures. "That is my airplane." "This is my car, the very latest model, you know." One is attached to whatever one possesses. Men have masculine attachments, women have feminine attachments; good people have the attachments of good people; bad people have the attachments of bad people. No matter what the attachments are, those who have them cannot let them go. They keep grabbing, taking, and hanging on, getting more and more attached. The process is endless. Pleasures such as good food, a fine home, exciting entertainment, and the like are usually considered beneficial, but it isn't certain that they are. Although you may not realize it, it is that very craving for pleasure that prevents your realization of Buddhahood. So the Buddha said, "It is only because of polluted thinking and attachments that living beings are unable to realize Buddhahood."

In the *Shurangama Sutra* the Buddha said, "Bodhi is the ceasing of the mad mind." The mad mind is explained as the false egocentric mind, the mind fond of status, the mind full of vain hopes and illusions, the mind that looks down on others and cannot see beyond its own achievements and intelligence. Even someone who is really ugly will consider himself to be very beautiful. Such strong attachments as these are dissolved when the mad mind is made to cease. That ceasing is bodhi. It is an awakening to the Way; it is an enlightenment that is a first step toward the realization of Buddhahood. If you can cause the mad mind to cease, then you are well on your way.

Of the three kinds of enlightenment, the arhats' and pratyekabuddhas' enlightenment of self distinguishes them from ordinary, unenlightened people. Pratyekabuddhas awaken to the Way by cultivating the twelve links of conditioned causation. Arhats awaken to the Way by cultivating according to the four sagely truths. Bodhisattvas differ from arhats and pratyekabuddhas in that they resolve to enlighten and to benefit others.

Ultimately, the arhats, the pratyekabuddhas, and the bodhisattvas are simply people who have cultivated to the point of realization. How many people are we speaking of? We could be speaking of one person who cultivates to become first an arhat, then a pratyekabuddha, and then a bodhisattva by means of the six paramitas and the myriad practices; such a person embodies all three levels.

Someone else, however, may cultivate to the level of arhatship, and then not want to go on. Once he himself has understood, such a person says: "I myself have already become enlightened. I understand. I can ignore everyone else." He is a selfish person. He comes to a halt at the accomplishment of arhatship and it does not occur to him to continue down the path to pratyekabuddhahood. Others continue to pratyekabuddhahood but do not consider progressing further. So one can say they are one person or one can say they are three people.

A bodhisattva, however – one who enlightens himself and others – cultivates the six paramitas and the magnificence of the myriad practices, and he can continue to progress until he reaches the perfection of the bodhisattva way. That stage is said to be the perfection of enlightenment and practice; it is the realization of Buddhahood. The Buddha's state of perfect enlightenment and practice distinguishes him from the bodhisattva.

These three kinds of enlightenment can be discussed at length. When one practices them, many distinctions appear; within realizations are further realizations; within distinctions are further distinctions. The process is extremely complex.

The **Summit** is the highest point. The crown of the head is its summit; above that is heaven. It is sometimes said of people that "the top of the head touches heaven and the feet touch the earth"; such people are indomitable. Together, the words "Crown of the Great Buddha" refer to the top of the great Buddha's head.

How big is the great Buddha? "The size of a six-foot-high Buddha-image?" you wonder.

No, a Buddha-image is like a mere drop in the ocean, or one fine mote of dust in a world-system. There is nothing greater than the great Buddha. He is great and yet not great. *That* is true greatness.

"Who is he?" you ask.

He is the Buddha who pervades all places. There is no place where he is and no place where he is not. No matter where you say he is, he is not there. Wherever you say he is not, he is there. What size would you say he is? There is no way to calculate how great he is, and so he is truly great – so great that he is beyond greatness.

"How can one be beyond greatness?"

No greatness can compare to his; his greatness is the most great.

"Who is he then?"

The great Buddha.

"Who is this great Buddha?"

He is you, and he is me.

"But I am not that great. And as far as I can tell, neither are you. How can you say he is you and me?" you ask. "How can you talk about it like this?"

If he did not have any connection with you and me, it would not be necessary to discuss him.

"How am I that great?" you ask.

The Buddha-nature is great, and it is inherent in us all. Just that is the incomparably great Buddha.

Now we are not only speaking of the great Buddha, we are referring to the crown of his head: his summit. And the great Buddha's summit refers to the appearance of yet another great Buddha.

"How big is that Buddha?" you ask.

That Buddha is invisible. He is referred to in the verse that we recite before reciting the Shurangama Mantra:

> The transformation atop the invisible summit
> poured forth splendorous light
> and proclaimed this spiritual mantra.

What is invisible can be said not to exist. How can one refer to the existence of a great Buddha when he cannot even be seen?

What cannot be seen is truly great. If it weren't so big as to be invisible, why do you suppose you couldn't see it?

"Little things are invisible, not big ones."

Really? The sky is big, but can you see all of it? No! The earth is vast, but can you see its entire surface? No. What is truly great cannot be seen.

The great Buddha's "invisible summit emits a light."

"How great is the light?"

Think it over. Could a great Buddha emit a small light? Naturally the light he emits is so great it illuminates all places.

"Does it shine on me?"

It has shone on you all along.

"Then why am I not aware of it?"

Do you want to know of it?

> When the mind is pure
> the moon appears in the water.
> When the thoughts are settled
> the sky is without a cloud.

If your mind is extremely pure, the Buddha's light will shine on you and illumine your mind like the moonlight deeply penetrating clear water. If your mind is impure, it is like a puddle of muddy water through which no light can pass. The mind in samadhi is like a cloudless sky, a state that is inexpressibly wonderful. If you can truly purify your mind, then you can obtain the strength of the Shurangama Samadhi.

Tathagata is a Sanskrit word; it means "Thus Come One." There is nothing which is not "thus," and nothing which is not "come." "Thus" refers to the basic substance of the Buddhadharma, and "come" refers to the function of the Buddhadharma. "Thus" refers to a state of unmoving suchness. "Come" means to return and yet not return. It is said,

> Thus, thus unmoving,
> Come and come again,
> Come and yet not come.

"Did he go?"

No.

"Did he come?"

No.

Therefore, it says in the *Vajra Sutra* that the Tathagata does not come from anywhere, nor does he go anywhere. He does not go to you nor does he come to me, yet he is right there with you and right here with me.

Tathagata is one of the ten names of the Buddha. Originally every Buddha had ten thousand names. In time these ten thousand names were reduced to one thousand because people got confused trying to remember them all. For a while every Buddha had a thousand names, but people still couldn't remember so many, so they were again reduced to one hundred names. Every Buddha had a hundred different names and living beings had a hard time remembering them, so they were shortened again to ten, which are:

1. Tathagata;
2. One Worthy of Offerings;
3. One of Proper and Universal Knowledge;
4. One Perfect in Clarity and Practice;
5. Well Gone One;
6. One Who Understands the World;
7. Unsurpassed One;
8. Great Regulator;
9. Teacher of Gods and People;
10. Buddha, World Honored One.

All Buddhas have these ten names. The first, "Tathagata," indicates that he has traveled the path as it truly is, and has come to realize proper enlightenment, that is, he has accomplished Buddhahood. The second, "One Worthy of Offerings," indicates that he is worthy of receiving the offerings of gods and people.

The **Secret Cause** is the basic substance of samadhi power[3] inherent in everyone. It is called "secret" rather than "manifest" because, although it is fundamentally complete in every person without exception, not everyone is aware of it. And so it is a secret. The secret is the basic substance of the Tathagata's samadhi power and in turn it is the basic substance of the samadhi-power of all living beings. The only difference is that living beings haven't uncovered it, and so for them it remains a secret.

Cultivation, His Certification to the Complete Meaning. The secret cause must be cultivated and certified. Although investigation of dhyana and mindfulness of the Buddha are both means of cultivation, the cultivation referred to here is exclusively that of investigating dhyana. Through exclusive cultivation of dhyana one can be certified to and obtain the complete meaning, which is just no-meaning.

"Is that to say it is meaningless?"

[3.] Concentration-power

The complete meaning is a complete certification to and realization of all worldly and world-transcending phenomena. There is no further practice that can be cultivated, no further practice that one can be certified as having attained. Great Master Yong Jia's "Song of Enlightenment" speaks of the complete meaning:

> Have you not seen the person of the Way,
>   who is beyond all learning
> And, in leisure does nothing?
> He neither casts out false thoughts
>   nor seeks reality…

The person of the Way does not do anything at all. He does not cast out false thoughts because he has already gotten rid of them. Only one who is not fully rid of them still needs to cast them out. The person of the Way does not seek after truth because he has already obtained it. Only those who have not obtained it need to seek it. These lines speak of the complete meaning.

The complete meaning, which is certified to, is also said to be "complete" because the principles spoken by the Buddha are so complete that an exhaustive study of them would reach to the end of all "meaning." When one has exhausted all the principles that the Buddha spoke, then they do not exist; the meaning is complete. An incomplete meaning still has "meaning" left in it. The complete meaning is without any "meaning" at all. It is pure. When it is reached, it is the secret cause, the basic substance of proper samadhi. Reaching the basic substance, you cultivate and are certified to the complete meaning. If you do not cultivate you cannot attain the realm of the complete meaning, the great meaning which encompasses all meanings.

"But you said the complete meaning does not exist," you say.

Yes, but that very non-existence is true existence. Relative existence is not true existence. When you have been certified as having understood the complete meaning, there are no further meanings for you to understand. You have arrived at the ultimate point.

"What is the ultimate accomplishment?"

It is the state of Buddhahood. But if you wish to reach the state of Buddhahood, you must continue to practice the bodhisattva way. Therefore, the title speaks of **all the Bodhisattvas' Myriad Practices.** "All" can refer to the incalculable number of bodhisattva's practices. In general there are fifty-five bodhisattva stages, which will be explained in detail later in the text. They include the ten faiths; the ten dwellings; the ten practices; the ten transferences; the four aiding practices; the ten grounds; and equal enlightenment, which comes before the wonderful enlightenment of Buddhahood. At each position are millions of bodhisattvas. The fifty-five stages do not refer to a mere fifty-five bodhisattvas, but rather to fifty-five levels through which limitless bodhisattvas pass.

The "myriad practices" are the numerous ways in which bodhisattvas cultivate. There are said to be 84,000 methods of practice, but the title simply refers to them as "myriad practices." In addition to their myriad practices, bodhisattvas also cultivate the six paramitas – also called the six perfections.

"Paramita," a Sanskrit word, literally means "arrived at the other shore." It means to completely finish whatever you do. If you decide to become a Buddha, then the realization of Buddhahood is paramita. If you want to go to a university and get a Ph.D., obtaining the degree is paramita. If you're hungry and want to eat, then to get full is paramita. If you're sleepy, then to lie down and go to sleep is paramita. The Sanskrit word "paramita" is transliterated into Chinese as *bo luo mi* (波羅蜜). *Bo luo* is Chinese for pineapple, and *mi* means honey. So the fruit of paramita is said to be sweeter than the pineapple.

Bodhisattvas cultivate the six paramitas. They are:

1. giving;
2. moral precepts;
3. patience;

4. vigor;
5. dhyana concentration;
6. prajna.

There are three kinds of giving: the giving of wealth, the giving of dharma, and the giving of fearlessness.

As to wealth: although money is one of the things people love most, it is also the dirtiest thing in the world. Just consider how many hands it passes through and how many germs it gathers. In Buddhism, money is considered unclean. First of all, its source is often unclean. It may have been stolen or embezzled.

"I've earned every penny of my money," someone may complain. "It's clean!"

Even if your money comes from legitimate sources, you still can't deny that the money itself is filthy and covered with germs. Even so, everyone still likes it. A lot of people spit on their fingers when they count money. Then they pass it back and forth, making it highly suspect as a carrier of infectious diseases. But in spite of its filth, no one is afraid of getting too much money. If you gave someone all the money in America, he would not think it was too much. But when you have a lot of money, you also have a lot of problems. You can't get to sleep at night. You are kept busy figuring out where to put it. Since money keeps you so preoccupied, it is basically not a good thing. But even though it is not a good thing, most people love it and cannot give it up. One who can give away money practices the paramita of giving and is cultivating the bodhisattva way.

It is not easy for people to give. Their hearts are the junction of *yin* and *yang*, the battleground of reason and desire. For instance, someone sees someone else in bitter straits without a bit of food and, being a principled person, he decides to give the poor person a dollar. He reaches into his pocket, but suddenly his desire seizes him and he starts to have second thoughts. "Wait a minute. I can't give him that dollar. It's the last bit of change I've got. If I give it away, I won't have any money for the bus and I'll have to walk. I can't do it." His first impulse was to be generous to someone else, but it was followed immediately by a second thought: his own welfare. So he puts the money back in his pocket and doesn't give it away. That's the way it goes. It happens the same way on a large scale as it does on a small scale, all the way from a penny to a million dollars. The first thought is to give, the second thought concerns oneself. The giving of wealth is not easy. Some people even go so far as to think, "I'd be stupid to give my money to you. Why don't you give yours to me?" It is easy to talk about giving, but when the time comes to do it, it is difficult.

Ever since I was young, I haven't known how to count. Whenever I got some money, I gave it away. If I had one dollar, I gave that, and if I had two dollars, I gave them both away. I didn't want money. Most people would consider my behavior very stupid, because I didn't know how to help myself out. I only knew how to help others.

By benefiting others one brings forth the heart of a bodhisattva, and those who bring forth the heart of a bodhisattva benefit others rather than themselves. They say, "It's all right if I have to suffer and endure distress, but I don't want others to suffer." Bodhisattvas always benefit others by practicing good conduct without bothering to figure out if they take a loss.

Some people spend all their time making sure they get a bargain. When they set out to buy something, they do a lot of comparison shopping until they come up with the best buy. But what they end up buying turns out to be cheap in more ways than one – things made of the "latest material" wrought from scientific experiments, things which look handsome enough but which break as soon as they are used. Although such people think they're getting a good deal, in the end they take a loss. Instead of indulging in such calculated selfish behavior, you should work for the good of others.

The lecturing of sutras and explaining of dharma are the giving of dharma. It is said:

> Of all the kinds of offerings
> The gift of dharma is the highest.

The money you give can be counted, but the gift of dharma can't be reckoned. If someone comes to a sutra lecture and hears something that causes him to become enlightened – to genuinely understand – can you imagine how great the merit derived from such a gift would be? Because the gift of a sentence of dharma can cause people to realize Buddhahood, it is the highest kind of giving.

The giving of fearlessness takes place, for example, when you bring calm to the victims of robbery or fire or any other catastrophe that causes them to be terrified or panic-stricken. You can calm them and comfort them by saying something like, "Don't be afraid. No matter what the problem is, it can eventually be resolved."

The second paramita practiced by bodhisattvas is keeping moral precepts. This refers to the precepts and rules, which are one of the most important aspects of the Buddha's teachings.

What are precepts?

Precepts are the rules of moral conduct that Buddhist disciples follow. The precepts stop evil and guard against mistakes. When you maintain precepts, you don't indulge in any bad actions, but instead you conduct yourself properly and you offer up your good conduct to the Buddha.

How many kinds of precepts are there?

Laypeople who have taken refuge with the Triple Jewel – the Buddha, the Dharma, and the Sangha – and who wish to make progress should take the five precepts. The five are not to kill, not to steal, not to commit sexual misconduct, not to lie, and not to take intoxicants. One vows to follow these rules for the rest of one's life. After receiving the five precepts, laypeople can make further progress by taking the eight precepts. Beyond the eight precepts are the ten precepts of a *shramanera* (novice)[4]. After receiving the

---

[4] See Part I of the Shramanera Vinaya by Tripitaka Master Hsuan Hua

shramanera precepts, to become fully-ordained – to become one who has left the home-life – one can take the two hundred fifty precepts of a *bhikshu* (monk) or the three hundred forty-eight precepts of a *bhikshuni* (nun). There are also the ten major and forty-eight minor bodhisattva precepts. The first ten are called "major" because one cannot repent and reform for violation of any of these ten. If one violates the minor precepts, it is still possible to change one's faults and begin anew.

When the Buddha was about to enter nirvana, his disciple Ananda asked him four questions, one of which was this: "When the Buddha was in the world, he was our master; after the Buddha enters nirvana, who will be our master?"

The Buddha told him, "After I enter nirvana, you should take the precepts as master." He was indicating that people who leave the home-life – all bhikshus and bhikshunis – should take the precepts as master.

Laypeople who seek to receive precepts should certainly seek them from one who has left the home-life. When the precepts are transmitted, the precept-substance must be bestowed upon the recipient by a bhikshu. According to the Buddha's precepts, bhikshunis cannot transmit precepts.

It is absolutely essential for people who want to cultivate the Way to receive precepts. If you can guard the pure precept-substance, then you are as beautiful as a gleaming pearl. Vinaya Master Dao Xuan ("Proclaimer of the Way"), who lived on Zhong Nan mountain during the Tang dynasty, held the precepts so well that gods made offerings of food to him. The virtue of the precepts is very great. If you study the Buddhadharma without receiving the precepts, you will be a leaky bottle. To keep the precepts is to patch the leaks. The human body has outflows. It leaks. If you maintain the precepts for a long time, eventually there will be no outflows.

This Shurangama assembly, in which the sutra is now being explained, offers a combination of study and practice. The schedule is strenuous, from 6:00 a.m. to 9:00 p.m. daily, much more rigorous than regular school – but this is a school for ending birth and death. It is a school of complementary practice and understanding. From the study of the *Shurangama Sutra* we derive understanding, and we practice by investigating dhyana. Through the combination of practice and understanding we can stride forward over solid ground and get the job done without carelessness or negligence. Through your efforts, you may solve the problem of birth and death and obtain extremely great benefit.

An example will help to illustrate the value of combining understanding with practice. A blind man and a cripple lived together in a family compound. There were several other people living with them and helping them out. One day, however, everyone else went out – fishing, shopping, doing the sorts of things people like to do. The blind man and the cripple were the only ones left at home. On that particular day a fire broke out in the house. The blind man couldn't see and had no way to get out. The cripple could see, but he didn't have any legs. What a predicament they were in! Both of them were certainly going to burn to death.

At that time a good and wise advisor gave them some advice. "You two can avoid dying. You can get out of this burning house. How? Cripple, let the blind man use your eyes. Blind man, let the cripple use your legs." They followed his advice. Did the cripple gouge out his eyes and stick them in the sockets of the blind man? Without a surgeon such a method would surely fail. To put the blind man's legs on the cripple without a physician would also be difficult. What did they do?

They made the best of the situation. The cripple climbed on the blind man's back and told the blind man where to walk. "Go left, go right, go straight ahead." The blind man had legs and, although he couldn't see, he could hear the cripple's instructions. Thanks to the timely advice, the two managed to save themselves.

When you hear this, don't mistakenly think that I am calling you blind or crippled. It is not you who are blind or you who are crippled. I am blind and crippled. But having understood the principle involved, I have spoken the analogy, which is not speaking of you or me and yet is speaking of you and me.

No one should be arrogant. Don't reflect on your singular understanding or the greatness of your wisdom. Why haven't you realized Buddhahood? It is because you are too arrogant. "I have so much knowledge," you think, but whatever you learn obstructs you. If you have a lot of knowledge, you are burdened with the obstruction of knowledge. If you have a lot of ability, your ability obstructs you so that you are unable to realize the Way. We should get rid of our thoughts of you, me, and him. Let the thoughts settle. Relax. Purify them. Empty your belly.

"What for?"

Then you can fill your belly with the wonderful flavor of clarified butter[5], the unsurpassed wonderful dharma. Once there was a young woman, a Ph.D. candidate, who admitted that her mind was full of garbage. Now we'll use her words and say, throw out the "garbage" from your mind, and then you can listen to sutras. Then each thing you hear will unfold into a thousand understandings.

The third paramita of the bodhisattva is patience. There are three kinds: patience with beings; patience with phenomena; and patience with the non-existence of beings and phenomena.

The fourth paramita is vigor. To be vigorous is to continually advance and never retreat. An example of extreme vigor is given in the *Wonderful Dharma Lotus Flower Sutra* in the *Chapter on the Past Deeds of Medicine King Bodhisattva*. This bodhisattva wrapped his body in cotton, saturated it with fragrant oils, went before the Buddhas, and burned his body as an offering.

"Why did he do that?" you ask.

Because he felt the Buddhas' kindness was so sublime, so profound, and so great that there was just no way to repay it.

---

[5]. The five periods of the Buddha's teaching are likened to stages of refinement of milk in one analogy. The clarified butter or "ghee" stage is the most refined.

Therefore, he used his own body, heart, nature, and life as an offering to the Buddhas.

"How long did his body burn?" you wonder.

For an extremely long time. There is no way to calculate for how long it burned.

When the Great Master Zhi Yi ("Wise One"), third patriarch of the Tian Tai school, read the *Chapter on the Past Deeds of Medicine King Bodhisattva*, he entered samadhi when he came to the passage that reads: "This is true vigor. This is a true offering of dharma." Within samadhi he saw that the assembly at Vulture Peak, where the *Dharma Flower Sutra* was spoken by the Buddha, was still there and had not yet adjourned.

Master Zhi Yi saw that Shakyamuni Buddha was still there speaking dharma, turning the great dharma wheel, teaching and transforming living beings. Thereupon Great Master Zhi Yi entered the Dharma Flower samadhi and obtained the once-revolving dharani. After experiencing this he withdrew from samadhi. By means of the great wisdom he had gained, he established and systematized the Tian Tai school. This response was evoked by the inconceivable merit and virtue of Medicine King Bodhisattva's vigor when he burned his body as an offering to the Buddhas.

Most people will react by saying, "If plucking out a single hair of my head would benefit the entire world, I still wouldn't do it." That's because they only know how to benefit themselves and not how to benefit others. They can't be called vigorous.

The fifth paramita is dhyana concentration, also called dhyana samadhi. There are four dhyanas and eight samadhis. The nine successive stages of samadhi are discussed in the text of the *Shurangama Sutra*, so they will not be dealt with in detail now. I will explain the four dhyanas briefly.

The first dhyana is called the "state of joy apart from production." In the first dhyana, one's pulse stops.

The second dhyana is called the "state of joy from achieving samadhi." Here one's samadhi is more solid than in the first dhyana. In the second dhyana one's breath stops, but this does not mean death; it is instead another realm of consciousness. The outer breath ceases and an inner breath comes to life. Ordinary people can use only their external breath. If a person can breathe internally, he can avoid death. He can live as many years as he wants. However, one can live so long as to turn into a useless corpse-guarding ghost obsessed with the need to protect his "stinking skin-bag" of a body.

The third dhyana is called the "state of wonderful bliss detached from joy." Most people who cultivate like to experience joy. However, the bliss experienced in the third dhyana, which is detached from joy, is extremely wonderful. In this dhyana, conscious thought ceases.

The fourth dhyana is called the "state of pure renunciation of thought." Here all thoughts are abandoned. One can know what is happening in the heavens and among people. But one should not become attached to the experience. Entering the samadhi of the fourth dhyana represents only a first step in cultivating the Way. One should not think that accomplishing the fourth dhyana is a special attainment. It is just the first step toward realizing Buddhahood. It is not even the accomplishment of the first stage of arhatship.

The sixth paramita is prajna. Prajna is a Sanskrit word that may be translated as wisdom. Most people consider mundane intelligence to be wisdom. It is not. Intelligence is worldly knowledge such as that derived from the study of science, philosophy, and the like. "Wisdom" refers to the world-transcending wisdom that realizes Buddhahood. This is prajna. The word prajna is not translated because it contains many meanings and thus falls within the five kinds of terms not translated, which are:

1. terms that are secret;
2. terms that have many meanings;

3. terms that refer to something not existing in the translator's country;
4. terms that traditionally have not been translated; and
5. terms that are honorifics.

This list was first drawn up by Tripitaka Master Xuan Zang in the Tang dynasty.

There are three kinds of prajna:

1. literary prajna;
2. contemplative prajna;
3. true-appearance prajna.

Literary prajna refers to the wisdom contained in the sutras. Contemplative prajna refers to the wisdom gained through returning the light and illumining within, through reversing the hearing to hear the self-nature. It arises when your eyes don't gaze outside but look within. With the light of wisdom of contemplative investigation, you can illumine and break through all darkness within you. When that happens you become very clear and pure inside and are no longer burdened with filth. True-appearance prajna, the most wonderful inconceivable kind of prajna, is synonymous with the "complete meaning" of which the sutra speaks. The true appearance has no appearance, and yet there is nothing left without an appearance. If you say that it has no appearance, everything thereupon appears. Thus it is the true appearance. If you understand this, you are right next to the Buddha; you are but a step away.

The *Vajra Sutra* says, "All that has appearance is empty and false. If you see all appearances as no appearance, then you see the Tathagata." Everything that has an appearance is false. If, while in the midst of appearances, you can understand that they have no appearance, then you see the Buddha. You understand the basic substance of the teaching and penetrate to its source. To see the source of dharma is to see the Buddha.

Such an experience is easy to talk about, but difficult to attain. You can't understand just by hearing lectures; you must think of a way to travel that road. For instance, one may say, "I'd like to travel to New York, but it's so far away and flying is very expensive. I guess I won't go." However, if you never go, you'll never know what New York is like. Realization of Buddhahood is the same way. On the one hand, you want to become a Buddha, but on the other hand, it's such a long hard pull that it would take forever to get there. It's just like looking at the sea and heaving a great sigh. "Studying the dharma is too difficult; I'll find something easier to do." If you take that attitude, you will never realize Buddhahood. If you don't want to become a Buddha, then there's nothing to talk about. But if you do then you must endure difficulties, because only through difficulty is ease attained. In China it is said, "If the winter's cold did not pierce to the bone, how could the plum blossoms be so fragrant?" The extremely sweet-smelling plum blossoms of China blooms in mid-winter. As a result of enduring the bitter cold, the blossoms have an exquisite fragrance.

Every living being is endowed with true-appearance prajna, but like the "secret cause" of this sutra, it is not yet manifest within them, and they are unaware of their own inheritance. We do not realize the prajna of our own nature, its inherent true-appearance, and so we are as if poverty-stricken within the dharma. Prajna is the wisdom we have always had. We should open this treasure-room of wisdom, and then our original face will appear. As long as we don't know that we are endowed with true-appearance prajna, we carry an undiscovered gold mine inside us. To discover the gold mine is not enough, however. We have to use manpower to mine the gold before it can be used. The sutras tell us that the gold mine of prajna exists within each one of us, but unless we mine the gold, it's not of much use to know about it. We must put in the work and vigorously resolve to cultivate. Then we can mine the prajna, and our inherent Buddha-nature will appear.

The Buddha said, "All living beings have the Buddha-nature and can realize Buddhahood." But one cannot say, "The Buddha said I am a Buddha, so I am a Buddha even without cultivating." This is to know the gold is there and yet not bother to dig it from the ground.

This has been a general explanation of the six paramitas of the bodhisattva. Everyone can decide to be a bodhisattva and cultivate the bodhisattva's practices. If you carry out the deeds of a bodhisattva, then you are a bodhisattva with an initial resolve. Bodhisattvas do not selfishly say, "Only I can become a bodhisattva. You can't be a bodhisattva. You can't compare to me." Not only can everyone become a bodhisattva; everyone can become a Buddha. I believe that everyone in this assembly will attain Buddhahood someday.

Foremost Shurangama. Shurangama is a Sanskrit word that means "the ultimate durability of all phenomena." "All phenomena" refers to everything – all the mountains, rivers, the great earth, buildings, people, and things, as well as all creatures born from wombs, from eggs, from moisture, and by transformation. When one plumbs all things to their unchangeable source, one obtains the basic substance of samadhi, the samadhi of the "secret cause." When one obtains the samadhi of the "secret cause," one can then be certified as having attained the "complete meaning." When one is certified as having attained the complete meaning, one then cultivates the six paramitas and the myriad practices of a bodhisattva and thereby attains the "great practice." When one has attained the great practice, one can then accomplish the samadhi of the ultimate durability of all phenomena, which is the "great result."

The Great Buddha's Summit, then, refers to the wonderful advantages of the four kinds of greatness: the great cause, the great meaning, the great practice, and the great result. They can also be called the wonderful cause, the wonderful meaning, the wonderful practice, and the wonderful result. However, "wonderful" doesn't describe them completely, and so the word "great" is used.

"The ultimate durability of all phenomena" refers to samadhi. Without samadhi, the body and mind are distracted and do not work in harmony. You may decide to go south, but your legs refuse to obey; you end up walking north. Or you may want to do good deeds, but you lose control and somehow end up committing crimes instead. A lack of consistency or constancy in carrying things out is also evidence of a lack of samadhi. In studying the *Shurangama Sutra* everyone should be firm, sincere, and constant. You should firmly resolve, "I am determined to study until I understand the principles of the *Shurangama Sutra*." You shouldn't stop in the middle of the road and turn around to go back; you shouldn't hit the drum to adjourn the meeting prematurely. Don't draw the line when you've come only half way. Don't say, "Ah, I've studied so many days and haven't understood yet. This is extremely difficult material. I don't think I'll study it any more."

With sincerity, you can study in earnest and can keep your mind on what you are doing. You are so delighted by study that all worries are forgotten. You study so industriously that you forget to eat. When you lie down at night to sleep no thoughts arise other than those of the doctrines in the sutra.

With constancy, you don't study for a few days and then back out, feeling that studying the Buddhadharma is dry and uninteresting. You don't decide to go play in the park or find some good entertainment. You don't think up excuses: "There's no practical value in studying this stuff. It's antiquated in this scientific age," and then run away. Without constancy, you lack ultimate durability.

With cultivation of these three – firmness, sincerity, and constancy – you can be "ultimately durable" and gain samadhi-power. With samadhi-power, you will not be "turned by states": you won't be controlled by your environment. This is a general explanation of the specific title of this sutra.

Sutra. To translate the Sanskrit word "sutra," the Chinese used the character that means "to tally," because a sutra tallies above with the principles of all Buddhas and below with the opportune circumstances for teaching all living beings.

"Sutra" is also defined as a "path," for it can lead ordinary people to the position of Buddhahood. "Sutra" has four further meanings: stringing together, attracting, constant, and method. A sutra strings together the meanings within it, like beads strung on a thread. It attracts the beings for whom the teaching will be opportune. The sutras present the practices appropriate to the particular needs of beings, as medicine is prescribed to cure specific illnesses. The sutra is like a magnet and living beings are like the iron filings which are attracted to the magnet. The *Shurangama Sutra* is like a magnet, and so it is called "durable." But the *Shurangama Sutra* is even stronger than a magnet. It can keep people from falling ever again. Thus it gathers in living beings so that they cannot possibly fall again into the realms of the hells, or turn into hungry ghosts, or change into animals. They are magnetized so that even if they want to run away they can't. Even if they want to fall they won't be able to. That's how wonderful the sutras are! People come to listen to a sutra lecture and once they've heard they become magnetized. They hear one passage and they want to hear the next. "This makes sense!" they exclaim. "I like the flavor. It's really sweet!" Sutras are said to be constant because from ancient times to the present day they have not changed. Not one word can be added or taken away. They are permanent and unchanging. The sutras are said to be methods, for they are revered by beings in the past, present, and future because they contain methods to cultivate the Way, realize Buddhahood, and teach and transform living beings.

The Buddhist canon is composed of twelve divisions. All twelve may be found within each sutra. The twelve divisions are:

1. prose;
2. reiterative verses;
3. bestowal of predictions;
4. causes and conditions;
5. analogies;
6. past events;

7. present lives;
8. broadening passages;
9. previously non-existent teaching;
10. unrequested teaching;
11. interpolations;
12. discussions.

The first of the twelve divisions consists of the prose sections of the sutras – in Chinese, literally the "long lines." The second division, the reiterative verses, consists of verses that rephrase the meanings expressed in the prose sections of the sutras.

The third division is bestowal of predictions. In the sutra Shakyamuni Buddha may tell a bodhisattva, "In such and such an age, you will become a Buddha. Your name will be such and such, your lifespan will be so long and in such and such a country you will teach living beings." An example is Dipankara ("Burning Lamp") Buddha's bestowing the prediction of Buddhahood upon Shakyamuni Buddha. In a former life, on the cause-ground, Shakyamuni Buddha cultivated the bodhisattva way so sincerely in his search for the dharma that once he "spread out his hair to cover the mud." Why did he do that? Once in a former life, when Shakyamuni Buddha was walking down a road, he noticed a bhikshu walking toward him. He didn't know the bhikshu was actually a Buddha. The road that lay between them was muddy and full of puddles. "If that old bhikshu walks through all this water, he's bound to get drenched," thought the future Shakyamuni Buddha, and out of his respect for the Triple Jewel, the ascetic lay down in the mud and water. He used his body as a mat on top of the water and invited the old monk to walk on his body to cross the puddles. There was a small portion of the puddle still exposed, and fearing the old bhikshu would have to step in the mud, he loosened his hair and spread it out over the mud for the bhikshu to walk on.

Who would have guessed that the old bhikshu was a Buddha! The Buddha, whose name was Dipankara, was pleased to witness such a sincere offering and he said, "So it is, so it is, you are this way and I am also this way." The first "so it is" meant: "You have now made an offering to me by lying down and allowing me to walk over the top of your body." The second "so it is" meant "In the past, I was this way, too. I also cultivated the bodhisattva way." His meaning was, "You are correct." And then Dipankara Buddha gave him a prediction, saying, "In the future you will become a Buddha named Shakyamuni." Why did Dipankara Buddha offer this prediction? Because he was moved by the sincerity of the future Shakyamuni Buddha's heart, and so although he usually paid no attention to other people's affairs, he took notice of this gesture and gave him a prediction of Buddhahood.

The fourth division of the sutra explains the causes and conditions that lie behind the speaking of various teachings. In the fifth division, analogies are used to make clear the wonderful aspects of the Buddhadharma. In past events, the sixth division, the sutras relate events in the former lives of Shakyamuni Buddha or of various bodhisattvas. Present lives, the seventh division, discusses events in Shakyamuni Buddha's present life or in the present lives of various bodhisattvas. Broadening dharma, the eighth division, refers to the universality of the dharma spoken. Previously non-existent teaching, the ninth division, refers to dharma that has never been spoken before. Without a request from anyone, the Buddha himself emits light, moves the earth, and speaks unrequested teaching, the tenth division. Interpolation, the eleventh division, refers to verses that express meanings that have no connection with the passages preceding or following. The twelfth division is discussions.

A verse says:

> Prose and reiterations;
> Interpolations;
> Bestowal of predictions;
> Unrequested teachings;
> Causes and conditions;
> Past lives; analogies;

Discussions; never been before;
This life; broadening passages
Make up twelve divisions;
The shastra of great wisdom
Explains them in roll thirty-three.

Each sutra has within it these twelve divisions. This is not to say that there are only twelve volumes in the Buddhist canon, but that every section of the sutra text falls under one of these divisions.

Causes and Conditions for the Arising of the Teaching

A2 The causes and conditions for the arising of the teaching.

Teachings are the transmissions of a sage – a Buddha or bodhisattva – in order to teach and transform living beings. The teaching arises from causes and conditions, and these come from living beings. If there were no living beings, there would be no Buddha. If there were no Buddha there would be no teaching. Therefore the teaching is established for the sake of living beings. The causes and conditions are the reasons for the teaching. They cause living beings to end birth and death. This is the reason Shakyamuni Buddha appeared in the world. The *Dharma Flower Sutra* says, "The Buddha appeared in the world because of the causes and conditions of one great matter." What is this matter? It is the problem of everyone's birth and death. Because people don't understand why they are born and why they die, they continue to undergo birth and death. Shakyamuni Buddha appeared in the world to cause living beings to understand why they are born and why they die.

> Where did you come from when you were born?
> Where will you go after you die?

Once born into the world, living beings are busy all their lives finding places to live, clothes to wear, and food to eat. They become so preoccupied with pursuing food, clothing, and shelter that they have no time to solve the problem of birth and death. This is how ordinary people carry on. They say, "We must work hard and keep busy to get two meals, clothes, and a place to live." Nobody is busy figuring out how to end birth and death. They don't think about it. They don't wonder, "Why did I come into this world? How did I get here? Where did I come from?"

When you meet someone, you say, "Where are you from? How long have you been here?" But people never ask these questions of themselves. They have forgotten where they came from, and they have forgotten where they are going. They forget to ask themselves, "Where am I going to go when I die?" It is just because people have forgotten to ask themselves this question that Shakyamuni Buddha came into this world to urge us to investigate the problem of birth and death.

The *Dharma Flower Sutra* says further that the Buddha appeared in the world to cause all living beings to give rise to the Buddha's knowledge and vision; to display the Buddha's knowledge and vision, to become enlightened to the Buddha's knowledge and vision; and to enter the Buddha's knowledge and vision. Originally all living beings inherently possess the Buddha's knowledge and vision. Their wisdom is identical to the Buddha's. But in a living being the wisdom is like the gold in the mine mentioned above. Before the mine is excavated the gold is not evident. Once you realize the existence of your inherent Buddha-nature, you can cultivate in accord with the dharma; you can excavate the mine and extract the pure gold that contains no slag or impurities.

"Where is our inherent Buddha-nature? Where is our inherent wisdom?"

The Buddha-nature is found within our afflictions. Everyone has afflictions and everyone has a Buddha-nature. In an ordinary person it is the afflictions, rather than the Buddha-nature, that are apparent. Afflictions are like ice. Our wisdom is like water. Our Buddha-nature is like moisture, which is present in both ice and water. So, too, the Buddha-nature is found within both wisdom and affliction. But while moisture is common to both ice and water, their physical properties differ. A small piece of ice is hard and can harm people if you hit them with it; in the same way you can injure people by giving rise to afflictions. But a small amount of water is harmless if you pour it over somebody; in the same way, a wise person, by the sound of his voice, can make people happy even when he's scolding them. If you use your affliction to make trouble for others, your great ignorance will ignite as soon as you speak to them. In fact, you may upset someone so much that the two of you come to blows, and certainly someone will be injured.

People can return to the original source if they can change their afflictions into wisdom. The change is analogous to the melting of ice. You can't say that the ice is not water, for the ice melts into water. You also can't say that the water is not ice, for water can freeze into ice. Their common quality is their moisture. In the same way, no one can argue that living beings are not the Buddha or that the Buddha is not a living being. The Buddha belongs to living beings, and living beings belong to the Buddha. You should understand this doctrine. You need only change and melt the ice. This is to be useful to people.

I say that water can't harm people; but someone may argue that everyone is aware of the danger of drowning and the danger brought by floods.

It is true that a lot of water can harm people; but in the analogy I referred to a small amount of water. If you want to come up with unreasonable objections, the possibilities are endless. You should grasp the meaning and not be obstructed by the particulars. Without faith your genuine wisdom won't ever manifest. Genuine wisdom arises out of genuine stupidity. When the ice turns to water, there is wisdom; when the water freezes into ice, there is stupidity. Afflictions are nothing but stupidity. If you are thoroughly clear, then you are without afflictions.

In lecturing the sutras, I refer to principle. Don't try to use specifics to criticize principles; the two are different. You should continue to listen, and when you have heard more of the teachings, you will understand. Having only heard a little, you are unable to put it together. "What is he talking about?" you wonder. "I don't understand." You've never heard it at all before; how could you understand? If you could understand the teachings without ever having heard it before, your wisdom would be truly exceptional. Perhaps you have heard it in the past; but this is the first time for you in this life. The first time you hear it, it seems familiar; but even then, hearing it is a gradual process. In the same way, if you meet someone for the first time, he may seem familiar to you, but it takes several meetings before you can easily recognize him.

Once you understand that your own nature is the Buddha-nature, you can change your afflictions into bodhi. To realize bodhi means to become enlightened: enlightened to the fact that you should not be attached to anything. If you have attachments, you cannot become enlightened.

A bodhisattva is not the same as you. Although he has attachments, he is not enlightened. If you had no attachments, you'd be enlightened. A bodhisattva is not enlightened because he doesn't want to be enlightened. He wants to be together with living beings. But your thoughts are not the same as the attachments of a bodhisattva, for he can't forsake living beings and he sees everyone as good. For this reason he doesn't want to be enlightened. One with the heart of a bodhisattva wishes for the welfare of others and is unconcerned for himself. A bodhisattva would willingly descend into the hells and undergo limitless sufferings if it would cause people to realize enlightenment. If there are good things to eat, he tastes a little bit and then gives the food to others. In the same way, he has already tasted a bit of the flavor of enlightenment and wants to give everyone a taste. To taste the flavor of enlightenment, you must sever your afflictions. When you are without afflictions and devoid of ignorance, wisdom comes forth and you become liberated. That is to give rise to the Buddha's knowledge and vision.

Once you give rise to the Buddha's knowledge and vision – once you've excavated the gold mine – then you need to display the

Buddha's knowledge and vision. You still need to work hard, just as it takes manpower to bring up the gold. First you must get rid of the dirt and then gradually you remove the gold from the sand. To display the Buddha's knowledge and vision, you instruct living beings in how to be truly vigorous.

Displaying requires cultivation – sitting in meditation and investigating Chan every day, until one day, while you are sitting, your contemplation will suddenly penetrate through, and you will become enlightened. You will understand, "Oh, originally it was thus. Originally it was all just this way." You will have truly solved the questions of human existence. This is to be enlightened to the Buddha's knowledge and vision.

The Buddha's knowledge and vision are not to be mistaken for the knowledge and vision of living beings. Living beings use their knowledge and vision to give rise to incessant false thoughts. Deep attachments cause them to become afflicted by the least impoliteness. "How can you be so mean to me?" you say. In fact, people will inevitably be good to you if you are truly good to them. It is not that people are not good to you but rather that you have not been good to them. If you understand this doctrine, then no one can be mean to you.

> One hand claps,
>   but makes no sound.
> Only two hands clapping
>   can make a sound.

Everyone bows to the Buddha with utmost respect because the Buddha is truly good. This is why no one is not good to the Buddha.

"I don't believe it," someone may say. "Some people slander the Buddha."

People who slander the Buddha can't even be counted as people. They simply don't understand how to be people and so they slander the Buddha, the Dharma, and the Sangha. They don't understand the basic question of their own lives. If they knew how to be human, they wouldn't slander the Triple Jewel.

We should enter the Buddha's knowledge and vision once we are enlightened to them. This also takes work. You must work to understand and then you must work some more. You must return the light and illumine inwardly. When your light illumines your heart and you become truly wise, then you will have entered the Buddha's knowledge and vision, with no duality, no difference. The Buddha spoke the sutras in order to cause beings to give rise to, to display, to become enlightened to, and to enter the Buddha's knowledge and vision.

In general, these are the reasons that Shakyamuni Buddha, in over three hundred dharma assemblies held for over forty-nine years, spoke the sutras and taught the dharma in the world. With particular reference to the *Shurangama Sutra*, six causes and conditions lie behind its being spoken.

The first of these six is:

1. The dependence on erudition and the neglect of samadhi-power.

The Buddha's disciple and cousin, Ananda, was very learned; he read widely and he was very knowledgeable. He followed the Buddha for several decades and could remember the teaching spoken at every assembly. His memory was so keen that once he heard something, he never forgot it. Ananda didn't have to force himself to remember, it came very naturally. Often, however, learned people force themselves to remember the principles they read in books and they come to rely upon their learning. "Look at me," is their attitude, "I know more than all of you. I have Ph.D.'s in science, philosophy, and literature. Why, I have more than a hundred Ph.D.'s!" Although Ananda's ability to learn came naturally, he also relied on it too much, and he neglected developing his samadhi-power. He thought samadhi was not important. "I know a lot of things and have wisdom. That's sufficient. Samadhi-power isn't important. It is said that through samadhi one develops wisdom, but I already have wisdom." So he forgot about samadhi.

The *Shurangama Sutra* was spoken for Ananda's sake, precisely because he didn't have sufficient samadhi-power. He had not done the work of meditation required to develop it. When others were sitting investigating dhyana, Ananda would go read a book or write instead. The wonderful quality of the Shurangama lecture and cultivation session, in which this sutra is being explained, is that it combines the actual practice of sitting in meditation with the understanding gained from the study of the sutra. You can practice meditation in accord with your new understanding. Through the application of effort, you can become enlightened. But it is essential both to develop samadhi and to acquire learning.

In other words, Ananda hadn't cultivated true-appearance prajna; he thought he could realize Buddhahood through literary prajna alone. He thought that since he was the Buddha's cousin, the Buddha, who had realized Buddhahood, would certainly help him realize Buddhahood, too. Thinking that it didn't really matter whether he cultivated or not, he ended up wasting a lot of time.

One day, as the *Shurangama Sutra* relates, Ananda went out to receive alms by himself. He took his bowl and went from house to house. While walking alone on the road, he encountered the daughter of Matangi. Ananda was particularly handsome, and when Matangi's daughter saw him, she was immediately attracted to him. But she didn't know how to snare him. So she went back and told her mother, "You absolutely must get Ananda to marry me. If you don't, I'll die."

Now the mother, Matangi, belonged to the religion of the Kapilas, the "tawny-haired," and she cultivated this religion's mantras and other methods of practice, which were extremely effective. Since Matangi really loved her daughter, she used a mantra of her sect – a mantra that they claimed had come from the Brahma Heaven – to confuse Ananda. Ananda didn't have any samadhi-power, so he couldn't control himself. He followed the mantra and went to Matangi's daughter's house, where he was on the verge of breaking the precepts.

The first five precepts prohibit killing, stealing, sexual misconduct, lying, and the taking of intoxicants; and Ananda was about to break the precept against sexual misconduct. The Buddha knew about it as it was happening. Realizing his cousin was in trouble, he quickly spoke the Shurangama Mantra to break up the former Brahma Heaven mantra of the Kapila religion. Ananda's confusion had made him as if drunk or as if he had taken dope – he was totally oblivious to everything. But when the Buddha recited the Shurangama Mantra, its power woke Ananda up from his confusion, and there he was wondering how he had gotten himself into such a situation.

He returned, knelt before the Buddha, and cried out in distress. "I have relied exclusively on erudition and have not perfected any strength in the Way. I haven't any samadhi-power. Please, Buddha, tell me how the Buddhas of the ten directions have cultivated so they were able to obtain samadhi-power." In reply the Buddha spoke the *Shurangama Sutra*. This was the first reason that it was spoken.

The second reason it was spoken was:

2. To warn about those with insane wisdom who cherish deviant thoughts.

There are many intelligent people in the world who, despite their intellectual ability, do not follow proper paths, but instead use their knowledge in ways that harm people. This is deviant thought. They harbor deviant thoughts and have no desire to put an end to them, because they think they are correct. They outsmart themselves and act in a very confused way. The sutra issues a warning about them.

There is a proverb that says:

> Intelligence is helped by hidden virtue.
> Hidden virtue leads you to enter the path of intelligence.

Those who do not practice hidden virtue,
but make use of intelligence alone,
Will be defeated by their own intelligence.

People are intelligent because in past lives they undertook virtuous practices. Perhaps they studied hard in past lives, or they read many Buddhist sutras. But intelligence is established by doing this good work in secret. It is "hidden virtue" that others do not see. Intelligence does not come to people who do a good deed and then strike the gong, beat the drum, and put an ad in the paper or on television saying, "I, so-and-so, have just now done something good." Such a person may have done good deeds, but this is not hidden virtue. Good deeds that are done unknown to anyone are hidden virtue; they are genuine good deeds. So it is said:

Good done hoping others will notice
 it is not true good.
Evil done fearing others will discover it
 is great evil.

People who want the good they do to be known haven't done genuine good; they're just being greedy for a good reputation. The very greatest kind of evil is done secretly in the fear that people will find out.

Hidden virtue practiced in the past may endow us with intelligence, but if we don't use our intelligence correctly, if we don't practice hidden virtue and do good deeds, but instead do evil, our intelligence defeats us and we defeat our intelligence. It becomes merely a petty knowledge, a petty intelligence, not true intelligence.

For example, the great general Cao Cao of the Three Kingdoms period in China was extremely intelligent, but as deceptive as a ghost. But great Emperor Yao of China was said to have divine wisdom. Wise people are sometimes even called gods. But, one should not view gods too highly in the Buddhadharma. They do not hold a very high position. They are simply dharma protectors whose job is to protect the Triple Jewel of the Buddha, the Dharma, and the Sangha.

One of great good who falls will join the ranks of evil. If someone who does great evil recognizes it and changes, he can be considered a person of great good because he has had the courage to change. However, when someone who ordinarily does good deeds decides to do evil and cheat people because he doesn't notice any particular response to his former conduct, he thereby becomes a very evil person since he is one who clearly knows what is right and intentionally does wrong.

A person with "insane wisdom" does upside-down things – improper things – and still feels he is correct. He may go so far as to commit murder and say: "If I hadn't killed that man, he might have killed others. But because I have killed him, he won't kill anyone else." In truth, the victim was not a potential murderer at all, but the killer had a grudge against him. This is deviant thought. Someone basically in error makes up a rationale for his behavior; he makes up a fine story to avoid the judgment of the courts. Although he is wrong, he is very convincing and he wins his case. This is insane wisdom. The *Shurangama Sutra* warns people against making arguments based on deviant thoughts. It warns people who do this not to cherish deviant thoughts, not to be convinced that they are right, but to change their ways and to correct their thinking so they may return to the proper path, to proper thought.

The third reason for the speaking of the sutra is:

3. To point to the true mind and manifest the basic nature.

The *Shurangama Sutra* points directly to our mind so we may see our nature and realize Buddhahood.

"What is this mind?"[6]

It is the true mind, which cannot be seen. The heart within your chest that you can see is merely the flesh-heart, the only function of

---

6. In Chinese the word for "mind" is also the word for "heart."

which is to keep you alive. It is not the true mind. It certainly cannot lead you to genuine understanding. If the heart within your chest were the true mind, it should be able to accompany you when you die. However, a person's body remains after death and the flesh heart is still within it. So the flesh heart is not your true mind. Your true mind is the Buddha-nature.

"Where is the Buddha-nature?"

It is "not outside or inside or in the middle." The sutra text will explain this principle in great detail. The sutra will also explain the "ten instances of manifesting the seeing-nature," that is, one's true mind. This is the third reason the sutra was spoken: to point out the pure nature and bright substance of the eternally dwelling true mind, which neither comes nor goes, neither moves nor changes. It is the basic substance, without defilement; its nature is pure, its substance, bright.

The fourth reason the sutra was spoken is:

4. To display the samadhi of the nature and to exhort us to actual certification.

There are many methods of practice in the cultivation of samadhi. Externalists also develop samadhis; but in cultivating samadhis, if one is off at the beginning even by a hair's breadth, one will miss the mark in the end by a thousand miles. Therefore it is necessary to cultivate proper samadhi, and to avoid cultivating deviant samadhi. The samadhis cultivated by externalists are deviant samadhis, not proper samadhis. Because their samadhis are not the proper samadhi of the true nature, they will never achieve sagehood, no matter how long they cultivate. It is said:

> When the nature is in samadhi,
>   demons are subdued and every day is blissful;
> When false thoughts do not arise
>   everywhere is peaceful.

Why do people have demonic obstacles when they cultivate? Why do karmic obstacles arise? It is just because people's natures lack samadhi. If the nature is in samadhi, all demons can be subdued.

There are many kinds of demons. This sutra explains fifty kinds of "skandha demons." Actually there are many, many demons: heavenly demons, earth demons, human demons, ghost demons, and weird demons. Heavenly demons are the demon-kings in the heavens who come to disturb your dhyana concentration. Earth demons that dwell on the earth, human demons, ghost demons, weird demons, and strange creatures also all come to disturb your dhyana concentration.

"Why do they do this?"

Because before you attain Buddhahood you are a member of the demons' family. When you decide to leave the family of demons, cultivate dhyana concentration, end birth and death, and break through the turning wheel, the demons are still fond of you. They love you and can't let you go. Therefore they come to bother your spirit and disturb your dhyana concentration.

If you have no concentration-power, you can be turned by the demon-states and end up following them. If you have concentration-power, you won't be turned. You will be "thus, thus unmoving / clear and eternally bright." To be "thus, thus unmoving" is to have concentration power. To be "clear and eternally bright" is to have wisdom-power. With the combined powers of concentration and wisdom, no demon can move you. But if you have no concentration or wisdom-power, you will follow the demons and become their children and grandchildren. It is extremely dangerous.

The reason externalists do not develop the concentration of the nature is because they apply effort to the branches, not the root; they work on the false shell of a body. Their mistake is to identify the sixth consciousness, the ordinary mind, with their true mind. As a result of their cultivation they get a little of the experience of still quiescence but what they experience is not actual. They force themselves to keep their thoughts from arising, but they haven't dug out the root of their polluted thinking, so they can't end birth and death. It is like trying to use a rock to prevent grass from growing. When the rock is removed, the grass grows right back. When cultivators of external religions relax their efforts, it is just like removing the rock. Their methods are not ultimate.

In dhyana cultivation, one investigates the meditation topic, "Who is mindful of the Buddha?" By investigating this topic one sweeps away all phenomena and leaves all appearances. In seeking for "who?" one penetrates to the root of all polluted thinking and rips it out. If you use this method, the day will come when your contemplation will suddenly penetrate through and you will suddenly become enlightened. Then you will know whether your nostrils are pointing up or down. At present you don't know whether your nostrils face up or down. Once you are enlightened, you will know, and then you're on your way.

When Shakyamuni Buddha spoke the *Shurangama Sutra*, there were in India various religious groups that did not discuss enlightenment. Rather, they imitated the behavior of cows or dogs. This strange practice came about because someone, while sitting in samadhi, had seen a cow reborn in the heavens, and this person concluded, "I should study the behavior of cows." He began to eat grass, to live outside in a cowshed, and to learn how to even sleep like a cow. When he wasn't sleeping he cultivated a bit of samadhi, but he had no genuine accomplishment; it was deviant samadhi.

Another religion of that time came about because someone had a confused dream in which a dog was born in the heavens. This person decided that if he imitated the behavior of dogs, he too would be born in the heavens. He modeled himself after a dog in every way; guarding the door, eating things dogs eat, and sleeping the way dogs do. But in the end such cultivation did not bring ultimate accomplishment.

Another old cultivator of another religion cultivated the no-thought samadhi, in which he didn't think of anything. He was without polluted thinking, and finally in his cultivation he was born in the no-thought heaven. But birth in the no-thought heaven is not ultimate, and eventually he fell. This too is considered a deviant samadhi. All these methods taught by externalists are not ultimate, not fundamental, they are not cultivation of the self-nature, our origin.

Using the ordinary mind and its false thinking to cultivate the Buddhadharma is like trying to make rice by cooking sand. It will never succeed. You can cultivate for countless ages, but you won't escape the turning wheel, you won't realize Buddhahood. It is essential for those of you who wish to cultivate to meet a master who has genuine understanding, in order for you to be able to attain genuine samadhi power. In order to attain real samadhi-power, you will certainly have to undergo the tests of demons, also. As I mentioned earlier, there are many kinds of demons: there are external demons and internal demons. The external demons are not too difficult to subdue, but the demons produced in your own mind are hard to defeat.

Certain demons that bring sickness are also hard to subdue. When I was about seventeen or eighteen, I studied the Buddhadharma and yet was very arrogant. My arrogance prompted me to say an insane thing: "Most people are afraid of demons, but I have no fear of them. In fact, demons fear me." Wouldn't you say that was an insane remark? "No matter what kind of demons they are – heavenly demons, earth demons, spirit demons, ghost demons, human demons – no matter what kind, I have no fear of them." After I finished spouting off, what do you suppose happened? I was attacked by a sickness demon, and then it was I who feared the demons, not the demons who feared me, because sickness inhibits one's movements like a yoke and chains. My body wouldn't obey my commands. I told it to walk, but it wouldn't; I told it to sit, but it couldn't. From morning to night I lay on the bed unable to eat or drink. The demon had me trapped. Then I realized what I had said was all wrong. I had boasted that I wasn't afraid of demons, but now when the sickness-demon caught me I was powerless. I was so sick that I was oblivious to everything. It seemed certain I would die. But just as I was lingering on for one last breath – when I was almost dead but not quite – another thing happened to me. I saw the three filial sons Wong of Manchuria: two monks – one a Taoist master and one a Buddhist bhikshu, and one a layman. The three came and told me to come out and play, and I followed them outside. It was very strange: just outside the door I started to walk, but my feet weren't touching the ground. Although I wasn't in an airplane, I was in empty space. It wasn't like mounting the clouds and driving the fog, however, it was like being enveloped in space. I walked on the tops of houses and soon they looked very small, and I could see lots of people below.

We went to all the famous temples, mountains, and great rivers. We went to the four sacred mountains in China: Wu Tai (Five Peaks), E Mei, Jiu Hua (Nine Flowers), and Pu Tuo. Wherever we went there were lots of temples and lots of people. We didn't stop with China, however, and soon were flying over foreign lands where the people were fair-haired and blue-eyed. We went from place to place so quickly that it was like watching a movie, where frame after frame flashes on the screen in a constant change of scene, except there was no projector or screen, and I actually went to the places I saw.

After seeing and hearing many things, I arrived back at my own front door. I opened the door and looked into my house, and there on the bed was another me. The moment I realized there were two of me I became one, and my breath and pulse returned. "He hasn't died!" exclaimed my father and mother, who were seated beside me. "He's alive!" Then I realized that when I had seen myself on the bed unable to move, I had been sick. I asked my father and mother about it, and they said I had been in a coma for seven or eight days, and had seemed dead. So, I am a living dead man. Even I myself thought I was dead, and then I was born anew. After that I wasn't so insane. I never said that I didn't fear demons or that demons feared me. Take my advice: whatever you do, don't say things like that. If you say, "I'm not afraid of anything," in the future you will encounter something that will frighten you. But to say "I'm afraid of everything" is also incorrect. In general, don't even bring up such useless topics.

Prior to my illness, I was an instructor at the Way-Virtue Society. I lectured on the advantages of benevolence, righteousness, the Way, and good conduct. Not only did I just exhort others to do good deeds, I myself also practiced benefiting others. I had cultivated to the point that I felt I had a little skill. One day I read an article about Zhang Xuan's exemplary way of life and I decided I wanted to be just like him. I vowed to heaven that I would practice the deeds of Zhang Xuan. But after I made the vow I regretted it. "Of what use is imitating him?" I wondered doubtfully. And, strangely enough, that very evening a demon came to test me to see if I really could keep my vow. If you make vows, the bodhisattvas may come to test you. The point is, don't speak arrogantly; take care to avoid something that pleases you or in time something will happen to cause you to be displeased.

Keep your mind on cultivation of the Way. Don't use the mind that ordinary people use but rather a mind that is intent on the Way. Cultivate the samadhi of the nature and seek actual accomplishment. Actual accomplishment is the opposite of what is empty and false. One whose accomplishment is empty and false may suddenly think, "I have just realized Buddhahood," and while sitting in dhyana he may feel that his body is like the Buddha's, emitting light and moving the earth. Actually there isn't anything going on at all. The experience is empty and false: it is not the accomplishment of the Way.

One may think: "Sitting here in dhyana, I saw the Buddha give me a prediction, saying, 'You will soon realize Buddhahood. Don't bother to cultivate. You are a Buddha already.'" This, too, is a false experience; it is not genuine accomplishment of the Way.

Shakyamuni Buddha accomplished the Way beneath the bodhi tree. He sat there for forty-nine days, and then one evening, he saw a star and awakened to the Way. "Strange indeed, strange indeed, strange indeed," he said, "all living beings have the Buddha-nature. All can become Buddhas."

However, before he had accomplished Buddhahood, a heavenly demon came to test him. It transformed into a beautiful woman who came before the Buddha and spoke seductively, trying to get him to abandon his cultivation and marry her instead. But the Buddha, from within his samadhi, was not moved by the sight of this exquisite creature. He just thought, "You think you are really beautiful, but actually you are an old hag. Countless wrinkles line your face and from your eyes and nose flow filthy tears and mucus. There is snot in your nose and phlegm and saliva in your mouth. Your whole body is filthy, and yet you still come and try to cheat me." The Buddha contemplated this thought from within samadhi and transformed the demon's power so that the demon turned into an old woman. Her hair turned white, her teeth fell out, and her nose began to run with snot. She looked wretched. "Look at yourself," the Buddha told the demon. The demon looked and was so ashamed that she ran away. Many such demons came to test the Buddha, but the Buddha was never turned. Since he was not turned by the demons, he accomplished the Buddha Way.

When people work hard cultivating the Way, they are likely, at crucial stages of development, to undergo the tests of demons. Before you have any skill the demons won't test you, but once you develop a little skill, they will try you out. If you don't recognize it as a test, then you may run off and join the retinue of demons. If you want to cultivate to the point of actual accomplishment, you must develop the samadhi of the nature. When you cultivate by working on the samadhi of the nature, and your nature is not moved, you will naturally have samadhi-power and your accomplishment will naturally be true and actual, not false. If you are moved by demons, then your samadhi is not true and proper but is rather a deviant samadhi, which will not lead you to Buddhahood.

Earlier I mentioned the deviant samadhis developed by people who studied the behavior of cows and dogs. How did the cow and dog they imitated happen to get born in the heavens? In a former life, the cow had cultivated the ten good deeds, but before that it had done many bad things. The retribution for the evil deeds caused it to be born as a cow and the reward for its cultivation of the ten good deeds led it, at death, to be reborn in the heavens. The same was true for the dog. Not knowing the past causes and conditions of the cow and the dog that led to their rebirth in the heavens, these people thought that it was merely being a cow or a dog in the present life that led to the heavenly reward. So they blindly imitated the behavior of cows and dogs. Nothing came of their cultivation, however, and they couldn't obtain actual accomplishment.

Actual accomplishment means the genuine realization of one's own perfect, clear inherent wisdom and samadhi-power, where samadhi aids wisdom and wisdom aids samadhi in a mutual, perfect, unobstructed interpenetration. It is to realize the true fundamental substance; it is to obtain one's own true mind.

The fifth reason the Buddha spoke this sutra is:

5. To destroy upside-down thoughts and dispel subtle delusions.

Upside-down thoughts are improper. People are really upside-down. Well, people aren't actually upside-down; their thinking is. When Ananda and Matangi's daughter returned to the Buddha, Ananda bowed and asked for instruction. After hearing it, he spoke a verse, which begins:

> The wonderfully deep dharani,
>   the unmoving honored one,
> The foremost Shurangama King
>   is rarely found in the world.

The "unmoving honored one" is the Shurangama Samadhi. The entire sentence refers to Shakyamuni Buddha. It is rare because, as the third line of the verse says, "It melts away my inverted thoughts gathered in a million kalpas." Life after life, for limitless, boundless kalpas, Ananda had been striking up upside-down thoughts, thinking of improper things. "Upside-down thoughts" refer to any of the thoughts worldly people have. The function of the *Shurangama Sutra* is to destroy and melt away these inverted polluted thoughts and to dispel our subtle delusions.

Subtle delusions may be so subtle that the eyes can't see them, the ears can't hear them, and the mind cannot form thoughts about them. As soon as we give rise to one unenlightened thought, the three subtle delusions arise, although the space of a thought is very short. Delusion can be likened to dust. If there is dust flying about in a room where there is a mirror, the mirror will immediately catch a lot of dust particles. These particles of dust will go unnoticed until they become so thick that they cloud the mirror. Our subtle delusions are like the dust on the mirror.

Fundamentally, our own nature is like a bright mirror – it is the great perfect mirror wisdom. But because of the production of these fine delusions, the bright mirror becomes coated and grows dimmer and dimmer. Great Master Shen Xiu's verse says:

> The body is a bodhi tree,
> The mind like a bright mirror stand.
> Time and again brush it clean;
> And let no dust alight.

Some people say this verse is incorrect. I say it is correct. Why? He is telling us to constantly cultivate, to time and again brush clean the mind so that it doesn't catch any dust. Brush it morning and night, for when you have cleared up the dust of the subtle delusions, the mirror of your own nature will shine brightly. Before one has become enlightened, one should honor this doctrine and cultivate in accord with it.

The Great Master, the Sixth Patriarch, said in reply:

> Originally bodhi has no tree,
> The bright mirror has no stand.
> Originally there is not a single thing,
> Where can the dust alight?

This verse was spoken by one who was already enlightened. One who is enlightened can understand and cultivate in accord with this verse.

It is said:

> When not one thought arises,
> the entire substance manifests.
> When the six roots suddenly move,
> one is covered by clouds.

When not one thought is produced, the Buddha-nature and samadhi appear. When your eyes, ears, nose, tongue, body, and mind suddenly move and take control, it is as if the sky has suddenly clouded over. So one must put an end to inverted false thoughts and dispel the subtle doubts and then one can very quickly realize Buddhahood. Unfortunately, though, no one wants to realize Buddhahood. People would rather flow along in the five turbidities, flowing along and forgetting to return. They take suffering as bliss, turn their backs on enlightenment and unite with defiling objects. Although they have not ended birth and death, they nonetheless think themselves pretty fine, saying, "Look at me, I am intelligent and handsome. Everyone who sees me likes me and I understand what others don't." Actually such people are just like mirrors attracting dust. The more dust that gathers, the dimmer the mirror gets until it reflects no light at all. They may think themselves smart in this present life, but wait and see: perhaps ten lives from now they will end up as stupid as pigs. Therefore, in this life we must decide where we will be going – we must recognize clearly what our destiny will be, what path we will take. Then there is hope.

The sixth reason the Buddha spoke this sutra is:

6. To clarify the two methods for the benefit of living beings of the present and future.

The two methods are the practice of equality, which is the actual method, and the use of expedients, which is the provisional method. Provisional method is not real, but is temporary and impermanent. Actual method is real and forever unchanging. There are two methods: provisional and actual.

The use of expedients, which is the provisional method, may be illustrated by the following event:

Once Shakyamuni Buddha saw a child toddling toward a well. The child was on the brink of falling into the water and would surely drown before anyone could reach it. The Buddha knew that if he called to the child to come back that it wouldn't listen, but would keep right on running. He said instead, "I have candy in my hand. Come back quickly and I will give my candy to you." When the child heard there was candy to eat it turned around and came back. Actually there wasn't anything in the Buddha's hand. But was the Buddha lying? Was he cheating the child? No. The child was just about to fall into the well. If the Buddha hadn't enticed it in such a way as to cause it to turn immediately, it would have drowned. The Buddha extended his empty fist and said there was candy in it. The child came because it wanted to eat candy.

The provisional method is used to teach and transform living beings. Basically there isn't anything at all, but the Buddha says to living beings, "I have treasures. Come to me and I will give you a jewel – a priceless gem – and other fine things." Because living beings are greedy, they follow along to reap the advantages. Ultimately they have been enticed by an expedient device. The provisional method, then, refers to the clever skill-in-means used to save living beings.

The practice of equality – the actual method – and the provisional method were both used in speaking this sutra. By means of these two methods living beings are led to separate themselves from suffering and to obtain bliss, so that they eventually may give proof to the result and realize Buddhahood.

The two methods benefit living beings of the present and future. The "present" here can refer to the time when the Buddha taught, and it can also refer to now. Living beings of the present and future can obtain the benefit of being enriched by the dharma. To make the two methods understood for the benefit of living beings of the present and future is the last of the six reasons for the arising of the teaching.

The Division and The Vehicle

A3 The division in which the sutra is included and the vehicle to which it belongs.

The "division" refers to the *tripitaka*, the three treasuries of the Buddhist canon: the *sutra* treasury, the *vinaya* treasury, and the *shastra* treasury. The three treasuries correspond to the three non-outflow studies: precepts, samadhi, and wisdom. The sutra treasury teaches samadhi, the vinaya treasury teaches precepts, and the shastra treasury teaches wisdom. In sutras one often sees the title "Tripitaka Master." This refers to one who has mastered all three treasuries.

Although sutras may include sections dealing with the vinaya or with wisdom, they predominately deal with the study of samadhi. For instance, the *Shurangama Sutra* teaches people how to cultivate dhyana concentration. This has already been mentioned as the fourth reason that the Buddha spoke this sutra: to display the samadhi of the nature and to exhort us to actual accomplishment. There is one section in this sutra known as the four unalterable aspects of purity, and this is an explanation of vinaya. But since the sutra is primarily devoted to a discussion of samadhi, it is not classed as vinaya, but as a sutra.

The "vehicle" refers to the two vehicles in Buddhism: the great vehicle (*mahayana*) and the small vehicle (*theravada*). The small vehicle is like a small cart, which can only seat a few people. It is the vehicle of the sound-hearers and pratyekabuddhas. The great vehicle is the bodhisattva vehicle, that is, like a limousine, which can seat many people. This sutra expounds great vehicle dharma for teaching bodhisattvas, of whom the Buddhas are protective and mindful. As instruction for bodhisattvas, it causes arhats to turn from the small and go toward the great, to resolve their minds on bodhi and cultivate the bodhisattva way. For instance, when Ananda returned from the house of Matangi's daughter to where Shakyamuni Buddha was, he respectfully requested the Buddha to instruct him in the "path to bodhi, which all Thus Come Ones of the past have cultivated." Shakyamuni Buddha's answer to his question is the *Shurangama Sutra*, a dharma cultivated by bodhisattvas. Therefore this sutra is classed as Mahayana rather than Theravada teachings.

The Depth of the Meaning and Principle

A4 The examination of the depth of the meaning and the principle.

To which of the teachings do the principles discussed in the sutra belong? The Tian Tai school describes the following four teachings:

1. the storehouse teaching;
2. the connecting teaching;
3. the separate teaching;
4. the perfect teaching.

The storehouse teaching, or *tripitaka* teaching, refers to the teachings of the small vehicle. It includes the *abhidharma* and the *agama* sutras. Agama is sometimes interpreted as "incomparable dharma" but even so it is still the teachings of the small vehicle.

The connecting teaching connects with the storehouse teaching that precedes it and with the separate teaching that follows it.

The separate teaching differs from what comes before and after it. It is not the same as the connecting teaching that precedes it nor the perfect teaching that follows.

The fourth of the teachings as described by the Tian Tai is the perfect teaching. Of these four, the *Shurangama Sutra* belongs to the separate teaching.

The Xian Shou school makes five divisions:

1. the small teaching;
2. the beginning teaching;
3. the final teaching;
4. the sudden teaching;
5. the perfect teaching.

The small teaching coincides with the storehouse teaching of the Tian Tai division. The beginning teaching includes both the connecting and the separate teachings of the Tian Tai. The final, sudden, and perfect teachings are all contained in the perfect teaching division of the Tian Tai. Although the names differ, the principles are the same.

The small teaching refers to the small vehicle teachings. The beginning teaching refers to the beginning of the great vehicle teaching. It was spoken for those who understood only the emptiness of people and had not yet realized the emptiness of phenomena. They were not yet free of their attachment to phenomena.

The final teaching is the great vehicle dharma. It is for those who understand the emptiness of people and the emptiness of phenomena, the doctrine of the great vehicle. Speaking of the emptiness of people and phenomena, I am reminded of a story that is on the public record.

When Shakyamuni Buddha lived in the world, people often asked him to accept vegetarian meal-offerings. Following the meal it was customary for the host to go before the Buddha, bow, and request dharma. If the Buddha was not present, then the host would ask the Buddha's disciples to accept the offering and in turn the disciples would speak dharma for the host.

One day the Buddha and his great bhikshus left the Jeta Grove at the city of Shravasti, where they were living, and went out to accept an offering of food, leaving behind only one small shramanera (novice monk) to watch the door. After the Buddha had departed, an upasaka (layman) came to the monastery to request that a member of the Sangha come and accept offerings at his home on behalf of the Triple Jewel. Finding that the bhikshus and the Buddha had all gone out, he said to the one small shramanera who was left, "That's okay, I'll invite you, shramanera, to come and accept my offering. Come with me." The small shramanera nervously consented to accompany him: nervous because he had never gone out by himself to accept an offering before. He had always gone with the other bhikshus. Once he found himself obligated to speak dharma, he realized he didn't have any idea what to say. Although this concern weighed on him, he accompanied the host who had so sincerely asked him to go and accept the meal-offering. After they had eaten, the inevitable happened. The host very respectfully turned to the small shramanera, bowed deeply, and requested dharma. As an expression of his sincerity, the host kept his head bowed as he knelt before the small shramanera, waiting for him to speak dharma. There sat the small shramanera staring at his host prostrate before him. And then what do you suppose happened? Without uttering a word, he slipped off his chair, tiptoed outside, and beat a hasty retreat back to the Jeta Grove. Naturally he felt ashamed at having eaten his fill and then run away without speaking the dharma.

For a long time the host knelt with his head bowed. But finally, having heard nothing, he lifted his head to steal a peek and he saw that there was no one in the seat before him. The small shramanera had disappeared. At the moment he saw that the shramanera was gone, he became enlightened. He awoke to the emptiness of people and the emptiness of phenomena. "Haaaa! So that's the way it is!" he exclaimed, and wished immediately to seek certification of his enlightenment. Naturally he headed for the Jeta Grove in search of the small shramanera.

Meanwhile the small shramanera, petrified that his host would pursue him in quest of the dharma, had run back to the Jeta Grove, headed straight for his room, slammed the door, and locked himself in. Who would have guessed that not long after he had locked the door, he would hear a knock? The little shramanera stood frozen with fear without making a sound on the other side of the door. He was totally panic-stricken. After all, he had eaten the host's food and now the host had come demanding the dharma. His nervousness reached such an extreme that at the height of his anxiety, suddenly he became enlightened and also awakened to the emptiness of people and the emptiness of phenomena.

This story illustrates that it is not certain under what circumstances one will become enlightened. Perhaps you will become enlightened by getting nervous. Or perhaps happiness will cause you to become enlightened. Any experience you stumble on may bring enlightenment. Some hear the sound of the wind and become enlightened. Some listen to the flow of water and become enlightened. Some become enlightened upon hearing a wind-chime; others upon hearing a bell ring.

"I have heard all those things many times. Why haven't I become enlightened?" you may ask.

How should I know why you haven't become enlightened? You must wait for enlightenment until your time arrives, just as you must wait for food to be cooked before you can eat it. You must wait for the opportunity to ripen. When the opportunities are ripe, then anything you run into can cause you to become enlightened. The patriarchs of the past in China have become enlightened under many different circumstances. It is only necessary that you continue to cultivate and investigate the Buddhadharma with determined and concentrated effort. If you do that, then one day you will become enlightened. If you are already enlightened, so much the better. If you aren't enlightened, you should go slowly and wait. Don't be nervous. Don't be so anxious that you can't sleep or eat.

The final teaching is for those who have awakened to the emptiness of people and phenomena. It is the entrance into the great vehicle teaching. The final teaching instructs bodhisattvas. It is not however the ultimate teaching. It is surpassed by the sudden and perfect teachings. The perfect teaching explains the unobstructed perfect interpenetration of all things. Everything is originally the

Buddha. The *Dharma Flower Sutra*, a perfect teaching, says that all living beings will become Buddhas in the future. That sutra says: "If people who are very scattered and confused enter a stupa or temple and say 'Namo Buddha' but once, they can all realize the Buddha's Way." When people enter stupas or temples to bow to the Buddha they should be sincere and intent upon what they are doing. But here, the *Dharma Flower Sutra* refers to an insincere person who enters a temple and casually recites "Namo Buddha." Due to just that one recitation of "Namo Buddha" he will become a Buddha in the future.

I am reminded of another story that is a matter of public record. When you recite the Buddha's name, you should transfer the merit to all living beings; you shouldn't just recite for your own sake. When you recite the name of a Buddha even once and dedicate the merit and virtue from your recitation to all living beings, you thereby increase the merit and virtue of the recitation, and you make it penetrate without obstruction.

Once, Shakyamuni Buddha went to a certain country to collect alms, accompanied by all of his disciples except Mahamaudgalyayana only to find that no one there would give them offerings. Neither the king, nor his government officials, nor the citizens made offerings to the Buddha or his disciples. Later, however, when Mahamaudgalyayana arrived in that country, there was a complete change of heart. The king, the officials, and all the citizens very respectfully gathered around to welcome Mahamaudgalyayana and to bow to him. They beseeched him to let them know what he needed so they could make offerings to him. The Buddha's disciples did not understand why the Buddha, one of such great virtue, received no offerings from the people of this country, while when the Buddha's disciple arrived, the whole town turned out to greet him and everyone made offerings to him. "What's the meaning of this?" the disciples asked the Buddha.

The Buddha told his disciples: "The great officials and the citizens made no offerings to me because in a past life I failed to set up conditions with them and consequently we have no affinity with one another. Once long, long ago, ages prior to this one, Mahamaudgalyayana was a firewood gatherer. One day while picking up firewood he bumped against a nest of bees, and they swarmed out to attack him. Mahamaudgalyayana simply recited the Buddha's name and made a vow saying, 'Namo Buddha. You bees, don't sting me! In the future when I have realized the Way, you will be the first ones I take across to Buddhahood. Renounce your evil thoughts and stop harming people.' As a result of this vow, the bees did not sting him. Eventually the queen bee became the king of this country and the drones and workers became the officials and citizens. When Mahamaudgalyayana, now a bhikshu, came to this city, the former bees whom he had to take across all bowed and welcomed him. Such is the power of his former vow."

Taking this situation to heart, we should always establish wholesome affinities by being kind to everyone. We should vow to lead all people and all creatures to Buddhahood. A vow is invisible, but living beings have the equivalent of a radio receiver in their minds, so they can tune in to it. A vow is not tangible or visible, but beings will instinctively know if you are good to them. You should resolve to rescue all living beings. Anyone who maintains this frame of mind will have affinities wherever he goes.

"I went to a certain place and no one came to my aid. Why was that?" someone may ask.

It is because you didn't develop any affinities with the people there in the past. Creating affinities is especially important for cultivators of the Way. So it is said, "If you haven't harvested the fruit of bodhi, first create affinities with living beings." How? By being good to everyone. Why is this necessary? Living beings are the Buddha. Being good to them is simply being good to the Buddha. If you're not good to them, you're not being good to the Buddha.

> Every thought ought to arise
> for the sake of living beings.

> Every good deed should be done
> for the sake of all living beings.

One should use all one's strength to do good deeds. Such is the resolve of a great vehicle bodhisattva. Don't be a small vehicle "self-ending" arhat who only takes himself across to enlightenment and doesn't take others across, too.

If you can see all living beings as Buddhas, living beings will see you as a Buddha. If you see all living beings as demon kings, living beings will see you as a demon king. It's just like putting colored glasses on. If you put on green glasses, everything you see is green. If you wear red glasses, everyone turns red. Not only that, but the way you see others is the way they see you. That's why I said earlier that living beings have radio receivers in their minds, which let them tune into each other. Don't think the other person is not aware of your bad thoughts. Although he may not actually know what you are thinking, his self-nature senses it. Being good to people is *yang*-light. Not being good to people is *yin*-shadow.

The meanings and doctrines of the *Shurangama Sutra* are as deep as the sea. Although some people claim to have fathomed the depths of the ocean, actually its depth varies so much from place to place that it's impossible to say just how deep it is. The doctrines of the *Shurangama Sutra* are the same way. It's not easy to fathom them. Each person gains his or her own particular advantages from the sutra. From person to person the advantages differ, but all come forth from the wisdom of the sutra. Because the sutra is deep, the wisdom we can obtain from it is great and the samadhi-power we gain is durable, and so it is called "the ultimate durability of all phenomena."

"If each of us obtains something from the sutra, are its meanings and doctrines diminished?"

No. The meanings and doctrines are like water in the sea. When someone goes to the shore and dips out a bucketful of water, the amount of water left in the sea is still great. If another person takes some water for his purposes, the water in the sea is still abundant.

The sea is inexhaustible and unending. The doctrines of this sutra are also inexhaustible and unending. When you become enlightened, the sutra's doctrines are still as complete as they were before your enlightenment. You can extract any amount of wisdom, but the wisdom obtainable from the sutra remains the same – it neither grows nor diminishes.

The Teaching Substance

<u>A5</u> The expression of the teaching-substance.

All dharmas spoken by the Buddha has a substance. What is the substance of this sutra's teaching? It consists of words, sentences, writings, and sound. Manjushri Bodhisattva suggests to the Buddha that when the Thus Come One appears in the world the "true teaching-substance of this region resides only in sound." The region meant is the Saha world, our world of suffering. However, sound alone cannot be considered the substance of the teaching. Wind and water also make sounds, but they cannot be called the substance of the teaching.

More specifically, then, the substance of the teaching consists of sound, words, sentences, and writings. The sound is that of the Buddha's first speaking this dharma. Once it was spoken, sound became words. And the words formed sentences, which were then written down. Once it was written down, the teaching became available. So the sutra's teaching-substance is composed of sound, words, sentences, and writings.

The teaching-substance can be divided into four doors. The first is the door of accompanying phenomena; in this case, the sound, words, sentences, and writings. The Shurangama's teaching-substance is based also on the door of consciousness-only, and on the door of returning to the nature, which is not concerned with appearances but returns directly to the nature. The sutra also takes the door of unobstructedness as its teaching-substance.

The door of consciousness-only discusses how the "three realms arise only from the mind and the myriad phenomena only from consciousness." Shakyamuni Buddha contemplated the conditions to see which teachings he should use to rescue beings. Then from within pure consciousness he spoke the dharma to teach and transform living beings, and their consciousness gained the benefit. This is the door of consciousness-only, taking consciousness-only as the substance of its teaching.

The door of returning to the nature is completely interpenetrated without obstruction. In it the consciousness disappears and returns to the nature. Returning to the nature is also the substance of the teaching.

What is the door of non-obstruction? The former doors include both phenomena and noumena, with the door of returning to the nature being noumena. When the four doors combine, phenomena and phenomena are non-obstructive. This non-obstruction, then – the perfect fusion and unobstructedness of all phenomena and of noumena – comprises this sutra's teaching-substance.

Individuals Able to Receive the Teaching

A6 The identification of the appropriate individuals able to receive the teaching.

This refers to the living beings who are taught and transformed. To whom is the teaching of this sutra directed? The *Shurangama Sutra* causes sentient and insentient creatures to perfect all-wisdom at the same time. Both sentient and insentient beings can realize Buddhahood. Those who are taught specifically here are the sound-hearers, ones enlightened to conditions, and those with something left to learn.

Sound-hearers, arhats, hear the Buddha's sound and awaken to the Way. They practice according to the four truths: suffering, accumulation, extinction, and the Way.

Ones enlightened to conditions are pratyekabuddhas born at a time when there is a Buddha in the world. They cultivate the twelve links of conditioned causation and awaken to the Way. When there is no Buddha in the world, pratyekabuddhas are called solitary enlightened ones. Solitary enlightened ones live deep in the mountains in the remote valleys where they hide away in caves. There they watch the myriad things between heaven and earth continually live and die. In the spring the hundred flowers open, in the autumn the yellow leaves fall. Watching these changes, they awaken to the Way.

Besides teaching the sound-hearers and the ones enlightened to conditions, this sutra also teaches those with something left to learn, which in this case refers to the bodhisattvas. The Buddha is the only one who has nothing left to learn. The sutra also transforms the fixed-nature sound-hearers, those who do not wish to turn from the small vehicle toward the great. A sound-hearer whose nature is flexible turns from the small toward the great and can pass from the position of sound-hearer through that of one enlightened to conditions on to become a bodhisattva. Although sound-hearers, ones enlightened to conditions, bodhisattvas, and fixed-nature sound-hearers can be said to be the primary recipients of the sutra's teaching, all living beings of the three realms – the desire realm, the form realm, and the formless realm – are the primary recipients of the teaching. This sutra accords with all opportunities and takes everyone across without exception.

Similarities, Differences and Determination of Time

A7 The similarities and differences between the principle and its implications.

The principle is that which is held in honor. What the principle leads us back to is called its implication. The teaching of the two vehicles (sound-hearers and pratyekabuddhas) is concerned primarily with cause and effect. This is a provisional teaching. The dharma the Buddha spoke includes both provisional and actual teaching. The provisional is temporary, the actual is everlasting. With the provisional teaching, cause is principle, the entering is its implication. When true appearance is reached, the provisional becomes actual. When the actual is reached, one is said to have awakened and entered. Thus the awakening is the principle, the entering is its implication.

When Ananda, the protagonist of this sutra, ran into trouble, the Buddha rescued him and then taught him to turn from the small toward the great. That is the principle. Ananda's arrival at the ultimate fruit is its implication. The principle and its implication thus penetrate to the Buddha Way, and are the way to Buddhahood, and are thus distinguished from the various small vehicle sutras which discuss only the small vehicle and cannot penetrate to the Buddha-position.

A8 The determination of the time.

This refers to the time when the sutra was spoken. The Buddha taught for forty-nine years. When he spoke the *Shurangama Sutra*, King Prasenajit was sixty-two years old, and since the Buddha and King Prasenajit were the same age, this would place the sutra in the prajna period. But if we judge the sutra by its teaching, it is classified as vaipulya. Vaipulya, a Sanskrit word, means "broadening passages" and refers to the third period of Shakyamuni Buddha's teaching, according to the Tian Tai classification. Therefore the previous classification of this sutra as a final teaching, according to the Xian Shou classification, was correct.

CHAPTER 2

The History of the Transmission and Translation

A9 The history of the transmission and translation.

After the great Tian Tai Master Zhi Yi read the *Dharma Flower Sutra*, he divided all sutras into three sections: the preface; the body, which embodies the principle and implication of the sutra; and the propagation, which is an exhortation at the end of the sutra that it be circulated throughout the world.

Later, when an Indian dharma master came to China and learned that Great Master Zhi Yi had divided all sutras into these three parts, he was amazed, and exclaimed, "That is just the same way the sutras of India are divided! The *Shurangama Sutra*, for instance is divided in exactly the same way!" When Master Zhi Yi heard of the existence of the *Shurangama Sutra*, which he had never seen, he was moved to bow to the west in the hope that he would one day see this sutra. He bowed to the west every day for eighteen years, but in the end he never had the opportunity to see the sutra. How superior must be the causes and conditions that allow us, who have never bowed to the sutra, to be able to encounter it now, to read it, and to recite it!

Eventually, the king of India proclaimed the *Shurangama Sutra* a national treasure because it was one of the sutras that Nagarjuna Bodhisattva brought back from the Dragon Palace. After the proclamation, no one was permitted to take the sutra out of the country. At that time, Dharma Master Paramiti was intent upon getting the sutra out of India into other countries, especially China. He set out for China carrying a copy of the sutra, only to be stopped at the border by customs officials who would not permit him to carry the sutra across the border. Since he was unable to take the sutra out of the country, he returned and tried to think of a way to get the sutra out of the country. Finally, he thought of a way. He wrote out the sutra in minute characters on extremely fine silk, rolled it up, and sealed it with wax. Then he cut open his arm and placed the small scroll inside his flesh. Next he applied medicines to the wound and waited for it to heal. Some people say he put the sutra in his leg, but I think that since it would not have been respectful to place the text below the waist, he probably chose some fleshly place on the upper part of his body and put the sutra there. When the wound healed, he again set out for China and passed through the border guards without incident since the sutra was well concealed. Eventually, he arrived in Canton province where he happened to meet the Prime Minister Fang Yong, who invited him to reside at a temple in Canton while he translated the sutra.

These were the difficulties encountered at the time the sutra was translated. How fortunate for us that the dharma master was so determined to take the sutra to China. From this account you can see how important this sutra is.

The Translator

B1 The translator.

Sutra:

Translated during the T'ang dynasty by Shramana Paramiti from Central India.

Commentary:

It was **during the Tang dynasty**, after Empress Wu Zai Tian retired, in the first year of the Shen Long reign period that Shramana Paramiti translated this sutra from Sanskrit to Chinese. He accomplished the translation very quickly, so that he could get back to India before the customs officials at the border were punished for letting him slip through with the sutra. Dharma Master Paramiti wanted to return to India and turn himself in so the guards would not be punished. After he finished his translation he went back to India, confessed to the king, and asked to receive whatever punishment the offense entailed.

This dharma master's merit with regard to this sutra is extremely great. Since it is due to his efforts at the outset that we now have the opportunity to investigate this sutra, we should first be thankful for this shramana's meritorious work.

Shramana is a Sanskrit word which means "diligent and putting to rest," that is, diligently cultivating precepts, samadhi, and wisdom, and putting to rest greed, hatred, and stupidity. The

Buddha is also called a shramana. Once in India, when the Buddha was in the world, the bhikshu Ashvajit ("Master of Horses") was walking down the road carefully attired in his robes. His awesome deportment was so striking that upon seeing him Maudgalyayana was moved to say, "You are so majestic, your awesome manner so well perfected, that certainly you must have a master. Whom do you study with?"

Bhikshu Ashvajit said, "All phenomena arise from conditions, all phenomena cease because of conditions. The Buddha, the Great Shramana, often spoke of this." When Maudgalyayana heard those words, he accompanied the monk back to the Jeta Grove in the Garden of Anathapindaka, bowed to the Buddha as his master, and left the home-life.

Each of us should study the conduct of a shramana. In order to cultivate precepts, samadhi, and wisdom diligently like the shramana, we should first take refuge with the Triple Jewel and then receive the five precepts: to refrain from killing, from stealing, from sexual misconduct, from lying, and from taking intoxicants. After receiving these precepts, we should actually put them into practice, which means we should never violate them. The five precepts are extremely important. Strict adherence to them will ensure rebirth in the realm of humans. If you cultivate the five precepts, you won't lose the opportunity to be born a person.

Someone may say, however, "I understand why one should not kill. After all, all living beings have the Buddha-nature, all can become Buddhas, so every living being's life should be spared. I also understand why stealing is not good and that it is important to refrain from indulging in sexual misconduct and lying, but why are intoxicants included within the five precepts? I've always enjoyed drinking and smoking. Everybody drinks. Everybody smokes. What's wrong with it? In fact, I'm seriously considering dropping my study of the Buddhadharma just because of this prohibition against intoxicants."

You should stop and think about it instead of just following the crowd. Others enjoy smoking and so you join them; others enjoy drinking and so you drink, too. You get caught up in such company and do the things they do until eventually you get the habit as well. Most people don't have great faults, but rather just slight faults and little problems. But just on account of these slight problems you would consider cutting short your study of the Buddhadharma. How stupid that would be! Do you want to know why there is a prohibition against wine? I'll tell you a true story to clarify this point.

There was once a man who liked to drink. He took the five precepts, but afterwards he didn't keep them. How did this happen? One day he thought, "Perhaps I'll have a little drink of wine." He took out a bottle and had a few swallows. He was accustomed to having something to eat with his drink, so he set the bottle down and went outside to look for something to eat. He noticed that his neighbor's chicken had strayed over into his yard. "Good," he thought, "it will make a good chaser," and he snatched up the pullet. At that point, he broke the precept against stealing. Once he had stolen it, he had to kill it before he could eat it, and so he broke the precept against killing. Once the chicken was cooked he used it to chase down his wine, and soon he was roaring drunk, thus breaking once again the precept against the use of intoxicants. About that time, there was a knock at his door. It was the neighbor woman in search of her chicken. "I haven't seen it," he blurted out, thereby breaking the precept against lying. A second glance at the neighbor woman revealed her beauty to him, and, aroused by an overwhelming sexual desire, he raped her. Afterwards he was sued. Now all this came about because he wanted to drink. Just because he had a few drinks, he subsequently broke the other four precepts and got into a lot of trouble. Intoxicants cause one to become confused and scattered, and so they are the object of one of the Buddhist prohibitions. A person who is drunk lacks self-control. With no forewarning he can find himself suddenly in the heavens, suddenly on earth. He "mounts the clouds and drives the fog." He'll do anything. Because it causes one to lose all inhibitions, it is included among the five precepts.

If you receive the five precepts and do not violate them, then you are protected by good dharma-protecting spirits who are connected with each precept. If you break the precepts, the good spirits leave and no longer protect you. This is why receiving the precepts is extremely important in Buddhism.

"How does one receive the precepts?" someone may want to know.

Merely reading in a book that one must not kill, steal, commit acts of sexual misconduct, lie, or take intoxicants does not count as taking precepts. Nor is it possible to go before the Buddhas, light some incense, and make some incense-burns on your body and receive the precepts in that way. No, it is not done that way. If a layperson wishes to receive the five precepts, he must certainly find a high Sangha member of great virtue to certify that he, the Sangha member, has transmitted the substance of the precepts to the layperson. The Sangha member tells the layperson that from now on he or she is one who has received the precepts. The merit gained by receiving and maintaining the precepts is inconceivably great and wonderful. But in order for it to be in accord with dharma, one must go before a Sangha member to seek and receive the precepts.

In addition to cultivating the precepts, a shramana cultivates samadhi. There are many kinds of samadhi that could be discussed, but in general, if you are not moved by any external experience, you are in samadhi.

"How can one obtain samadhi?"

First you must become quiet by sitting in meditation and investigating dhyana. The reason most people go restlessly back and forth, east today and west tomorrow, is that they have no samadhi. In the morning to the gate of *Qin*, in the evening to the court of *Chu*: they run all over, because they don't have any samadhi. To obtain samadhi, you must work hard, and as you do, you may have many different experiences. But in the midst of these experiences, you should take care not to let them turn you around. That is samadhi. If an experience changes your state of mind, you have no samadhi. For instance, if you receive a letter containing bad news and it makes you worry, you have no samadhi. You don't pass the test. Or if you encounter some happy situation and you go chasing after it, you have no samadhi. If you are faced with a displeasing experience and you get angry, you also have no samadhi. You should be neither happy nor sad, neither exhilarated nor mournful. To have samadhi is to do things without getting emotional, but to use your Way mind instead.

By cultivating samadhi, you can open your wisdom. If you have no samadhi-power then you have no wisdom-power. Without the strength of wisdom, how can you study and practice the Buddhadharma?

"Where do samadhi-power and wisdom-power come from?" you ask.

They come from precepts. Every day you must protect and keep the precepts until eventually there comes to be a mutual response between the teachings and your cultivation of it. When you have established this kind of relationship with the dharma you can obtain nourishment from it.

A shramana diligently cultivates precepts, samadhi, and wisdom and puts to rest greed, anger, and stupidity. These three poisons, greed, anger, and stupidity, are precisely the reason you have not realized Buddhahood. If you can put a stop to the three poisons you will quickly become Buddhas.

Greed is the feeling of "the more the better" whenever you encounter something you like. Anger is the feeling that arises when you encounter a situation that doesn't please you. Stupidity is the polluted thoughts of the stupid mind that cause you to go about things in a confused way. If you can simply put an end to those three poisons, you can be in mutual response with the Way. Then it is very easy to accomplish your work in the Way.

There are four kinds of shramanas:

1. A shramana victorious in the Way. He has cultivated and accomplished either arhatship or bodhisattvahood.

2. A shramana who speaks of the Way. He propagates the teachings for the benefit of living beings.

3. A shramana who lives the Way. He maintains the precepts with purity and great vigor and is careful never to break them.

4. A shramana who defiles the Way. He doesn't eat pure food and he breaks the precepts; he turns his back on them. Not only does he defile himself, but he defiles the Buddha's teaching. He makes a bad impression on people. When they see a person who has left the home life but does not keep the precepts, they lose their faith in the Buddhadharma. Since he causes others to lose faith, he is said to defile the Buddha's teaching.

Paramiti, the shramana who translated the *Shurangama Sutra*, represents the first three kinds of shramana: he is victorious in the Way, he speaks of the Way, and he lives the Way. Paramiti in Sanskrit means "extreme amount," indicating that his talent and his wisdom were both extremely ample and full. Dharma Master Paramiti translated the *Shurangama Sutra*, and as director of translation, he stood at the head of more than two hundred dharma masters who had assembled to work on the translation. The work was done at Zhi Zhi monastery, a large monastery in the city of Canton. Because of the great merit and virtue involved in directing the translation of the sutra, the translator and the history of transmission and translation are discussed as the ninth door, before the text itself is explained.

The Reviewer, Certifier and Editor

B2 The reviewer.

Sutra:

Reviewed by Shramana Meghashikara from Uddiyana.

Commentary:

Dharma Master Paramiti was assisted by a shramana from Uddiyana, a place in India. Before it was converted to housing, Uddiyana had been the imperial flower garden, so in transliterating the word into Chinese, the character for carambola, a kind of flower, was used. Meghashika means "able to subdue," which indicates that he could subdue afflictions, demon-obstacles, or anything of the sort. Having left Uddiyana for China, Meghashika revised the translation, paying particular attention to what expressions in Chinese would be used. He was one of the highest dharma masters to take part in the work.

B3 The certifier.

Sutra:

Certified by Shramana Huai Di from Nan Luo Monastery on Luo Fu Mountain.

Commentary:

Often copies of the sutra text do not list this dharma master's name, but his name is listed in earlier editions and should be added to later ones if it has been omitted. **Luo Fu Mountain** is a famous mountain in Canton province. **Nan Luo Monastery** is the place where **Shramana Huai Di** ("Cherishing Progress") dwelt. Probably when Huai Di's master gave him that name, it was in the hope that he would work hard and vigorously. The "Di" of his name means to "progress," the meaning being that he should continually be vigorous in his cultivation, that he should not rest, that he should not be lazy. This dharma master was extremely well-educated. He concentrated on the study of the teachings of the sutras, so he was very clear about the doctrines contained in them. Because he also understood Sanskrit, he was the dharma master appointed to certify the translation. Since both Dharma Master Paramiti and Dharma Master Meghashika understood Sanskrit thoroughly, why did someone else from China certify the translation? Although these two dharma masters had mastered both Sanskrit and Chinese, they had just come to China, and it was to be feared that they did not completely understand Chinese, so someone from China was called upon to certify the translation. This was Dharma Master Huai Di.

I haven't looked into why contemporary editions of the sutra don't list Dharma Master Huai Di, although former editions all do. But I wanted to mention him so that it would be known who certified the translation.

B4 The editor.

Sutra:

Edited by Bodhisattva-precepts Disciple Fang Yong of Qing He, former Censor of State, and concurrently Attendant and Minister, and Court Regulator.

Commentary:

The **Bodhisattva precepts** should be taken by both people who have left the home-life and laypeople. The sutra that sets forth the bodhisattva precepts, the *Brahma Net Sutra*, says, "Whether as king of a country or as a great official, when one is initiated into one's position, one should take the bodhisattva precepts." Because Fang Yong understood the Buddhadharma, he took the Buddha as his father and the bodhisattvas as his brothers, and took the ten major and forty-eight minor bodhisattva precepts. Afterwards, he referred to himself as a **disciple**.

He received the bodhisattva precepts and then he became the **Censor of State**, which means whenever the country was in error he reported it. He criticized. "Of State" indicates his official capacity within the government. The text says **former**, indicating that at the time he edited the *Shurangama Sutra* translation, he was no longer in that position. **Concurrently** means that he held two positions: **Attendant and Minister**. As attendant, he looked after the emperor's affairs and carried out imperial commands. As minister, he was involved in the government of the country and in that capacity issued his own commands. His duty as **Court Regulator** was to make sure the affairs of court were in equilibrium.

His family name was Fang; his given name was Yong. Yong means "perfectly fused." He was from Qing He.

Edited by means he used his brush to write out the text. He polished the language, making it even more eloquent, so that the style and technical perfection of the writing is of unsurpassed excellence. Why? Official Fang Yong was a great writer, an extremely well-educated man. That he himself, with his own brush, polished this text makes the *Shurangama Sutra* text particularly fine. If you wish to study Chinese, you can memorize the *Shurangama Sutra*; it is a paragon of Chinese composition. Even many Chinese are unable to read and understand it.

Now that the first nine doors of explanation are complete, the specific explanation of the meaning of the text follows.

CHAPTER 3

The Testimony of Faith

A10 The specific explanation of the meaning of the text.
B1   The preface.
C1   The testimony of faith.
D1   An explanation of the six fulfillments.

Sutra:

Thus I have heard.

Commentary:

Thus expresses faith. Ananda, the Buddha's cousin and the foremost in learning of all his disciples, edited and compiled the sutras. At the beginning of each sutra he says, "Thus I have heard," indicating that the words to follow are the Buddha's words. "Thus" means "Dharma such as this, the eight volumes of the *Shurangama Sutra*, is what I, Ananda, have heard. I, Ananda, myself heard the Buddha speak this." Therefore, dharma that is "thus" can be believed; dharma that is not "thus" cannot be believed. "Thus," then, refers to the text of the sutra.

"Thus" satisfies the fulfillment of faith. All sutras spoken by the Buddha begin with the six fulfillments: the fulfillment of faith; the fulfillment of hearing; the fulfillment of time; the fulfillment of a host – one who speaks the dharma; the fulfillment of a place; and, the fulfillment of an audience.

1. The fulfillment of faith.

"Why must one have faith?" someone may wonder.

Faith is the source of the Way
And the mother of merit and virtue
Because it nourishes all good things.
Such is its great importance.

It is said,

The Buddhadharma is like a great sea;
Only through faith can one enter it.

There is no other way to enter the sea of dharma except by faith. Only by means of faith can one "deeply enter the sutra treasury and have wisdom like the sea." One should have faith that the *Shurangama Sutra* is extremely fine. Believe in the sutra. That is to have faith. That is what is meant by the fulfillment of faith.

2. The fulfillment of hearing.

Those with the fulfillment of faith still must come to listen to what is said. If you have only the fulfillment of faith, then when lecture time comes you may be off in the park or at a coffee house and miss the lecture entirely. That would be a case of there being no realization of hearing. But if instead you aren't out drinking coffee while sutras are being lectured – what is more, if you aren't even thinking about food though you've skipped dinner and are thus making absolutely certain that you hear the sutra – you have achieved the fulfillment of hearing. Since you have all come to listen and have brought about the fulfillment of faith with your sincerity, I will realize the fulfillment of hearing for you.

3. The fulfillment of time.

If you have faith and hearing, but you don't have the time, then there's no way to hear the sutra. There must be an appropriate time. Usually, you are either going to school or going to work and have no time to come and listen to sutra lectures. But now we have found the time to assemble and investigate the sutra.

4. The fulfillment of a host.

You must also have a host to speak the dharma. If, for instance, you want to listen to sutras, you must find someone to lecture them for you. However, if you were to request one of your "do-it-yourself dharma masters" (laypeople who use this title even though they have not left the home-life in the orthodox tradition) to lecture, you would find that you might as well lecture yourself. You already understand what they lecture. Therefore you must find a host who can speak the dharma. It was for this reason that you pulled me out of the grave. Basically I'm known as the "Monk in the Grave," but you have brought me out to lecture sutras and speak dharma for you.

"Who is the host of the sutra?"

Shakyamuni Buddha spoke the *Shurangama Sutra*; he represents the fulfillment of a host.

5. The fulfillment of a place.

"Once there is a host to speak the dharma, then everything is ready for dharma to be spoken, right?" you ask.

No, you still need a place to lecture the sutras.

"What about the park? It's big enough. We could go there for lectures."

That might work for a day or two, but by the third day the authorities would prevent it. "This is a public park," they would say. "You can't occupy it like this." So you have to find somewhere appropriate to bring about the fulfillment of a place.

6. The fulfillment of an audience.

Finally, there must be people who come to listen. If there's no audience for the sutra lecture, you can go ahead and lecture to the tables and chairs, but can they listen? No, an audience is necessary.

For the *Shurangama Sutra*, the place is the Jeta Grove, in the Garden of the Benefactor of Orphans and the Solitary, at the city of Shravasti, where the Buddha dwelt with his disciples.

In this sutra, the audience is composed of the great bhikshus and bodhisattvas who came to listen.

When Ananda says, "Thus I have heard," the "I" refers to the "hypothetical self" of the bodhisattva. There are four kinds of self:

1. Ordinary people have an "attachment to the self" which comes from their attachment to the body.
2. Non-Buddhist religions speak of a "divine self." They maintain that there is a God-head, or say that they themselves are God.
3. Bodhisattvas follow worldly custom and manifest a "hypothetical self."
4. The Buddhas have the "true self" of the dharma body.

The ordinary person is attached to his body and feels that it is his real self. Actually the body is but a temporary dwelling, like a hotel. You can live in a hotel for a while, but eventually you will have to move. You can't stay forever. Ordinary people do not understand this principle. They think, "My body is me," and they strive to feed it well and dress it beautifully. They look for pleasure to indulge it in. They want an elegant home and beautiful surroundings. They busy themselves dressing well, eating rich food, and living high – all only to help out their "stinking skin-bags."

The human body is merely a stinking skin-bag. You don't believe it? Take a look. Unclean matter oozes from your eyes. Your ears discharge wax, which is also unclean. Your nose is full of filthy mucus and your mouth is full of unclean saliva and phlegm. If you don't bathe for four days, your body begins to stink, and if you perspire, it becomes foul in just a day or two. Feces and urine are also filthy. Impurities are constantly being discharged from the nine bodily apertures of the eyes, ears, nostrils, mouth, anus, and urethra – they're all unclean. What is there to love about your body? You may dress it in finery; dab it with perfume; slave for it all day applying lipstick, rouge, and powder as some women are wont to do – all for the sake of the false shell of the body. No matter how good the food, it still turns into excrement. Decorating the body is just like decorating a toilet with beautiful material. No matter how elegant the toilet turns out, it is still a place to deposit filthy things. Would you say the insides of a human body are clean?

Tell me, what's so good about your body? When the time comes to die, it retains no sentiment for you. It doesn't say, "You've been so good to me, I'll live a few extra days and help you out." It can't do it. So what good is the body after all? Nonetheless, the ordinary person is attached to his body and takes it as himself. "This is MY body," he says. "You hit ME! I can't allow that! How dare you insult ME!"

Ultimately, who is that "me?" He doesn't even know who he is, and yet he says others are insulting him or hitting him. He hasn't recognized his original face and thinks the flesh body is "me." The spirit and the self-nature are the true self, but he has not found them. He can't see them. He doesn't even know enough to look for them. He just assumes he's doing the right thing by slaving for the sake of his body.

If your primary concern is to get the better half of things for yourself, you haven't figured out life right. Anyone like that won't be able to make things add up. He is busy for the sake of himself to the exclusion of all else. Therefore, a bodhisattva is never busy for himself. He is busy for the sake of others. If people want his help, he will give it to them, regardless of the circumstances.

Non-Buddhist religions speak of a "divine self." "What is the self?" they say. "It is God." There are many varieties of this kind of self, but they will not be discussed at this time.

What is the "hypothetical self" of the bodhisattva? Ananda says, "Thus I have heard." However, Ananda is enlightened; at the time he recalls the Buddha's words for us, he has already attained arhatship, and so he no longer has any "I" – any ego. In saying "I have heard," he is simply following worldly custom and assuming a hypothetical self in order to be comprehensible to ordinary people who have an attachment to the self.

Bodhisattvas do not have the characteristic of a self. They recognize the ordinary attachment to the self as false, and they seek the true self of one's own nature. It is from the false self that you can arrive at the true self, for only if you recognize the false can you find the true. If you don't recognize the false as false, how can you find the truth? Why are we now investigating the Buddhadharma? It is because we are searching for true principle. Why do we seek true principle? Because we know that everything in the world is false, and we want to find the truth within falsity. What is the true self of one's own nature that the bodhisattva seeks? It is the Buddha. The Buddha is the true self. Before you have realized Buddhahood, your "I" is false. The bodhisattva knows the self is false, but the ordinary person says, "You say the self is false, but as I see it, my body is excellent. It is strong, tall, well-proportioned and handsome. You may say it is false, but I think it is true." He can't see through it, and so he can't put it down. Unable to put it down, he cannot become truly independent.

The phrase "I have heard" indicates the fulfillment of hearing.

"Now, basically," you may say, "the ears hear. Why doesn't it say, 'Thus the ears heard,' instead of 'Thus I have heard'?" Actually, the ears cannot hear. They are merely the organ of hearing. What hears is the nature, which is eternally present. It is the mind that heard. What it heard was the dharma which is "thus."

"Which dharma is 'thus'?" you ask.

It is the *Shurangama Sutra* that Dharma Master Paramiti wrote out on sheer silk, placed in an incision he made in his arm, carried to China, and translated into Chinese. Now it has come to America, where it has been translated into English. It is what Ananda himself heard the Buddha speak. It is what the Buddha has transmitted to China. It is not something that Ananda as an individual put together and made. It is the dharma the Buddha spoke.

All sutras that the Buddha spoke begin with the four words "Thus I have heard." There are four reasons for that.

1. To put the doubts of the assembly to rest.

After the Buddha had entered nirvana, and it came time to compile the sutras, Ananda ascended the high seat to speak dharma. He immediately manifested the appearance of entering samadhi and sat there for perhaps five minutes without speaking. Once he had entered samadhi, his appearance became identical with the Buddha's. He was endowed with the thirty-two marks and eighty subtle characteristics of a Buddha; he emitted light and moved the earth. The great assembly of disciples immediately gave rise to three doubts:

a) Some thought that Shakyamuni Buddha had come back to life because they saw that Ananda had taken on the perfect features of the Buddha. The disciples had probably been thinking so much about the Buddha that their brains were a bit murky, and so they jumped to this conclusion.

b) Some thought that the reason Ananda now had such perfect features was that he, Ananda, had himself realized Buddhahood.

c) Some thought a Buddha had come from another region. "It isn't Shakyamuni Buddha, and Ananda hasn't become a Buddha," they thought. "Perhaps it is a Buddha from the north, south, east, or west, from one of the ten directions."

But as soon as Ananda said, "Thus I have heard," the three doubts of the assembly were suddenly resolved.

2. To honor the Buddha's instruction.

When the Buddha was about to enter nirvana, he announced his intent to his disciples, and they began to cry. Ananda, who was the Buddha's cousin, cried hardest of them all. He sobbed and wept, probably until his tears washed his face clean. Finally the Venerable Aniruddha approached him and said, "Don't cry. You can't cry. Since the Buddha is about to enter nirvana, you should ask him what to do about things after he is gone."

"What things should I ask about?" Ananda said.

The Venerable Aniruddha replied, "In the future, the sutras will be compiled. You should ask what words to begin them with. Second," Aniruddha continued, "when the Buddha is in the world, we live with the Buddha. When the Buddha enters nirvana where will we dwell? Ask the Buddha that. Third, we now rely on the Buddha as our teacher. After the Buddha enters nirvana, whom should we take as our teacher? We have to have a teaching and transforming guide, a teaching host. Fourth, when the Buddha is in the world, he is able to discipline and subdue the bad-natured bhikshus. After the Buddha enters nirvana, how should they be dealt with? The proper thing for you to do is to go ask the Buddha these four questions."

Ananda agreed. He went to the Buddha and asked, "When the Buddha is in the world, we take the Buddha as our master. After the Buddha enters nirvana, whom should we take as master?"

The Buddha answered, "Take the precepts as your master." Bhikshus and bhikshunis should take the precepts as master.

"When the Buddha is in the world, we dwell with the Buddha," Ananda said. "When the Buddha enters nirvana, where shall we dwell?"

"When the Buddha leaves the world, you should dwell in the four applications of mindfulness," the Buddha answered. The four applications of mindfulness are: contemplate the body as impure; contemplate feelings as suffering; contemplate thoughts as impermanent; and contemplate phenomena as being without self. If you contemplate the body as impure, you won't love the body. If you contemplate feelings as suffering, you can't be greedy for pleasure. If you know thoughts are impermanent, you won't become attached to the polluted thoughts that arise in your mind. The phenomena that are without a self are the five skandhas, or heaps: form, feeling, thinking, activity, and consciousness.

Third, Ananda said, "In the future when the sutras are compiled what words should we begin them with?"

The Buddha answered: "Use these four words: 'Thus I have heard.'" These words and the six fulfillments represent the completeness of the sutra's meaning and certify that the sutra was spoken by the Buddha.

"I have just one more question," said Ananda. "When the Buddha is in the world he can control the bad-natured bhikshus. But when the Buddha enters nirvana, what is to be done about them?"

The Buddha said, "As to the bad-natured bhikshus, ignore them and they will go away. Pay no attention to them. Don't talk to them. Don't sit with them. In general, treat them as despicable; ignore them. If no one pays any attention to them, they won't be able to do anything, no matter how evil they may be."

Bad-natured bhikshus are people who have left the home-life and who say and do unprincipled things. When the Buddha was in the world, there were six bhikshus who were very bad. You shouldn't think that every person who leaves the home-life is good. There are also many unruly people among the Sangha. The Buddha instructs us to "ignore them and they will go away." Keep silent and pay no attention to them. In that way you can subdue them.

3. To resolve the assembly's disputes.

The Buddha had many disciples who were old cultivators – senior members of the assembly who had much more Way-virtue than Ananda. Ananda had just recently attained the fourth stage of arhatship, while among the assembly were many who had long been fourth-stage arhats. If Ananda had simply spoken the sutras, most of them would not have paid him due respect. But by saying "Thus I have heard," he made it clear that what they were about to hear was not a sutra spoken by Ananda himself, but rather a sutra he heard the Buddha speak. Therefore, no one could argue. Everyone knew that Ananda had the most excellent memory and could remember in their entirety all the sutras the Buddha had spoken during his forty-nine years of teaching without getting them confused or mixed up in any way. Ananda was born on the day of the Buddha's enlightenment. He heard everything the Buddha taught during the last twenty-nine years of his life and remembered every single word of it.

"But how could he remember what the Buddha taught during the first twenty years?" someone may ask. "He wasn't even there to hear the teaching." Remember that Ananda was the Buddha's personal attendant and never left the Buddha's side. He used every opportunity to question the Buddha about the earlier teachings and in this way he learned all the dharma the Buddha had spoken during those first twenty years. The Buddha's teaching was like a great river. Every drop of it flowed into the ocean of Ananda's mind. Not a single drop escaped. That is why it is said that everything the Buddha taught during all the forty-nine years – from his enlightenment to his nirvana – was perfectly preserved in Ananda's memory. Thus, the disputes of the assembly were quelled.

4. To distinguish Buddhist sutras from the writings of other religions.

Non-Buddhist texts begin either with the word *O*, "existence," or the word *E*, "non-existence." They say that all phenomena are either existent or non-existent. But Buddhist sutras speak of true emptiness and wonderful existence, the doctrine of the Middle Way. They avoid the extreme doctrines of existence and non-existence, being and non-being. They begin with "Thus I have heard" to distinguish them from non-Buddhist texts.

Sutra:

At one time the Buddha dwelt at the city of Shravasti in the sublime abode of the Jeta Grove.

Commentary:

At one time refers to the time when the *Shurangama Sutra* was spoken. It was the appropriate time to speak the sutra.

"Why wasn't the specific year, month, day, and time recorded?" you ask.

Since the calendars of India and China did not coincide, there was no way to fix the time the *Shurangama Sutra* was spoken, so the simple phrase "At one time" was chosen. Of the six fulfillments, "At one time" brings about the fulfillment of time, and **the Buddha** as the host who speaks the dharma is the fulfillment of a host.

If you want to become a Buddha, you must learn what a Buddha is like.

"What is a Buddha like?"

A Buddha is happy from morning to night. He doesn't worry. He doesn't give rise to afflictions. He sees all living beings as Buddhas, and so he himself has realized Buddhahood. If you can see all living beings as Buddhas, you too are a Buddha.

"What does the word Buddha mean?"

The word Buddha means "enlightened." The Buddha has perfected the three kinds of enlightenment: enlightenment of self, enlightenment of others, and the perfection of enlightenment and practice. This has been explained above.

In this sutra the terms for the three kinds of enlightenment are called basic enlightenment, initial enlightenment, and ultimate enlightenment, but these are simply different names for the enlightenment of self, the enlightenment of others, and the perfection of enlightenment and practice. In Buddhist sutras there are many places where the names vary but the meaning is the same. You should not fail to recognize something just because the name is different. If someone changes his name, you won't know he is being referred to when someone mentions him by his new name, but when you meet him face to face, you'll say, "Oh, it's you!" The three kinds of enlightenment of the Buddha are the same way. If you haven't investigated the Buddhadharma deeply, then you won't know what basic enlightenment, initial enlightenment, and ultimate enlightenment are, but if you have studied the Buddhadharma you know that they are the same as the three enlightenments.

That is a general explanation of the word Buddha. If the word Buddha were discussed in detail, it could not be completely explained in three years, let alone three months. Now I have no alternative but to explain it for three minutes and let it go at that. That is because Americans like speed. They want everything to be done fast. So now in lecturing the sutra I will do it fast, like a rocket going to the moon. In a rocket, Zut! – you're there. Although basically I hold to the old ways, I can't use antiquated methods.

The Buddha **dwelt at the City of Shravasti**. Shravasti, a Sanskrit word, was the name of the capital city in which King Prasenajit lived. The Buddha taught and transformed many living beings there while he dwelt in the sublime abode of the Jeta Grove; which was near the city. Shravasti was different from other cities, in that it was unusually full of pleasures involving the five objects of desire: forms, sounds, smells, tastes, and objects of touch. All were extremely fine. As to forms, there were probably many beautiful women, and the city itself was undoubtedly very colorful. As to sounds, the music was probably extremely beautiful. As to smells, there was Indian curry, for instance, which we also have in this country and which can be smelled for quite a distance when it is cooking. As to flavors, there was ghee, a delicious milk product. As to objects of touch, they probably had the finest silks – the epitome of elegance – in Shravasti.

The city had abundance and affluence, and the people had the virtues of education and freedom; thus Shravasti is interpreted as meaning "abundance and virtue." The people were well-educated, well-read, and experienced. They were endowed with intelligence, penetrating insight, and scholarship. They were also a free people; they were not bound by others.

Once there was a dharma master who went to seek instruction from an elder dharma master. When he arrived, he put on his robe and sash, opened his kneeling cloth, knelt before the elder dharma master, and asked for instruction.

"What instruction do you want from me?" asked the old master.

"I am seeking freedom," came the reply.

"Who's binding you up?" the old master asked.

As soon as he heard the question, the young dharma master realized that no one was binding him, and he immediately became enlightened. "I am already free," he realized. "What am I doing seeking further freedom?" That realization brought about his enlightenment.

"If I were to seek instruction in how to obtain freedom, and someone were to tell me that I'm not bound up, would I become enlightened?" you ask.

That's different. Your time has not yet arrived. Your potential has not yet matured. When it does, one sentence will cause you to awaken, to connect suddenly and penetrate through to enlightenment.

The people of Shravasti were free, which means that their cultivation made it easy for them to realize the Way. Because Shravasti was so well-endowed with abundance and virtue, the Buddha dwelt there.

The sublime abode of the Jeta Grove is the "Jeta Grove in the Garden of the Benefactor of Orphans and the Solitary" mentioned at the beginning of the *Vajra Sutra*.

In Shravasti there lived a great elder named Sudatta, who was endowed with many blessings. No one knew the extent of his wealth. One day a friend said to Sudatta, "The Buddha is at such-and-such a place speaking dharma." The moment Sudatta heard the word "Buddha," his hair stood on end and he was beside himself.

"I want to go see the Buddha right now," he said; "Immediately!" Because of his wish to see the Buddha, the Buddha shone his light on Sudatta, although he was a good distance away. It was the middle of the night, but because the Buddha's light was shining on him, Sudatta thought it was already dawn, so he arose and set out to see the Buddha. Since it was actually the middle of the night, the city gates were still locked, but by means of the power of the Buddha's spiritual penetrations, the gates opened of themselves when Sudatta arrived and closed behind him again as he went out. He reached his destination, saw the Buddha, and, hearing the

Buddha speak dharma, was inexpressibly happy. Then he asked the Buddha, "You have so many disciples; where do they live?"

At that time there wasn't any sublime abode in the Jeta Grove. The Buddha said, "I haven't any permanent residence."

"I will build you a monastery!" said the elder. "I will make a place for you." Since he was wealthy, he could speak with authority. "As soon as I return I will find a place and begin construction."

When he got back to Shravasti he looked everywhere until he eventually found Prince Jeta's garden, which was about a mile and a half outside the city. He saw that the garden was the most appropriate place to give the Buddha. But it belonged to the prince, so he went to negotiate.

"Why do you want to buy my garden?" Prince Jeta asked.

"I'm going to build a place to invite the Buddha to live in," replied the elder.

"All right," Prince Jeta said in jest, "cover the grounds of the garden completely with gold coins, and I will sell it to you."

It never occurred to the prince that Sudatta would actually do it. Who would have guessed that Sudatta would return and take all the gold coins from the family storehouses to the gardens to be laid out on the grounds?

"I was just kidding!" cried the prince when he saw the gold-laden ground. "How could I sell you my garden? You shouldn't have taken me seriously!"

"You are a prince now," replied the elder Sudatta. "In the future you will be the king. A king does not speak in jest. You can't joke with me. Whatever you say should be just as it is. You can't refuse to sell."

When the prince heard that, there was nothing he could do. "Very well," he said. "You have covered the ground with gold coins, but you didn't cover the trees. Here's what we will do. We will divide it. The ground you covered is yours, but the trees are mine. However, I don't want them for myself. I'll make a gift of them so you can provide a place for the Buddha."

The elder Sudatta had no choice but to accept Prince Jeta's conditions. So the place was named the "Jeta Grove in the Garden of the Benefactor of Orphans and the Solitary." Sudatta was also known as Anathapindaka, "the benefactor of orphans and the solitary," because he took pleasure in helping widows, widowers, orphans, and the solitary, that is elderly couples who had no children. His virtuous deeds earned him a title awarded to elders of great virtue.

"How is Prince Jeta's name explained?"

Prince Jeta was born on the day his father, King Prasenajit, returned victorious from a battle with a neighboring country, so the child was given the name Jeta, "Victorious in War," by his father, the king.

This is the history of the "sublime abode of the Jeta Grove." Sudatta invested large additional sums of money in the construction of the sublime abode.

D2 A broad explanation of the fulfillment of an audience.
E1 Sound-hearers.
F1 Listing their number.

Sutra:

With a gathering of great bhikshus, twelve hundred fifty in all.

Commentary:

The **gathering** of great bhikshus, together with the great arhats and the bodhisattvas of the ten directions mentioned below, bring about the fulfillment of an audience.

The sutras spoken by the Buddha are not confused or disconnected. They weren't spoken casually. Every sutra has its six fulfillments at the beginning, because only when these six are brought about can a dharma assembly be established and the dharma be spoken.

Great bhikshus are different from small bhikshus. Great bhikshus are at the stage in their cultivation where they are just about to attain enlightenment. "Bhikshu" is a Sanskrit word that has three meanings: mendicant, frightener of Mara, and destroyer of evil.

A bhikshu is a mendicant who takes his bowl out into the streets to collect alms. He does not go only to the wealthy and avoid the poor, or vice-versa. A bhikshu must practice equality in his alms-rounds, which means he must go strictly from door to door, and to no more than seven houses. So it is said, "One should not avoid the poor and go to the rich, nor ignore the lowly and seek out the honorable."

When someone ascends the precept platform to receive the bhikshu precepts, he faces three masters and seven certifiers. The three masters are the precept transmitter, the karmadana, and the teaching transmitter. The seven certifiers act as guarantors that, as a monk, the bhikshu will not violate the rules of pure eating or break the precepts. When the precepts are transmitted, the karmadana asks, "Have you already resolved to attain bodhi?"

The answer is, "I have already resolved to attain bodhi."

He also says, "Are you a great hero?"

The answer to be given by the preceptee is, "Yes, I am a great hero." When the questions have been answered in this way, an earth-traveling rakshasa ghost, a being of our world who records good and evil, says, "Now the Buddha's retinue has increased by one, and Mara's retinue has decreased by one." The earth-traveling rakshasa transmits this news to a space-traveling yaksha ghost, who in turn transmits the news through space to the sixth desire heaven, where Mara dwells. When Mara, who is king of the heavenly demons, hears the news, he is terrified. That is why the second meaning of bhikshu is frightener of Mara.

A bhikshu is also a destroyer of evil, because he breaks up the evils of ignorance and afflictions.

Since the word bhikshu has three meanings, it falls in the category of "terms not translated because they contain many meanings," and, according to the rules of translation as set down by Dharma Master Xuan Zang during the Tang dynasty in China, it is left in Sanskrit.

Actually, there were twelve hundred fifty-five great bhikshus in the Jeta Grove assembly, but the number is rounded off to **twelve hundred fifty in all**. These disciples comprised the Buddha's constant following. Formerly most of them had adhered to non-Buddhist paths, but, upon receiving the Buddha's teaching, they were transformed. Moved by the Buddha's deep kindness, they constantly dwelt with him thereafter.

Of the twelve hundred fifty, the Buddha first took across Ajnatakaundinya and the other four of the five bhikshus in the Deer Park. Next he converted the three Kashyapa brothers, who had been fire-worshipers. When they took refuge with the Buddha, they brought their thousand disciples along with them to also take refuge. That makes one thousand five disciples. Maudgalyayana and Shariputra each had a hundred disciples: they brought the total to one thousand two hundred and five. Then Yashas, the son of an elder, and his disciples took refuge for a total of fifty people, which makes one thousand two hundred fifty-five disciples in all.

What is meant by a "gathering?" One person cannot be called a gathering, nor can two, nor three. It takes four or more to form an assembly. In this case, however, the gathering consisted of more than twelve hundred fifty.

This is how Ajnatakaundinya became the first of Shakyamuni Buddha's disciples. In a former life, the Buddha was a patient immortal cultivating the Way in the mountains. He cultivated the practice of patience in the face of insult. One day the king of Kalinga went to the mountain on a hunting expedition, bringing with him a party of concubines, palace girls, ministers, and officials. While the king hunted, the concubines went for a stroll on the mountain and encountered the old bhikshu, the patient immortal. The concubines, who rarely left the palace, had never before seen a person with such a long beard and such hair as his. Although he was a cultivator, the concubines thought he was a freak, and so they crept closer and asked him, "What are you doing?"

"I am working at cultivating the Way. I am practicing the Buddhadharma," replied the old cultivator. The concubines had never heard of the Buddhadharma or even of the Buddha and were completely puzzled by his answer. Their curiosity got the better of them, and each one had to come closer for a peek at the old cultivator. They crowded around him in a circle.

By then the king of Kalinga had returned from his hunting, only to find that his beautiful concubines had disappeared. He went looking for them and found them standing in a circle around a long-haired, bearded man. The sight ignited the king's jealousy. He thought to himself, "This man has seduced my beautiful women! They won't pay any attention to me, and yet he's managed to seduce them." Aloud he asked, "What are you doing?"

"I am cultivating patience," replied the old cultivator.

"What do you mean by patience?"

"Patience means that no matter what you do to me, no matter how impolite you are to me, no matter how badly you treat me, I can bear it."

"Really?" said the king of Kalinga. "Is that truly the way you are? I don't believe you can do it. If you truly have patience, why did you seduce my women? Now that they have become so involved with you and have fallen in love with you, in the future they will certainly run away from the palace."

"No, I wouldn't seduce your women. I have been speaking dharma for them, teaching them to be patient."

"Patient!" spit back the king. "So you can be patient, eh? All right, I'll try you out. Let's see if you can be patient..." and he chopped off the old cultivator's ear. "Can you bear it?" he shouted. "Are you angry?"

"I'm not angry," replied the old cultivator.

Next the king sliced off the cultivator's nose. "Are you angry?" he asked. "Are your afflictions welling up? Don't you hate me?"

"I haven't given rise to affliction," replied the old cultivator, "nor am I angry with you."

"Is that true? Are you really not angry?" screamed the king. "Very well, I'll cut off your hand," which he did in one blow. "You still don't hate me?"

The old cultivator, this previous incarnation of Shakyamuni Buddha, said to the king of Kalinga, "I don't hate you."

"Then I will cut off the other hand!" and the king brought his sword down once again on the old cultivator. "Are you angry?"

"I'm still not angry," replied the old cultivator.

"Ah, you don't know truth from falsehood. Here, I'll cut off your foot. Now, are you angry?"

"I'm not angry."

The king cut off his other foot, which meant that he had severed all four of the old cultivator's limbs. "You still don't hate me?" he asked.

The old cultivator replied, "I still don't hate you."

"You're lying!" cried the king. "There isn't a person in the world who wouldn't get angry upon having all four limbs sliced off his body. I don't believe you really can be this way."

At that time the old cultivator made a vow. "If I have not given rise to any anger," he told the king, "then my four limbs will grow back and my body will be whole once more. But if I have gotten angry, my hands and feet won't rejoin my body, and my nose and ear won't grow back." As soon as he finished speaking, his hands, feet, ear, and nose, which had been completely severed, grew back again.

"What kind of weird monster are you?" the king of Kalinga cried. "What kind of freak can make his hands and feet grow back on his body? A demon!" the king concluded, addressing his party of ministers and concubines. But as soon as these thoughts arose, the dharma protectors and beneficent gods let loose a hail-storm that came beating down on the king.

Then the old cultivator made another vow. "Please, dharma protectors and good spirits, don't punish him. I forgive him," he said. Then he told the king, "In the future, when I realize Buddhahood, I will take you across to Buddhahood first." As a result of that vow, when Shakyamuni Buddha realized Buddhahood, the first person he took across was Ajnatakaundinya, who was none other than the former king of Kalinga.

Upon realizing Buddhahood, the power of his vow led him immediately to the Deer Park to save the five bhikshus, of whom the first was Ajnatakaundinya. When someone makes a vow, a connection is created. Therefore you should make vows to be good to people and to rescue them, and you should be careful not to make vows to kill people. If you vow to kill people, in the future, people will vow to kill you, and there will be no end to the cycle of killing. If you make vows to take living beings across to Buddhahood, then we can all realize Buddhahood together, and everyone will obtain the bliss of the eternally still, bright, Pure Land. Be good to people, even if they are not good to you. We should have the kind of vitality that the patient immortal had when, far from getting angry, he vowed to save his attacker who was cutting off his limbs. Students of the Buddhadharma should imitate this spirit of magnanimity.

F2 Praising their virtues.

Sutra:

All were great arhats without outflows, disciples of the Buddha, dwellers and maintainers. They had fully transcended all existence, and were able to travel everywhere, and to accomplish the awesome deportment.

Commentary:

These great bhikshus were not just great bhikshus; they were bodhisattvas appearing in the bodies of bhikshus. So it is said,

"Inwardly they secretly practiced the bodhisattva-conduct. Outwardly, they appeared in the bodies of sound-hearers." Though all were bodhisattvas at heart, though the fundamental nature of the great vehicle was contained in their hearts, they outwardly practiced the dharmas of the small vehicle and appeared as **great arhats without outflows**. A person who has attained the first fruition of enlightenment is called a "small" arhat, while one who has attained the fourth fruition is called a "great" arhat. However, if an arhat who has attained the fourth fruition does not continue to progress in his investigation, does not advance in his cultivation, he is called a "fixed-nature sound-hearer"; he remains fixed on that level. He obtains a little and is satisfied. Although what he has is not much, he thinks it is sufficient and does not consider making any further progress. If he continues to advance in his cultivation, he can attain the position of a bodhisattva. This was the case with the great arhats of the Shurangama assembly.

As explained above, "arhat" is a Sanskrit word with three meanings: worthy of offerings, without birth, and killer of thieves. While bhikshus can receive the offerings only of people, small arhats are worthy of the offerings of people and gods, such as kings of countries or of heavens. Great arhats are worthy of receiving the offerings not only of people and gods, but also of those who have transcended the world – that is of those who have reached states beyond the six desire heavens. Great arhats can receive the offerings of bodhisattvas, because they have cut off afflictions beyond the triple realm, whereas small arhats have cut off only the afflictions within the triple realm. So great arhats can be said to be bodhisattvas. Although they manifest as bhikshus and do not practice the bodhisattva way, within their hearts they have the magnanimity of bodhisattvas, and they can gradually attain the level of bodhisattvahood. In past lives, they had already realized Buddhahood. Wishing to help Shakyamuni Buddha propagate the Buddhadharma, they appeared in the bodies of bhikshus to act as arhats. Basically, these arhats are great bodhisattvas.

An arhat also is said to be without outflows. This means he has already attained the state of being patient with the non-existence of beings and phenomena. An arhat is also called a "killer of thieves," because he has completely killed the thieves of ignorance.

People who have attained the fruition of the Way have no outflows; no outflows of desire, no outflows of existence, and no outflows of ignorance. Being "without outflows," they do not fall into the three realms: the realm of desire, the realm of form, and the formless realm. We people all now dwell in the realm of desire; although we live on earth, we are actually a part of the heavens of the desire-realm. It is called the desire-realm because the people in it have thoughts of desire and longing, which they are unable to stop. There are two kinds of desire: the desire for material objects and the desire for sex. By the desire for material objects is meant greed for all enjoyable things. For instance, if you don't have a house, you want to buy a house. Once you have a house, you think about buying a better one. That is the desire for houses. Or perhaps you want a good car. At first, perhaps you buy a beat-up car, but when you drive it around, people look down on you so you decide to buy a better car, but you still do not invest in the latest model. Once you compare your car to the newest model, however, you feel your present car isn't good enough, so you invest in a new one. That is the desire for cars. Eventually your desire reaches the point that once you have the latest model car, you decide to buy an airplane. Once you have an airplane, you decide to invest in ships. The desire for material objects never ends. You never say, "I've had enough; I'm satisfied. I don't want any more. I'm not greedy for any more things."

"Where does desire come from?"

It comes from ignorance.

Desire for sex is something you would probably understand without my speaking about it. It refers to being greedy for beauty. It, too, cannot be satisfied. One wife is not sufficient; he has to have two. Then two are not enough; he needs three. Some men keep ten or twenty wives. How do you suppose one person can respond to so many? Emperors often had several hundred or several thousand women gathered in the palace. Wouldn't you say that was extremely unfair? Now in democratic countries men are allowed only one wife. The practice of polygamy is prohibited, but there are still many people who sneak out and become involved in illicit affairs. Driven by their desire for sex, many men and women sneak out to carry on wanton relationships; they do not follow the rules.

Besides the outflow of desire there is the outflow of existence. This outflow occurs in the heavens of the form-realm, which are beyond desire. By existence is meant the existence of everything and anything. People who are greedy for existence and cannot maintain control have outflows whenever there is a lot of something.

The greatest of the three kinds of outflows is the outflow of ignorance; ignorance is the basic root of affliction. With the outflow of ignorance, the outflows of existence and of desire arise. If ignorance disappears the other two are also cut off.

Disciples of the Buddha. The Chinese word for disciple can also mean son, but here it refers not to Rahula, the Buddha's son, but to the great bhikshus, the great arhats spoken about above. The *Brahma Net Sutra* says:

> When living beings receive the Buddha's precepts,
> They enter the Buddha's position,
> When their state is identical to great enlightenment,
> They are truly the Buddha's disciples.

Living beings who have received the Buddha's precepts have the qualifications necessary to realize Buddhahood. When their enlightenment comes, they are called disciples of the Buddha.

The *Dharma Flower Sutra* says,

> "Because they come forth from the Buddha's mouth and are born by transformation from the dharma, they are called disciples of the Buddha."

"What does it mean to be born by transformation from the Buddha's mouth?" you ask.

As a result of being taught and transformed by the Buddha, they became enlightened and thus were born from the Buddhadharma. For example, the day you took refuge with the Triple Jewel was your new birthday, the beginning of a new life. Those of you who have taken refuge with the Triple Jewel are the Buddha's disciples.

As **dwellers** they dwelt within the Buddhadharma, and as **maintainers** they relied on the Buddhadharma in their cultivation. Specifically, in terms of the *Shurangama Sutra*, they dwelt in the treasury of the Tathagata and maintained the Ultimately Firm Samadhi. You should protect and maintain the Firm Samadhi and not allow it to become scattered or lost.

The term "abbot,"[7] one who heads a monastery, literally refers to someone who dwelt in and maintained the Buddhadharma, because it is his work to cause the Buddhadharma to continue and not to be cut off, to hand it down and to allow it to spread; to perpetuate the Buddha's wisdom-life, like the great arhats of the Shurangama assembly.

The arhats **had fully transcended all existence**, that is, the twenty-five realms of existence found in the triple realm, **and were able to travel everywhere, and to accomplish the awesome deportment**. They had the ability to live in any land in the ten directions, not just in our Saha world. Because they were arhats and had spiritual penetrations and transformations, they could fly or walk as they pleased.

"If they could go anywhere, why haven't I ever seen any in America?" you may ask.

Even if they had come to America you wouldn't have been able to see them or know of it, because at the time the Buddha was in the world you hadn't even been born yet!

[7.] *zhu chi,* 住持

They were able **to perfect the awesome deportment** wherever they went; they had an awesomeness that people feared and a deportment that people wished to imitate. They were deserving of respect because they differed from the ordinary in every way, and they were respected by everyone they met. "Ah, that person is truly fine, truly deserving of respect and admiration!" Wherever the great bhikshus went, they did not look at improper things. They wouldn't peer around like someone intent upon stealing something. Their eyes constantly regarded their noses, their noses regarded their mouths, and their mouths regarded their hearts. When they walked, their gaze did not extend beyond three feet in front of them. In this way they returned the light to illumine within. So awesome was their bearing that they never indulged in rowdiness or horseplay, never giggled or joked. They were very refined and stern.

Sutra:

They followed the Buddha in turning the wheel and were wonderfully worthy of the bequest. Stern and pure in the vinaya, they were great exemplars in the three realms. Their limitless response-bodies took living beings across and liberated them, pulling out and rescuing those of the future so they could transcend all the bonds of dust.

Commentary:

These four sentences praise four kinds of admirable virtues that characterize the practice of the arhats. The first sentence praises the arhat's virtue of wisdom; the second praises the maintenance of the precepts and rules; the third praises the virtue of kindness; and the fourth, the virtue of compassion.

They followed the Buddha in turning the wheel. The arhats constantly followed the Buddha, not just to serve the Buddha or provide for him; not just to offer the Buddha a towel or to bring the Buddha a cup of tea in order to be filial to the Buddha. It's not simply that they attended upon the Buddha. They helped him turn the wheel. This does not refer to the turning wheel of the six paths, but rather to the great dharma wheel.

"Why is it called a wheel?" you ask.

For one thing, a wheel can grind; a mill-wheel grinds rice and other grains. The dharma wheel grinds up all the "dead-end sects and externalist paths" and pulverizes and destroys their erroneous and improper teachings.

A wheel also transports. Just as a boat transports cargo from Europe to America, so, too, the turning dharma wheel transports living beings from this shore of birth and death to the other shore of nirvana. The speaking of dharma is like a ship that transports living beings from this shore of birth and death to the other shore of nirvana. The speaking of dharma is like a ship that transports people from one place to another.

They **were wonderfully worthy of the bequest**. They had all attained inconceivable states and so were wonderfully worthy. "Worthy" means that, because of the inconceivable states they had accomplished, they were capable of receiving and had the authority to receive the Buddha's final bequest, that is, the last instructions he gave everyone about what to do after his nirvana. It is like an ordinary family; when the father is about to die, he tells his sons and daughters what they should do in the future, how they should cultivate and handle matters. The Buddha also commands his disciples, telling them, "You should work in this way; you should go to that place and turn the dharma wheel to teach and transform living beings." That is called the bequest.

The great bhikshus were worthy to receive the Buddha's final instructions because they all had an inconceivable wisdom and could turn the dharma wheel to benefit themselves and benefit others. This sentence praises the wisdom that enabled them to teach and transform other people and cause them also to have wisdom. This sentence praises the arhat's virtue of wisdom.

Stern and pure in the vinaya, they were great exemplars in the three realms. "Stern" means severe in demeanor, exacting, and not the least bit haphazard. It means they were honorable and awesome; they were forbidding, so that when you were in their presence you dared not laugh or be rambunctious or disobedient. You also did not dare let your eyes wander around, because the great arhats were so severe.

They were clear and pure because they had ended evil and had rid themselves of all bad habits. "Pure" can also mean that they had severed the delusions arising from views, the delusions arising from thoughts, and the myriad subtle delusions like dust and sand, and it means they were also without ignorance. Pure and clear, clear and pure, they had no filth left; they were devoid of evil.

"How can one become devoid of evil?" you wonder.

"Cut off evil," it is said. However, the purity referred to here is free even of the concept of cutting off evil. If you still remember how you cut off evil, then you are not yet pure. If you remember that on such and such a day you cut off a certain amount of evil, and at such and such a time you also cut off a certain amount of evil, then you are not yet pure. Why? You still have dirty things in your mind. If you are pure, all these things are forgotten. When they are absolutely non-existent, you have attained purity.

"Vinaya" is a Sanskrit word which means "good healing." It is fully able to cure your faults. "Stern and pure in the vinaya" means the great arhats, through actual practice, had perfected and attained the method for curing faults.

"They were great exemplars," unsurpassable standards in the three realms: the desire realm, the realm of form, and the formless realm. They were guides and masters of gods and people. And so this sentence praises the great arhats' virtue of maintaining the precepts.

Their limitless response-bodies took living beings across and liberated them. "Response-bodies" are also called transformation-bodies. Originally the great arhats didn't have response-bodies, but they created them by transformation in infinite amounts. There might be three thousand of them, then at another time five thousand, or ten thousand, a hundred thousand, a million, a billion. Why are response-bodies brought forth? Is it so that the great arhats can go about displaying spiritual penetrations to let people know that they have them? No. The great arhats create the response-bodies to teach and transform living beings who need to be taken across to enlightenment. For living beings who should be taken across by a Buddha, they manifest the body of a Buddha and speak dharma for their sake. For living beings who should be taken across by a pratyekabuddha, or by a Brahma king or by Shakra, or by a bhikshu or a bhikshuni, they manifest those response-bodies to take those beings across. Like Guan Shi Yin Bodhisattva, who is extremely kind to those with whom he has karmic ties, and greatly compassionate toward those who are at one with him, great arhats manifest numberless response-bodies to cause beings to leave suffering and to obtain bliss. They enable them to be at peace and to experience the bliss of obtaining what they like. Kindness can bestow happiness, and the great arhats were extremely kind and compassionate.

Pulling out and rescuing those of the future so they could transcend all the bonds of dust. What is meant by "pulling out?" Say, for example, that someone gets both feet stuck in the mud so that each time he pulls one foot out, the other foot gets stuck deeper, until eventually he can't take another step. Then you extend your hand and pull him out of the mud. Or someone may be caught in flood waters, unable to get out until you go in and rescue him. The great arhats extricate and rescue "those of the future," and so we now have hope, because we are those of the future. If you can but believe the dharma the arhats speak for you to hear, you can be rescued and crossed over. You and I are numbered among those of the future.

Why can't you fly now? Why can't you go into empty space? You have too many burden, that's why. They weigh you down and make your body very heavy. That is to speak of the earth's gravitational pull. But if you are free of burdens, then the force of gravity does not bind you, and you can gain your independence. The transient dust burdens us. It is because your burdens pull at you and cling to your clothing that you can no longer fly, although originally you could. However, the great arhats can think of ways to enable all living beings to transcend their troublesome burdens so they can no longer be tied down, so the earth's gravitational force can no longer hold them. Once free, you can drift off into space like a balloon, you can go wherever you wish – to the moon, to the stars. It's not easy to travel this way. This kind of travel is very convenient. There's no need to buy a plane ticket. Wherever you want to go, you can just go there. If you can reach that level, you are said to have transcended your troublesome burdens.

Just as the previous sentence praises the great arhats' virtue of kindness, which brings happiness, this last sentence praises their virtue of compassion, which can rescue living beings from their distress.

F3   Listing the names of the leaders.

Sutra:

The names of the leaders were: the greatly wise Shariputra, Mahamaudgalyayana, Mahakaushthila, Purnamaitreyaniputra, Subhuti, Upanishad, and others.

Commentary:

Shariputra's name may be translated in three ways: "son of the body," because his mother's body was extremely beautiful; "son of the pelican," because his mother's eyes were as beautiful as a pelican's; and "son of jewels," because his mother's eyes shone like jewels, and Shariputra's eyes were like his mother's. Shariputra was foremost in wisdom among the sound-hearers. In fact, **greatly wise** Shariputra's wisdom was evident even before he was born. **Mahakaushthila**, Shariputra's uncle used to debate with his sister, Sharika. He never had any trouble defeating her until she became pregnant with Shariputra, and then she outwitted him every time. Realizing that his sister's newly acquired skill in debate must be due to the presence of an exceptional child in her womb, Mahakaushthila set out to school himself in all the teachings of all the non-Buddhist religions in preparation for the day when he would meet his nephew in debate. He spent many years in southern India pursuing his studies, and when he returned to seek out his nephew, he learned that the greatly wise Shariputra had left the home life to follow the Buddha after having defeated all the master-debators from the five parts of India in debate when he was only eight years old.

Mahakaushthila was displeased to learn that his nephew was a disciple of the Buddha, because he had naturally hoped that after all his years of study and with his unsurpassed debating-powers, he would win the respect and loyalty of the child. He decided to challenge the Buddha, proposing that if he won a debate with the Buddha, the Buddha would relinquish Shariputra to him. And just to show his confidence, he blatantly added that he would chop off his head as an offering to the Buddha if he lost the debate.

Once he went before the Buddha, however, his confidence wavered and he searched frantically through his teachings for a tenet of doctrine to form the basis of this all-important debate. Finally the Buddha said, "Well, speak up. Establish your principle and I will consider your request."

"Basically, I do not accept any principle," said Kaushthila finally and a bit triumphantly, thinking that this would render the Buddha speechless.

"Oh?" replied the Buddha without hesitation. "Do you accept that position?"

Bewildered, Shariputra's uncle thought, "If I say I don't accept the position of having no position, I will have destroyed my own doctrine and will lose the debate. But if I say I do accept it, my acceptance will be in direct opposition to my basic tenet." Caught in the horns of this dilemma, Kaushthila hesitated a fraction of a second and then, without a word, turned on his heels and ran as fast as he could out of the room, out of the Buddha's Way-place, out of the gardens, and down the road for several miles without stopping. Eventually, he regained some self-control, recalled that he was a man of his word, and realized that he must return to the Buddha and offer him his head. When he arrived and asked the Buddha for a knife, however, the Buddha explained that in the Buddhadharma things are not done that way. Then the Buddha spoke dharma for Mahakaushthila and enabled him to open his dharma eye. Once his dharma eye was opened, he could see clearly the fallacies in the teachings of the non-Buddhist paths that he had studied so rigorously, and he requested permission to leave the home life and follow the Buddha. Mahakaushthila's name means "big knees." Some say his ancestors' kneecaps were big, and some say that Kaushthila's own kneecaps were big. In general, large kneecaps were a family trait. Mahakaushthila was first among the Buddha's disciples in debate.

Mahamaudgalyayana's name means "kolita tree" because his father and mother prayed to the spirit of that tree for a son. He was foremost among the disciples in spiritual penetrations.

Purnamaitreyaniputra, another Sanskrit name, means "son of fullness and compassion." "Purna," which means "full," refers to his father's name, which meant "fulfilled vows." "Maitreyani," which means "compassionate woman," was his mother's name. "Putra" means "son." What was his particular talent? Whereas Shariputra was foremost in wisdom, and Mahamaudgalyayana was foremost in spiritual penetrations, Purnamaitreyaniputra was foremost in speaking dharma. No one else could explain the sutras with such subtlety and in such a deep and moving way. When Purna spoke the sutras, heavenly maidens scattered flowers, and golden lotuses welled up from the earth. Whoever would like to be foremost in speaking dharma can recite "Namo Venerable Purna," over and over, and Purna will use his wisdom and eloquence to aid you in speaking dharma so that you will be able to move people. How will they be moved? They won't doze off when you are lecturing sutras. When Purna spoke dharma, no one was able to go to sleep. He expressed the characteristics of all phenomena well and so was said to have unobstructed eloquence.

Subhuti, another of the ten great disciples, was foremost in understanding emptiness. His name has three meanings: "born to emptiness," "splendid apparition," and "good luck." When Subhuti was born, all the wealth in his household – all the gold, silver, and precious gems – disappeared. The treasuries stood empty. No one knew where it had all gone, but since the disappearance of the wealth coincided with the birth, the infant was given the name "Born to Emptiness."

Seven days after his birth, all the riches reappeared, and so the child was renamed "Splendid Apparition." His parents wanted to find out whether their child was good or bad, so they went to a diviner soon after his birth. In India there was no *Book of Changes* (I Ching). Instead they used the diviner to figure out whether their child was good or bad. He came up with "good" and "lucky," so the child was renamed "Good Luck."

Subhuti was foremost in understanding, and so in the *Vajra Sutra* he is the Buddha's interlocutor; that is, it was he who asked Shakyamuni Buddha to explain the doctrine of prajna.

Upanishad, also Sanskrit, means "dust-nature." Upanishad awakened to the Way when he saw that the nature of all external objects is fundamentally empty; he awakened to the doctrine of impermanence as it is embodied in the nature of external objects.

And others means that these six bhikshus were not the only ones in the assembly. There were at least twelve hundred fifty disciples in the assembly, but these six held seniority and sat in the highest positions. Thus, they are mentioned by name to represent the assembly of great arhats and great bhikshus.

E2　Those enlightened to conditions.

Sutra:

Moreover limitless pratyekas who were beyond learning and those with initial resolve came to where the Buddha was to join the bhikshus' pravarana at the close of the summer retreat.

Commentary:

The **numberless pratyekas** were the pratyekabuddhas, who belong to the vehicle of those enlightened by conditions. This vehicle and the sound-hearer vehicle of the great arhats mentioned above are often referred to together as the two vehicles.

They had reached a level of being **beyond learning**. Upon attainment of the fourth fruit of arhatship, cultivators reach a position of being beyond learning. The term "pratyekabuddha" can be interpreted as meaning "solitary enlightened ones," referring to those who were enlightened by themselves at a time when no Buddha was in the world, but it also has come to refer to "those enlightened by conditions" during a time when a Buddha is in the world.

Those enlightened by conditions follow the Buddha in cultivating the twelve links of conditioned causation and thus awaken to the Way. The twelve links of conditioned causation are:

1. Ignorance, which conditions activity;
2. Activity, which conditions consciousness;
3. Consciousness, which conditions name and form;
4. Name and form, which condition the six sense organs;
5. The six sense organs, which condition contact;
6. Contact, which conditions feeling;
7. Feeling, which conditions love;
8. Love, which conditions grasping;
9. Grasping, which conditions existence;
10. Existence, which conditions birth;
11. Birth, which conditions;
12. Old age and death.

When ignorance is extinguished, activity is extinguished; when activity is extinguished, consciousness is extinguished; when consciousness is extinguished, name and form are extinguished; when name and form are extinguished, contact is extinguished;

when contact is extinguished, feeling is extinguished; when feeling is extinguished, love is extinguished; when love is extinguished, grasping is extinguished; when grasping is extinguished, existence is extinguished; when existence is extinguished, birth is extinguished; when birth is extinguished, old age and death are extinguished. Thus the twelve links of conditioned causation can be extinguished.

Pratyekabuddhas who live at the time when a Buddha is in the world are called "those enlightened by conditions"; nevertheless, in the Shurangama assembly there were cultivators who are properly called "solitary enlightened ones." How can that be? There were sages who had cultivated the Way in the mountains before Shakyamuni Buddha had realized Buddhahood, when there was no Buddha in the world. In the springtime, they watched the many flowers blossom. In the autumn, they saw the yellow leaves fall. They observed the myriad things being born and dying; and by themselves, they awakened to the Way. Then after Shakyamuni Buddha realized Buddhahood, they left their caves in the crags deep in the mountains and desolate valleys, and came forth to help Shakyamuni Buddha propagate the Buddhadharma. Limitless numbers of them became part of that influential assembly.

Besides pratyekabuddhas who were beyond learning, there were also pratyekabuddhas **with initial resolve**, arhats with initial resolve, and bhikshus with initial resolve, who had not yet become mature in the Way. All **came to where the Buddha was to join the bhikshu's pravarana at the close of the summer retreat**. In Buddhism, there is a rule that those who have left the home-life must pass the summer in retreat. This rule came about because for a period of ninety days, from the fifteenth of the fourth lunar month to the fifteenth of the seventh lunar month, the members of the Sangha lived in one place and did not go anywhere; they didn't go traveling or take a vacation. There were two reasons for this. First, the weather was very hot and made for especially uncomfortable traveling. That was particularly true in India. Second, insects and other small creatures are particularly abundant on the earth in summer. To avoid stepping on them and squashing them to death, to nurture compassion for all living beings and to protect them, the bhikshus, the bhikshunis, and the Buddha lived in one place and did not go out.

At the close of the summer retreat refers to the end of the ninety-day period of seclusion. During the three month retreat, people might have committed offenses and broken rules, and so at the close of the retreat, at the end of the ninety days, it was necessary to hold a communal examination during which everyone was encouraged to confess his offenses frankly. This was the "pravarana." If anyone had committed offenses without realizing it, then others in the assembly were expected to question him and help him see his mistakes. Nothing was held back, and everyone was expected to answer the questions he was asked and to admit his faults without argument. This discussion was carried on in an open, orderly fashion without anyone giving rise to afflictions or becoming angry when his errors and faults were pointed out. In this way they rid each other of their faults. This kind of communal examination was designed to cause people to change their errors and move toward the good. Everything that had happened before became a dead issue, and everything that happened from that day onward was like a new life. People were encouraged to do things that benefit body and mind and not to do things that do not benefit body and mind.

E3 Bodhisattvas.
F1 First, the pravarana assembly gathers.

Sutra:

Bodhisattvas from the ten directions who desired counsel in order to resolve the doubts in their minds were respectful and obedient to the Awesome but Compassionate One as they prepared to seek the secret meaning.

Commentary:

Besides the two vehicles of sound-hearers and those enlightened by conditions, there were also **Bodhisattvas from the**

ten directions in the Shurangama assembly. The "ten directions" are north, south, east, west, northeast, southeast, northwest, southwest, and above and below.

"I would expect there to be bodhisattvas from the eight directions and from above," you may say, "but do bodhisattvas also come from below?"

Yes, Earth Store Bodhisattva, for example, watches exclusively over things below us.

I discussed the word "bodhisattva" in the introduction, so now the explanation will be brief. Bodhisattva is a Sanskrit word; "Bodhi" means "enlightenment" and "sattva" means "sentient being." A bodhisattva is one who enlightens those with sentience. He himself is a sentient being who was originally just like ordinary people, but who afterward became enlightened.

Bodhisattvas have attained the enlightenment of self and can enlighten others. They can benefit themselves and benefit others. But their enlightenment is not yet perfect, so they are called bodhisattvas.

"How many bodhisattvas came from the ten directions?" you ask.

An incalculable number.

"What did they get together for? Did they come together to cause a commotion? To see a play? To go to a fair?"

No, they came because there were some things they did not understand. They **desired counsel in order to resolve their doubts in their minds**. They had questions. They wanted to ask about doctrines they could not understand.

"What doctrines in particular?"

The doctrine of the **secret meaning**, which refers to the "secret cause" spoken of in this sutra.

They **were respectful and obedient to the Awesome but Compassionate One as they prepared to seek the** secret meaning. The bodhisattvas did not understand the doctrine of the secret cause. Therefore they came wishing to learn of the principle of the secret cause that leads to the complete meaning.

"Do you mean that the *Shurangama Sutra* that is now being explained is a sutra which even bodhisattvas don't understand?" you ask.

It is true that the bodhisattvas desired counsel to resolve their doubts because they did not understand the doctrines of the sutra, but if you now understand and become enlightened, then you are bodhisattvas, too. Don't disdain yourselves. Don't say, "How can I understand doctrines which bodhisattvas didn't understand? I'd better quit now." It is just because these are doctrines that bodhisattvas don't understand that you are now being taught to understand. We have karmic connections with Shakyamuni Buddha and with the dharma that he proclaimed and that remains in the world. So we now have the opportunity to come to understand doctrines that even the bodhisattvas had not understood. We are now in an advantageous position, even though we have been born after Shakyamuni Buddha spoke the dharma. Who knows how long a road those bodhisattvas in the Shurangama assembly had to travel to get there? Not from our north, south, east, and west, perhaps, but from great distances from numberless other worlds. Now we have encountered this sutra. We have great good roots and great affinities that enable us to listen to this dharma. Don't be afraid and think that since bodhisattvas didn't understand it, you shouldn't attempt to study it. That's a mistaken attitude.

Sutra:

Then the Tathagata arranged his seat, sat quietly and peacefully, and for the sake of everyone in the assembly proclaimed the profound and mysterious. Those in the pure assembly at the banquet of dharma obtained what they had never obtained before.

Commentary:

Then refers to the time when the *Shurangama Sutra* was spoken. It was a time when the conditions were appropriate – a time when the Shurangama Mantra was about to be proclaimed.

The Tathagata arranged his seat. "Tathagata," one of the ten titles of the Buddha, has been explained already.

Arranged his seat means that he opened his sitting-cloth, spread it out, and sat down on it.

Sat quietly and peacefully means the Tathagata sat "in purity," in the manner of one absorbed in dhyana, that is, "still consideration." "Peacefully" means at ease; he did not knit his eyebrows together straining to display the pose of one meditating but was very relaxed, with the faint trace of a smile on his face, making those who saw him feel happy. This quiet peaceful style pleased those who looked at him and made them become resolved to learn from him.

And for the sake of everyone in the assembly. Why did the Buddha arrange his seat and sit quietly and peacefully? It was because he wished to enter samadhi, and, in peace and quiet, contemplate the basic natures of living beings. In the "assembly" there were twelve hundred fifty bhikshus, countless pratyekabuddhas who were beyond learning, bodhisattvas from the ten directions, and many more, countless hundreds of thousands of myriads of millions who circumambulated the Buddha. Although the number of people attending our dharma assembly is not nearly as great, the assembly is still vast because there are limitless, boundless numbers of ghosts and spirits who have come to join us. Countless ghosts are outside listening to the dharma, and vast numbers of spirits are standing outside protecting this place. If you don't believe it, take a look; you won't be able to count how many there are.

Proclaimed the profound and mysterious. "Proclaim" means to explain clearly and teach. "Profound" refers to the deep "secret cause." "Mysterious" and wonderful refer to the "complete meaning." He teaches the principle of the secret cause that leads to the complete meaning. If the Buddha did not speak about the secret cause, you would have no way to know of it. If the Buddha did not explain the complete meaning, you wouldn't be able to understand it. The mysterious and wonderful is whatever you don't know.

What you already know you consider quite ordinary, but if you see something you have never tasted before, you'll want to have a taste of it no matter what.

The bodhisattvas came desiring to understand the doctrine more fully, and Shakyamuni Buddha, knowing what was in the minds of those in the dharma assembly, proclaimed the profound and mysterious principle.

Those in the pure assembly at the banquet of dharma obtained what they had never obtained before. Speaking dharma is compared to giving living beings flavorful dharma to taste. When you have eaten your fill of flavorful dharma, you will realize Buddhahood. The banquet does not refer to an ordinary feast where wine is drunk and the like.

"Pure assembly" means that not one being who came to the assembly was unclean. All were pure in body and mind, without defilements. They did no evil and respectfully offered up good conduct. Since they did not engage in any improper or unwholesome behavior, they are referred to as the "pure assembly." This is the first time they had heard the wonderful dharma, and so what they obtained was unprecedented. Unprecedented teaching also refers to the ninth of the twelve divisions of the Buddhist canon, dharma that has never been spoken before.

F2 The assembly that arrived later after hearing the Buddha's voice.

Sutra:

The Immortal's kalavinka-sound pervaded the ten directions and bodhisattvas as numerous as the sands of the Ganges gathered at the bodhimanda with Manjushri as their leader.

Commentary:

Kalavinka is Sanskrit for "wonderful sound"; it is the name of a bird whose cry can be heard at a great distance, even while it is still in the egg. Once the bird is hatched, its call can be heard even more clearly, and the sound is very pleasing to the ear. Here the reference is not to the bird's call but to the sound of the Buddha's voice, which is as pleasing, clear, and penetrating as the kalavinka's.

The Buddha is called **the Immortal** because in the past, Shakyamuni Buddha cultivated as a patient immortal and upon realizing enlightenment, he was known as the Great Enlightened Golden Immortal.

The Buddha's voice **pervaded the ten directions**: it can be heard everywhere. For example, the Buddha spoke dharma in India and we in America can hear it. Under the right conditions, it can be heard more clearly than a radio, and it arrives faster than a telegraph message.

Once, the Buddha's disciple Mahamaudgalyayana, who was foremost of the Buddha's disciples in spiritual penetrations, became curious to know just how far the Buddha's voice reached. So he used his spiritual penetrations to travel east through numberless unreckonable lands, through hundreds of thousands of millions of Buddhalands. But when he had reached a land an enormous distance away, he still could hear the Buddha speaking dharma as if it were spoken right into his ear. It was still perfectly clear.

The inhabitants of that far-off eastern land were huge. The shortest of them was thirty or forty feet tall. Maudgalyayana arrived at lunch time, and the bowls they were using were as large as our houses. The amount they ate far surpassed what we consume. Maudgalyayana perched on the edge of one of the bowls and stood watching the giants eat. Eventually one of them noticed him and exclaimed, "Oh? Where did that human-headed bug come from?" He was so tiny that they called him a human-headed bug.

But the Buddha of that far eastern land told them, "You must not speak like that. That is Maudgalyayana from the Saha world. He is foremost in spiritual penetrations among Shakyamuni Buddha's disciples. Don't ridicule him. He's not a human-headed bug." The disciples of that land were surprised indeed to learn that Shakyamuni Buddha's disciples were the size of insects.

Bodhisattvas as numerous as the sands of the Ganges gathered at the bodhimanda.[8] The Ganges River in India is about fifteen miles wide and its sands are as fine as flour. So they are used as an analogy for the unreckonable number of bodhisattvas who came to the dharma assembly. The bodhisattvas came to protect the place where Shakyamuni Buddha spoke the *Shurangama Sutra*. The Way-place referred to is also this present Way-place where the *Shurangama Sutra* is now being explained. The bodhisattvas from the former assembly are also here. You should not look lightly on this place just because the room is small. There are also many great bodhisattvas here listening to the sutras, protecting this Way-place, and enabling it to become more flourishing every day. Would you like to meet them? I will tell you that they have **Manjushri as their leader**. Manjushri is a Sanskrit name that means "wonderful virtue," referring to his subtle, wonderful, inconceivable virtuous practices. He is also called "wonderfully lucky," because every place he goes becomes auspicious. Every time he comes to a Way-place, the Way-place becomes very auspicious.

In China, the bodhimanda of Manjushri is at Wu Tai mountain. He is referred to as the Greatly Wise Manjushri because he is foremost among the bodhisattvas in wisdom. Among the arhats, Shariputra is foremost in wisdom, but his wisdom is small compared to that of the bodhisattvas.

---

[8]. "Bodhimanda" is Sanskrit for "place of enlightenment," a "Way-Place."

CHAPTER 4

Ananda's Fall

C2 The prologue.
D1 The king and officials prepare offerings.

Sutra:

Then King Prasenajit, for the sake of his father, the late king, arranged on the day of mourning a vegetarian feast and invited the Buddha to the side rooms of the palace. He welcomed the Tathagata in person with a vast array of superb delicacies of unsurpassed wonderful flavors and himself invited the great bodhisattvas.

Commentary:

King Prasenajit, whose name means "moonlight," was born in India on the same day the Buddha was. When the Buddha entered the world, a light illumined the entire country. King Prasenajit's father thought the light was connected with the birth of his son, so he named him "Moonlight." The child later succeeded the father to become the ruler of a country in India.

For the sake of his father, the late king. The fifteenth day of the seventh lunar month marked the close of the summer retreat for people who had left the home-life. On the fourteenth, fifteenth, and sixteenth days of the month the pravarana is held, as I explained earlier. The fifteenth marks the Ullambana festival. The fifteenth day of the seventh month was also the day King Prasenajit recognized to be the anniversary of his father's death. It is referred to indirectly as **the day of mourning**, since one did not speak explicitly of one's father's death because of the pain and sorrow involved. Filial people find it very difficult to be reminded of their parents' deaths; remembering how good their parents were to them and how they have been unable to be sufficiently filial in return, they experience deep regret. Although mention of the anniversary of King Prasenajit's father's death was avoided, everyone knew of it, and the king chose that day to make offerings to the Triple Jewel and to do various good deeds. One does good deeds and makes offerings on such a day in order to rescue one's father and mother from the hells and secure for them rebirth in the heavens.

When Mahamaudgalyayana first obtained the six spiritual penetrations, he went exploring to find out where his mother was and discovered that she had fallen into the hells. Why had his mother fallen into the hells? It was because when she was alive she liked to eat seafood, and most especially enjoyed fish-eggs. How many lives do you suppose there are in a mess of fish-eggs? A vast number. Because she ate quantities of fish-eggs, thereby taking a vast number of lives, and because she did not believe in the Triple Jewel – because she did not believe in the Buddha, did not believe in the Dharma, and did not respect the Sangha – she fell into the hells upon her death. And then even Maudgalyayana with his six spiritual penetrations could not save her.

It upset Maudgalyayana to see his mother in the hells enduring so much suffering. His samadhi-power was shaken. And so he used his spiritual penetrations to go to the hells, and he took with him a bowl of rice, which he gave to his mother. When his mother was alive, she had been very stingy. If she was asked to give a little money, her heart and liver began to ache and her very flesh hurt. It is said that parting with money is like cutting off a piece of one's own flesh. That's the way it was with her. She couldn't bear to give it up. As a result of her stingy habits, what do you suppose she did when her son brought her the bowl of food? She grabbed it with her left hand and covered it with her right arm. Why did she cover it? She was afraid someone would steal her food. The place was full of ghosts, but she found a spot where there were none, and she stealthily took a bite of food. Who would have guessed that as soon as she put the food in her mouth it would turn to burning coals so that she couldn't eat it? Why was this? She was a hungry ghost, and – like all such ghosts – had a stomach as big as a bass drum and a throat as narrow as a needle. As a result, she couldn't eat. Even when she tried, her karmic obstacles caused the food to turn to fire. Confronted with this situation, Maudgalyayana, despite his spiritual penetrations, was powerless. He had no mantra to recite. And so he returned to his teacher. He used his spiritual penetrations to bring himself before the Buddha; he knelt and said, "My mother has fallen into the hells. I have come seeking the Buddha's compassion to help me rescue her."

The Buddha answered, "Your mother has fallen into the hells because she slandered the Triple Jewel, was not respectful toward the Triple Jewel, and did not believe in the Triple Jewel. You can't save her by yourself, Maudgalyayana. You must rely on the united strength of the Sangha of the ten directions in order to save your mother. On the fifteenth day of the seventh month you should make an offering of the finest vegetarian foods and drinks that have not been tasted by anyone before being offered to the Buddha and the Sangha. By making this offering, the Way-karma of the virtuous high Sangha-members of the ten directions will then be able to save your mother. Otherwise there is no way you can save her."

On the appointed day Mahamaudgalyayana did as the Buddha had instructed; he asked the great virtuous high Sanghans of the ten directions to come and rescue his mother. He prepared a vast array of superb delicacies of unsurpassed wonderful flavors, and made offerings to the Buddha. His mother was reborn in the heavens as a result of the strength of the greatly virtuous ones of the ten directions. Since that time, the Ullambana festival has become an annual celebration, a day upon which anyone can rescue his parents of seven lives past.

Ullambana is a Sanskrit word which means "rescuing those who are hanging upside-down." This refers to the extreme suffering of the ghosts in the hells who are as tormented as one hanging upside-down would be. The Ullambana is performed especially for releasing those undergoing the painful suffering of being hungry ghosts and enabling them to be reborn in the heavens.

The fifteenth day of the seventh month is the day of the Buddha's rejoicing and the Sangha's pravarana. On that day the merit and virtue derived from making offerings to the Triple Jewel is several million times greater than that derived from offerings made on ordinary days. That was the day King Prasenajit chose to offer **a vegetarian feast** to the Buddha and to make offerings to the Triple Jewel on behalf of his father.

No meat was served, nor any of the five edible members of the allium family – onions, leeks, garlic, chives, or shallots – for all of those foods make people murky and confused.

He **invited the Buddha to the side rooms of the palace**. Why wasn't the banquet held in the main hall? The main hall was where orders were signed, governmental matters were carried on, and where humane and beneficent policy-making took place. The side rooms were reserved for banquets.

He welcomed the Tathagata in person with a vast array of superb delicacies of unsurpassed wonderful flavors. The king himself went out to welcome the Buddha. The banquet consisted of the finest array of foods and drinks – vegetarian dishes that were cooked to perfection – and their flavors were the finest to be had.

And himself invited the great bodhisattvas. The king himself signed the invitation, or perhaps he himself went to invite them, saying, "I wish to request the presence of all the great bodhisattvas to come and accept my offerings." He invited all the great bodhisattvas, as many as the sands in the Ganges River. How much food do you suppose he had to prepare for such a gathering? It must have taken a lot of money, but King Prasenajit was probably not stingy like Maudgalyayana's mother, so he prepared a great offering.

Sutra:

In the city were also elders and laypeople who were also prepared to feed the Sangha at the same time, and they stood waiting for the Buddha to come and receive offerings.

Commentary:

The king wasn't the only one who was prepared to make offerings to the Buddha. There were also elders and laypeople in the city.

These are the ten virtues of an elder:

1. honorable name;
2. lofty position;
3. great wealth;
4. heroic deportment;
5. deep wisdom;
6. maturity in years;
7. pure practice;
8. perfect propriety;
9. the praise of their superiors;
10. the trust of those below them.

They are perhaps of royal blood or of otherwise noble birth. They hold high-ranking positions as officials. They are really rich. Their awesome air is stern and severe; their sanguine energies are powerful and sure. They are courageous, awesome, magnanimous, and forthright. They are decisive and never procrastinate. Their wisdom is great and profound. Elders are usually between fifty and seventy years old. They conduct their affairs in a clean, undefiled, correct, and straightforward manner, and their integrity is impeccable. They are very lofty in their ideals. They are extremely courteous to everyone, never arrogant or condescending. Although their manner is heroic, they do not bully people. When meeting someone they first bow from the waist and then ask after his health. They are never in the least bit crude. They are spoken of highly by their superiors. The people put their trust in the elder. They all wish the best for him – wish him to be a great official, hope he will be wealthy, hope that all good things come his way. Why? He in turn will use his wealth and position for the good of the people. He enjoys giving; the more money he has, the more it pleases everyone. As a great official his every effort is bent on pleasing the people, and the masses look up to him.

Laypeople refers to cultivators who are householders. They cultivate in their households.

The elders and laypeople **were also prepared to feed the Sangha at the same time**. The elders and laypeople were also aware of the merit and virtue derived from making offerings to the Triple Jewel on such an important day, the day of the Buddha's rejoicing, the day of the Sangha's pravarana. Probably the vegetarian food they prepared in no way compared to the delicacies offered by the king, however, so the text makes no mention of superb or wonderful flavors.

And they stood waiting for the Buddha to come and receive offerings. They stood in their doorways waiting for the Buddha to come and receive their offerings, speculating among themselves, "He'll come to my house today." "He's going to receive my offerings."

Not only did they wait for the Buddha, they also were waiting for the lofty and virtuous members of the Sangha to come and accept their offerings, and so sincere were they that they remained standing during their wait.

Today in Thailand, Burma, and Sri Lanka, donors kneel to make their offerings to the Sangha. When a member of the Sangha comes along, they add their offering to his bowl and then bow to him. Then he returns to the monastery to eat.

D2 The Buddha and Sangha go to accept the invitation.

Sutra:

The Buddha commanded Manjushri to assign the bodhisattvas and arhats to receive offerings from the various vegetarian hosts.

Commentary:

The Buddha commanded Manjushri. Kings can issue commands and so can the King of Dharma. Thus, the text says that the Buddha "commanded" Manjushri Bodhisattva **to assign the bodhisattvas and arhats.** How were they assigned? That would depend upon how many bodhisattvas there were. Perhaps they were assigned to go on the rounds individually or perhaps they were divided into groups of twos and threes.

The great bhikshus and the great arhats, as well as the bodhisattvas, were commanded **to receive offerings from the various vegetarian hosts.** This means that they went to the homes of the elders and laypeople and received their offerings. Although the Buddha has millions of transformation bodies, he would never display his spiritual penetrations just for the sake of a meal and go to the various donors' homes to appear as transformation Buddhas and seek alms at each door. It would never be done that way. If the Buddha were like that then spiritual penetrations would be cheaper than bean curd. And so he said to Manjushri, "You assign the bodhisattvas and great arhats so that they can go to each home and receive offerings."

D3 Ananda's fall is revealed.
E1 The circumstances leading to his fall.

Sutra:

Only Ananda, who, having accepted a special invitation earlier, had traveled far and had not yet returned, was late for the apportioning of the Sangha. No senior-seated one or acharya was with him, so he was returning alone on the road.

Commentary:

Only Ananda. This is the whole reason he got into trouble. He was alone. What had Ananda done? He had **accepted a special invitation earlier**. Perhaps a month or so in advance, someone had made an appointment and said, "On the fourteenth day of the seventh month you certainly should come and receive offerings from us."

So he went. In fact, he went early. And so on the fifteenth day of the seventh month, the day when everyone was receiving offerings, he **had traveled far and had not yet returned**. Basically, bhikshus should not accept special invitations. For instance, if there are ten Sanghans here and you invite only one to go to your home to eat, you are issuing a special invitation. The one who has received the special invitation should not go. Why? The rule in Buddhism is that all the Sanghans of a Way-place should be invited for the offerings together; but sometimes people who like good food ignore the rule and accept the special invitations they are given, thinking, "Why should I look after all of you? What counts is that I get my fill. My special invitation is a response to my blessings and virtue." They pay no attention to others.

Ananda probably had a bit of fondness for eating good food. Now think about it; during the close of the summer retreat it was absolutely impermissible to travel, and yet Ananda had accepted a special invitation and went out to receive offerings. And so he had already gone against the rules; he had already committed an offense. He was invited for the fourteenth of the month, and so he probably went on the thirteenth. After eating on the fourteenth he stayed the night, planning to return early the next day, and he **was late for the apportioning of the Sangha**. He didn't make it in time.

No senior-seated one or acharya was with him, so he was returning alone on the road. People who have left the home-life should go in twos and threes. The three would perhaps consist of a young bhikshu, a senior bhikshu and an acharya. A "senior" is one who has held the precepts purely for more than twenty years, and therefore is seated in the front of the assembly. "Acharya" is a Sanskrit word, which means "a teacher who exemplifies the rules." He is a master who follows the rules and understands them. There are five kinds of acharya:

1. an acharya under whom others may leave the home-life;
2. an acharya who transmits the precepts;
3. a karmadana acharya;
4. an acharya upon whom others may rely;
5. an acharya who transmits the teachings.

One person can be all five kinds of acharya. A person who is qualified to lecture the sutras and speak dharma is an acharya who transmits the teachings. He may also have a Way-place where people may draw near him to study and practice, which makes him an acharya upon whom others can rely. He may also teach people the rules and transfer merit to them every day before the Buddhas, asking the Buddhas to wash away their karmic offenses and to cause their good roots to increase. That makes him a karmadana acharya.

He may teach others how to request the precepts, what to say when they receive them, and how to reveal violations of precepts or other offenses before he bestows the precepts upon them. Then he is an acharya who transmits precepts. He may receive people as left-home disciples, in which case he is an acharya under whom others can leave the home-life.

An acharya is one who helps you realize the Way. He aids you in your cultivation of the Way. He stands beside you and admonishes you, "Don't commit offenses." That is an acharya. But Ananda didn't have a senior-seated one or acharya with him in order to help him "guard the mind and be apart from offenses," and so he walked right into trouble. The worst thing he did was to be out returning alone on the road.

Basically, people who have left the home-life should always travel in pairs. If you truly have samadhi-power, then to do things on your own is not a problem. But if your samadhi-power is not sufficient, then it is very easy to encounter a demonic-obstacle. It is very easy to be affected by external states. These days there are many young monks who travel around by themselves, and that's very dangerous.

Still we should all thank Ananda. If he hadn't gone out alone and gotten into trouble, how could he have come to understand the *Shurangama Sutra*? We wouldn't have any opportunity to understand the sutra ourselves because Shakyamuni Buddha wouldn't have been presented with the opportunity to speak the *Shurangama Sutra* to teach us how to cultivate samadhi. The fact remains that Ananda benefited us a great deal by his action.

Sutra:

On that day he had received no offerings, and so at the appropriate time Ananda took up his begging bowl and, as he traveled through the city, begged in successive order.

Commentary:

Since he had failed to return in time for the apportioning of the Sangha for that day's vegetarian offering, **he had received no offerings, and so at the appropriate time Ananda took up his begging bowl**. Bowl is *patra* in Sanskrit, meaning "a vessel of appropriate measure." It contains enough, but not more than enough, to satisfy one's needs.

As he traveled through the city, he **begged in successive order**. He went from house to house in Shravasti, from door to door. Since some give more and some give less, it is necessary to stop at more than one house, but according to the rules one does not stop at more than seven houses. If after stopping at seven houses one has not received any offerings, one must do without food that day.

Sutra:

As he first began to beg, he thought to himself that down to the very last danapati who would be his vegetarian host he would not question whether they were clean or unclean;

whether they were ksatriyas of honorable name or chandalas. While practicing equality and compassion he would not merely select the lowly but was determined to perfect all living beings' limitless merit and virtue.

Commentary:

As he first began to beg, he thought to himself that down to the very last danapati who would be his vegetarian host. When Ananda took up his bowl and went to receive food offerings, his very first thought was about his donors: "From the very first to the very last *danapati* who becomes my vegetarian host." "Danapati" is a Sanskrit word which is transliterated into Chinese by two characters which also shed light on its meaning: the first, *tan* (檀), represents the Sanskrit *dana*, and means "to give," and the second, *yue* (越), means "to transcend." The meaning of danapati as based on that transliteration, then, is "one who gives so that he can transcend birth and death." A layperson who gives offerings to people who have left the home-life is called a danapati, "one who gives in order to transcend."

By the "very last donor" Ananda meant the one whose offerings would give him the final amount of food necessary for that day.

He would not question whether they were clean or unclean; whether they were ksatriyas of honorable name or chandalas. He would not notice if they were poor or rich. Kshatriyas are the noble or royal class of India. Chandalas are butchers, interpreted in Chinese to be "those who kill pigs," because in India the killing of cattle is forbidden. This caste also included other classes of India, trades such as removing dead bodies, butchering animals, and so forth. And so when chandalas walked down the road, most people would not walk with them. They had to walk on separate roads. In order to identify themselves as being lower than ordinary people, they were required to ring bells and hold banners as they walked down the road.

While practicing equality and compassion he would not merely select the lowly but was determined to perfect all living

beings' limitless merit and virtue. He paid no attention to how honorable might be the person from whom he was receiving offerings, nor did he receive offerings exclusively from the lowly. He intended to give all living beings the opportunity to plant blessings.

When donors make offerings, they plant blessings that will grow and ripen in the future. Thus people who have left the home-life are called "fields of blessings." One who has the reward of many blessings is in all ways content. So if you feel your reward of blessings is not sufficient, you should make offerings to the Triple Jewel and plant more blessings.

Ananda was determined that every wish of every living being be fulfilled. His hope was that the boundless merit and virtue which living beings seek would be completely fulfilled through him.

Sutra:

Ananda already knew that the Tathagata, the World Honored One, had admonished Subhuti and great Kashyapa for being arhats whose hearts were not fair and equal, and he regarded with respect the Tathagata's instructions on impartiality, to save everyone from doubt and slander.

Commentary:

Why did Ananda want to practice equality and compassion in receiving offerings? Earlier, he had heard Shakyamuni Buddha admonish Subhuti and Mahakashyapa and call them arhats, meaning arhats of the small vehicle, not great arhats of the great vehicle. Why did he do that? It was Subhuti's opinion that he should seek alms exclusively from the rich. "Rich people should plant more blessings," he said. "If they continue to do good deeds, then in their future lives they will continue to be wealthy. If they don't give now, they won't be rich in the next life. In order to help the rich, I seek alms from them."

Subhuti's method was an example of "avoiding the poor and favoring the rich." In complete contrast to him, Mahakashyapa sought alms exclusively from the poor. He thought, "Poor people should plant blessings and do good deeds, so that in their future lives they can be wealthy and honored. If I don't help them out by receiving alms from them, then in the next life and on into the future, they will continue to be poor." And so they were both small arhats. I believe there was another reason underlying their behavior. It seems fairly certain that Subhuti liked to eat good food, and great Kashyapa, foremost among the disciples in his practice of asceticism, ate what others couldn't eat, endured what others couldn't endure, bore what others couldn't bear, and yielded where others couldn't yield. Evidently he was unconcerned about what kind of food he ate, so he sought alms from the poor and gave them the opportunity to plant blessings. The gifts of food and drink offered by poor people are never as fine as those given by the wealthy. The food the rich throw out on the streets is bound to be better than the offerings of the poor.

Shakyamuni Buddha knew that these two disciples did not practice equality and compassion in their alms-rounds. He was aware of the discriminations they made, and so **the Tathagata, the World Honored One, had admonished Subhuti and great Kashyapa for being arhats whose hearts were not fair and equal**.

Ananda **regarded with respect the Tathagata's instructions on impartiality, to save everyone from doubt and slander.** He was extremely respectful of this method of practicing equality, which advised against choosing among donors. Minds that make such discriminations do not belong to the great vehicle dharma but to selfish people. Remembering the reprimand Subhuti and Great Kashyapa had received from Shakyamuni Buddha, Ananda did not want to imitate them, and so he carefully practiced equality and compassion.

Shakyamuni Buddha's dharma-door was a wide-open expedient free of the slightest obstruction, devoid of any limitation. If one begs exclusively from the rich or from the poor, one can easily arouse people's doubts and cause them to slander the dharma. Collecting alms impartially makes everyone's doubts and slander melt away and disappear altogether. Everyone can happily plant blessings and have his wishes fulfilled.

E2 The incident of the actual fall.

Sutra:

Having crossed the city moat, he walked slowly through the outer gates, his manner stern and proper as he honored with propriety the method of obtaining food.

Commentary:

Shravasti was surrounded by a moat just like those found around some ancient cities in China. Water was kept in the moat at all times to form a protection for the city. Once Ananda had crossed the moat, he arrived within the confines of the great city of Shravasti.

Having crossed the city moat, he walked slowly through the outer gates, his manner stern and proper as he strictly respected the rules for obtaining vegetarian food.

Ananda was dignified, with eyes straight ahead, and at the same time extremely respectful. In this way he slowly passed through the outer gates of the city. He exhibited an awesome manner and model deportment; he didn't look at improper spectacles, nor did he eavesdrop. All the time that he held his bowl, he displayed the utmost propriety and respect for the method of receiving food, not daring to be the least bit casual or lax as he traveled through the streets.

Sutra:

At that time, because Ananda was begging in sequential order, he passed by a house of prostitution and was waylaid by a powerful artifice. By means of a mantra of the Kapila religion, formerly of the Brahma Heaven, the daughter of Matangi drew him onto an impure mat.

Commentary:

At that time Ananda was being stern and proper, honoring with propriety the method for obtaining food. Because Ananda was

begging in sequential order – by going door to door, house to house – **he passed by a house of prostitution and was waylaid by a powerful artifice**. It was not real, but was something conjured up. **The daughter of Matangi** had urged her mother to make use of a mantra, which allegedly had come from the gods of the Brahma Heaven and had been brought down to the human realm. But it was phony; it was empty and false, so it is called an "artifice."

Matangi is a Sanskrit name, interpreted to mean "vulgar lineage," indicating that she was not honorable. Her daughter's name was Prakriti, which is Sanskrit for "basic nature."

Ananda was snared by **a mantra of the Kapila religion, formerly of the Brahma Heaven**. Matangi had learned her false mantra from members of the tawny-haired religion. In fact, the mantric device was falsely named, because it was not really a transmission from the Brahma Heaven. Its proponents just claimed it was, and in that way got people to believe in them. However, the recitation of the mantra was able to turn Ananda's spirit and soul upside-down and he fell into a stupor as if asleep, dreaming, or drunk. Without realizing what was happening he went into the house of prostitution. The mantra "which came from the Brahma Heaven," had rendered him totally oblivious and had totally confused his self-nature.

"Basically Ananda was a sage who had been certified as having attained the first fruition. Then why was the mantra purported to have come from the Brahma Heaven able to confuse him?" you wonder.

He became confused because he had concentrated on studying the sutras and had not been attentive to samadhi-power; and so although he had attained the first fruition; his samadhi-power was still insufficient. Therefore when he encountered this kind of demon he was confused by her, and the daughter of Matangi **drew him onto an impure mat**.

Ananda was extremely handsome. His features were almost as perfect as the thirty-two fine marks of the Buddha. Ananda's skin was snowy white and glistened like silver, sparkled like frost. Most Indians had dark complexions but Ananda's skin was extremely soft, supple, smooth, and especially fair. That is why Matangi's daughter was infatuated with Ananda the moment she laid eyes on him and went running to tell her mother that she wanted Ananda.

"He's a disciple of the Buddha," her mother said. "How can you want him? He's a bhikshu and cannot marry. You can't have him."

"That doesn't make any difference to me," replied her daughter. "Mother, you're going to have to think of a way to trap Ananda for me. If I can't marry Ananda I won't go on living," she said obstinately.

Her desire was so overpowering that it was a matter of life and death.

"Ah," thought Matangi, "She loves him so much. I'll have to think of a way to do what cannot be done." So she used the mantra, a deviant artifice from the Kapila religion, and recited until Ananda became hypnotized. He followed her in a daze like a drunken beggar, in such a stupor that he couldn't tell east from west, or north from south. He went right into the house and followed Matangi's daughter into her room and onto the bed.

Sutra:

With her licentious body she stroked and rubbed him until he was on the verge of destroying the precept-substance.

Commentary:

This was a dangerous spot to be in! **With her licentious body she** caressed him until **he was on the verge of destroying the precept-substance**. He still hadn't broken it. This is an important point. When one receives the precepts one becomes endowed with a certain substance, which, if destroyed, is as serious as if your very life had been cut off. It is extremely important for people who have left the home-life not to break precepts. If precepts are broken, you might just as well die. As for Ananda, if the text said that his precept-substance was "already" destroyed, it would mean it would be all over for him, Ananda would have fallen, and in the future he would have had a great deal of difficulty in cultivating successfully.

Why did Matangi's daughter have such a compelling attraction for Ananda? It stemmed from the fact that Ananda and Matangi's daughter had been married to one another in five hundred former lives. Because they had been a married couple in so many former lives, as soon as she saw Ananda this time, her old habits took over, and she fell madly in love with him. Ananda had been her husband before and she was determined to have him for a husband again. Because of those seeds passed down life after life, she was now willing to sacrifice everything – even her very life – for the sake of her love for Ananda.

D4 The Tathagata compassionately rescues him.
E1 He quickly returns and speaks the mantra.

Sutra:

The Tathagata, knowing Ananda was being taken advantage of by the indecent artifice, finished the meal and immediately began his return journey. The king, great officials, elders, and laypeople followed along after the Buddha, desiring to hear the essentials of dharma.

Commentary:

Whenever the Buddha accepted an offering he always spoke the dharma after the meal for the sake of the vegetarian host. Only after speaking the dharma would he return to the sublime abode of the Jeta Grove. But this time there were special circumstances. **The Tathagata, knowing Ananda was being taken advantage of by the indecent artifice, finished the meal and immediately began his return journey.** Knowing that Ananda had met with difficulty and was on the verge of destroying the precept-substance, the Buddha ate quickly, and as soon as he finished he immediately returned to the sublime abode of the Jeta Grove. In fact, I imagine he did not eat very much, since his beloved disciple and cousin and personal attendant was in trouble. The Buddha thought, "Ah, my attendant is being waylaid by demons. He's been captured by demons. How can this be?"

The king, great officials, elders, and laypeople followed along after the Buddha, desiring to hear the essentials of the dharma. Everyone knew that there was some important reason why the Buddha had not spoken dharma for the vegetarian host after the meal. They thought that the reason for the hasty retreat would certainly be announced, so everyone – the king, the officials, the elders, and the laypeople – followed the Buddha back to the sublime abode of the Jeta Grove. Why? Everyone had forgotten everything else but the single-minded desire to understand whatever important principle of dharma was about to be spoken. They didn't know what had come up that was so unusual. Everyone was anxious to hear what the Buddha would say.

Sutra:

Then the World Honored One emitted a hundred rays of jeweled and fearless light from his crown. Within the light appeared a thousand-petalled precious lotus, upon which was seated a transformation-body Buddha in full-lotus posture, proclaiming a spiritual mantra.

Commentary:

Shakyamuni Buddha, **the World Honored One, emitted a hundred rays of jeweled and fearless light from his crown**. The hundreds of rays can represent the hundred realms. **Within the light appeared a thousand-petalled** jeweled **precious lotus**, which can represent the thousand suchnesses. These meanings can be investigated gradually. Now it is enough to understand the passage in general. **From his crown**, the crown of his head, were emitted a hundred rays of jeweled light and from these lights radiated fearless lights. The rays of "fearless lights" showed possession of a great awesome virtue. Fearing nothing, they were able to subdue all heavenly demons and externalists. No mantra whatever could withstand them. Not even one "purported to have come from the Brahma Heaven."

The hundred rays of jeweled light also brought forth a thousand-petalled jeweled lotus, **upon which was seated a transformation-body Buddha in full-lotus posture**. In "full lotus-posture" you sit with your legs crossed over one another, your feet resting on the tops of opposite thighs. There is a great deal of merit and virtue involved in sitting in full lotus.

This transformation-body Buddha was **proclaiming a spiritual mantra**. He pronounced the Shurangama Mantra. For Shakyamuni Buddha to have a transformation-body Buddha speak the mantra represents the secret cause within the secret cause, the king of kings of mantras. The Shurangama Mantra is extremely important. If you who study the Buddhadharma can learn the Shurangama Mantra in this life, you will not have been a human being in vain. If you do not learn the Shurangama Mantra, it will be like climbing a mountain made of the seven jewels – gold, silver, crystal, lapis lazuli, mother-of-pearl, red pearl, and carnelian – and coming back down empty-handed. You arrive at the top of the mountain and you think about picking up some gold or perhaps some pearls, but then wonder if you should take silver instead. In the end you can't decide which ones it would be best to take and so you come away without any at all. That is the situation of people who can't memorize the Shurangama Mantra. So I hope that everyone will at the very least study hard enough so that they are able to recite it from memory. Not to speak of several weeks' effort, it is worth several years' effort if needed. It is extremely valuable. And this opportunity you have now to encounter it is extremely rare, very hard to come by. It is "the unsurpassed, profound, subtle, wonderful dharma." There is nothing higher, nothing deeper. The Buddha used the Shurangama Mantra to save Ananda, who had already attained the first fruition of arhatship. Now, if you ordinary people do not rely on the Shurangama Mantra, how can you end birth and death? Therefore each of you should resolve to take my advice in this.

I will tell you a story that illustrates the merit of sitting in full lotus-posture. Once there was a bhikshu who did not cultivate, but concentrated instead on reciting sutras and repentances for the dead for money. Whenever someone died, he would accept requests to take the deceased across the sea of suffering by reciting sutras and performing repentances.

One day he was returning to the monastery after having spent the day reciting sutras for the deceased. He passed a house with a dog in the yard. The dog began to bark at him, and he overheard the wife inside the house say to her husband: "Go see who it is." Then the bhikshu saw the husband peer out the slit in the curtain and reply, "Oh, it's just that ghost who peddles sutras and repentances."

He passed on by, but the words echoed in his ears. Why had that man called him a "ghost who peddles sutras and repentances?" Why hadn't he called him a "Buddha" who peddles sutras and repentances? Or an "immortal sage" who peddles sutras and repentances? As he continued on his way to the monastery, it suddenly began to rain and he took shelter under a bridge. "I guess I'll sit in meditation," he thought, and he pulled up his legs in full lotus-posture. After he had sat for a while, two ghosts came by. When they reached the spot where he was sitting they suddenly stopped, and one said to the other, "There's a golden pagoda! Hurry up! Let's start bowing. The sharira (relics) of the Buddha are kept in golden pagodas! If we bow to the Buddha's relics our offenses will soon disappear." With that the two began to bow. After they had bowed for a while, the legs of the "ghost who peddled sutras and repentances" started to hurt, and in order to be more comfortable, he released the full lotus-posture into half-lotus, that is, with the left leg above, the right leg beneath, and the left foot resting on the right thigh. The next time the two ghosts came up from a bow they noticed something strange. "Hey," said one to the other. "That golden pagoda just turned into a silver pagoda! Do you see that?"

"So what?" said the other. "Silver pagodas are still something special. We should keep bowing." So the two of them kept bowing. They bowed for about half an hour or an hour, or maybe it was only twenty minutes; there was no clock, so there's no way to know. Soon enough the bhikshu's legs hurt again. He unfolded them and lazily stretched them out, just like some people do when they are tired of sitting in meditation. "I think I'll lie down," he thought. But just then the two bowing ghosts caught a glimpse of their pagoda turning into a pile of mud. "Hey! Look at that!" one cried. "Quick! Let's clobber it." Realizing the ghosts were about to beat him up, the bhikshu froze in fear and slipped neatly back into full lotus just in the nick of time. "Oh!" the two ghosts cried in unison. "It does have the Buddha's relics in it! It's going through all kinds of weird changes. One minute it's a golden pagoda, the next a silver pagoda, and then it turns into mud. We'd better just keep bowing no matter what happens next," and they continued non-stop until dawn.

The incident had a lasting effect on the "ghost who peddled sutras and repentances." He sat there thinking, "If I sit in full lotus there is a golden pagoda, if I sit in half lotus there is a silver pagoda, and if I don't sit at all there's nothing but a pile of mud. I had better start to cultivate and stop peddling sutras and repentances." He buried himself in the task at hand and worked diligently at his cultivation. After he had cultivated, he eventually became enlightened and was given the name Dhyana Master Gui Bi, "Pressured by Ghosts," because if it hadn't been for those two ghosts who were threatening to beat him up, he might have continued to procrastinate and never gotten around to cultivating.

E2 The messenger is sent and Ananda is rescued.

Sutra:

He commanded Manjushri to take the mantra and go provide protection, and, when the evil mantra was extinguished, to lend support, and to encourage Ananda and Matangi's daughter to return to where the Buddha was.

Commentary:

It takes a person with great wisdom to rescue a stupid person. Although Ananda had certified to the first fruition of arhatship, his samadhi-power was not enough to keep him from being confused by Matangi's false mantra. To save him, the Buddha manifested a hundred rays of jeweled light, and a thousand-petalled lotus, and a transformation-body Buddha who spoke the Shurangama Mantra.

Still, Ananda was a long way off, and so the Buddha needed a member of the Sangha to take the mantra and go save Ananda. So Shakyamuni Buddha **commanded Manjushri to take the mantra and go provide protection**. He was to go to the house of prostitution, the home of Matangi, and rescue and protect Ananda. Within the Shurangama Mantra are several phrases that are specifically directed at breaking up externalist teachings; in this its efficaciousness is unsurpassed. As soon as Manjushri went to Matangi's house and recited the Shurangama Mantra, the evil mantra was dispelled. The "mantra purported to have come from the Brahma Heaven" was no longer efficacious. Ananda woke up.

The Bodhisattva Manjushri then needed **to lend support, and to encourage Ananda and Matangi's daughter to return to where the Buddha was**. Ananda had been confused by the mantra-trick and had just "come to," so he was disoriented and had no idea where he was; it was as if he had just awakened from a dream. So Manjushri Bodhisattva lent him support, took hold of him and pulled him up.

"Why did he encourage Matangi's daughter?" you ask.

If he had not encouraged her at that time, her own life would have been in danger and perhaps his as well. She was so distraught she might have tried to kill Manjushri Bodhisattva for having taken away the one she loved so much. Had he not reassured her at that point, she would have been beside herself. Who knows what she might have done out of her jealousy?

Manjushri Bodhisattva said, "You are a very beautiful girl. I can see you are a good woman. Come along with me and we will go talk things over with the Buddha and find out if your wishes can be fulfilled. I'll put in a good word for you. It will all work out, I'm sure." He chose his words carefully, expediently, being discreet and tactful so as not to arouse her anger or cause her to harm or kill herself. With Manjushri supporting Ananda and encouraging Matangi's daughter, they returned to where the Buddha was, to the sublime abode of the Jeta Grove.

From "Thus I have heard" to this point in the text is called the "preface." The preface includes the "testimony of faith," that is, the section that fulfills the six fulfillments, and certifies that the sutra can be believed.

The entire preface is also called the "postscript," although it comes at the beginning of the sutra.

"Isn't that a contradiction?" one may ask. "How can it be both a preface and a postscript?"

When the sutra was first spoken, this initial section of text did not exist. It was written by Ananda at the time the sutras were compiled, and for this reason is called the "postscript."

The preface is also called the "general preface" because other sutras also have similar prefaces. It is called the "foreword" as well, because it is placed at the beginning of the sutra, even though it was written after the sutra was spoken.

The second part of the preface is called the "prologue." It explains the causes and conditions involving Ananda and Matangi's daughter that led to the speaking of this sutra.

It is important for those who study the Buddhadharma to be able to distinguish the various sections of the sutra text. In this way one can come to "deeply enter the sutra treasury." Boring your way in you will come to have "wisdom like the sea." In fact you should think like this: "It is I who spoke this sutra. Its principles have come forth from my heart." If you can be like that, in such a way that the sutra and your basic substance become one, then there will be no deep and no shallow. You will no longer feel that the study of sutras is difficult, but will take it as a matter of course.

The text of the *Shurangama Sutra* is extremely well written. Of all the Chinese classics, such as the *Four Books* and the *Five Classics*, none is a finer piece of literature. I regard the *Shurangama Sutra* as the ultimate in literary texts, wonderful to the extreme. People who wish to study Chinese should not miss the opportunity to penetrate the *Shurangama Sutra* text. Anyone who does so will have a thorough foundation in the Chinese language and will be able to understand all of Chinese literature.

B2 Text proper.
C1 A complete explanation of the wonderful samadhi for accomplishing Buddhahood.
D1 Ananda requests samadhi.
E1 He regrets excessive learning and requests samadhi.

Sutra:

Ananda saw the Buddha, bowed, and wept sorrowfully, regretting that from time without beginning he had been preoccupied with erudition and had not yet perfected his strength in the Way. He respectfully and repeatedly requested an explanation of the very first expedients of the wonderful shamatha, samapatti, and dhyana, by means of which the Tathagatas of the ten directions had realized bodhi.

Commentary:

Manjushri Bodhisattva had used the Shurangama Mantra to rescue Ananda, and after a time on the road, during which a gentle breeze probably sprang up, brushing softly against their faces and bringing Ananda awake from his dream, they reached the Jeta Grove.

Ananda saw the Buddha, bowed, and wept sorrowfully. His grief was extreme. Sorrow welled up from deep within him and he wept silently, out of remorse. The finest word in this section of text is the word **regretting**, because it indicates that Ananda had awakened. If he hadn't been regretful, then upon returning to the Jeta Grove he still would not have been able to be honest about what had happened. He would have returned to where the Buddha was and acted as if nothing had happened. He would have put on a front. The very best thing about Ananda was that he didn't put on a front. He came back, faced the Buddha and bowed, without any pretences, because he knew he had to correct his errors and change his ways. He wanted the Buddha to teach him new paths. Because of this, he was able later to realize enlightenment.

From time without beginning means not just this time in this present life, but many lives, many eons past, from the time Ananda very first became a person. No one could say when that was, so it is referred to as time without beginning.

He had been preoccupied with erudition. Life after life, time after time he had concentrated on his studies, so that he had developed "great learning and strong memory"; but he had neglected to develop, **had not yet perfected his strength in the Way**, that is his samadhi-power. His samadhi-power was very meager, extremely immature. Fortunately, Shakyamuni Buddha had rescued him, so he placed himself on the ground in obeisance, paying deference with his body and mind. **He respectfully and repeatedly** bowed over and over again, without being the least bit lazy about it.

He **requested** of Shakyamuni Buddha that the Buddha explain the principle by which **the Tathagatas of the ten directions had realized bodhi**. He didn't ask the Tathagatas, the Thus Come Ones of the ten directions to speak; you should not misread the text at this point. If Ananda was asking the Buddhas of the ten directions to speak, what was Shakyamuni Buddha doing there? He was Shakyamuni Buddha's disciple; would he have ignored what was right before him and gone seeking instead for some distant Buddhas of the ten directions? No; the text means that he turned to Shakyamuni Buddha and asked him to explain what doctrine the Tathagatas of the ten directions had relied on to become enlightened. Ananda didn't know what skill he ought to develop in order to realize Buddhahood; but he had heard of three kinds of samadhi – **shamatha, samapatti, and dhyana**; so he brought them up and referred to them each as **wonderful**, in order to emphasize them.

As soon as Shakyamuni Buddha heard his request, he knew Ananda was an outsider: that he didn't know about the samadhi for realizing Buddhahood. And what is the samadhi for the realization of Buddhahood? It is the Shurangama Samadhi. It was just because Ananda didn't understand the Shurangama dharma-door that he proceeded to bring up a lot of arguments, as the text describes below.

The very first expedients. Ananda wanted to know about expedient dharma-doors for the beginner, the easiest way to start cultivating, the simplest methods of practice.

Some people have immediately become prejudiced. "Ananda concentrated on erudition and almost ended up by falling," they say. "Obviously it is useless to study a lot. I'm going to cultivate samadhi exclusively, and not study at all." This one-sided view is not in accord with the Middle Way. The principle of being in accord with the Middle Way is to be neither too far to the left or too far to the right, or too far in front or too far behind. Ananda was also prejudiced because he concentrated on learning and neglected samadhi. But if you concentrate exclusively on samadhi and neglect learning, your wisdom won't develop. You must study to gain understanding, and you must also practice to gain samadhi, and then the two will be integrated. At the Buddhist lecture hall we both investigate sutras and meditate. By putting aside everything else and not letting your mind wander to the north, south, east, and west, you can concentrate your whole attention on the Buddhadharma. Don't waste valuable time. Don't just chatter on at random or do things which are of no benefit. You can't make squares and circles if you don't have a compass, and in the same way, you have to follow the rules in your daily practice. In the Chan hall, when the wooden fish is hit three times it is a signal to stop and be still. During that period no one should talk. Those who do may receive a beating from Wei Tuo Bodhisattva's jeweled pestle.

"He hasn't hit me yet," you say.

He hasn't gotten angry yet. But when he does, things get serious fast. So everyone should take care to genuinely follow the rules. When the rules are followed, there can be successful accomplishments. Don't be so casual.

The people in this assembly are basically very well-behaved, but just in case some may have forgotten the importance of the rules

I am mentioning them once again. During the period set aside for study of the *Shurangama Sutra*, all should single-mindedly apply themselves to the study of the sutra and to their meditation. If you do, I can guarantee there will be a response and you will have some accomplishment. If you do not become greatly enlightened, you will certainly gain a little enlightenment. You won't miss out on the merit and virtue. If you are sincere and single-minded during this period of study and practice, you will certainly gain some advantages. I am not cheating you. However, if you don't follow the rules you'll be like the Mongolian who goes to the opera and misses out altogether.[9] You've come from far away for no other reason than to study the dharma, and that makes me very happy – so much so, that no matter how hard I have to work I don't fear the suffering. During the dharma assembly I am determined to research and explain the sutra, do everything in my power to bring the sutra out in the open for you. It is my hope that all of you will obtain the advantages to be gained from the Buddhadharma. However, although I say this, whether you listen or not is still up to you. If you chose not to listen, there is nothing I can do, because I am not you and you are not me.

You can also say that you are me and I am you. How? We are connected to one another in that we breathe the same air. Thought of it in this way, everyone becomes one identical substance, and so you shouldn't obstruct me and I shouldn't obstruct you. Everyone investigates the Buddhadharma together and becomes enlightened together. If there is one who has not yet become enlightened, then I will not have fulfilled my responsibility.

Pay no attention to whether the Buddhadharma seems deep or shallow. You should resolve: "If I understand, I will investigate further, and if I don't understand, I want to investigate even more." Understanding a little is a lot better than not understanding anything at all. You should say to yourself: "If I understand one

---

[9]. When someone is totally out of it, the Chinese use this phrase to describe him, saying he's like the Mongolian who goes to see a Chinese opera and comes away without having understood a word that was said.

word of the sutra the dharma master is lecturing, that's one word which I never understood before, and that makes it worthwhile; I've obtained advantage." The value of that single word is inexpressibly great.

Why was Ananda unable to resist the mantra "formerly of the Brahma Heaven," since he had after all reached the first stage of arhatship? It was because in the past, in cultivating samadhi, he had used his conscious mind. The conscious mind is subject to production and extinction and is not ultimate. A samadhi which is developed by using the thought-processes of the conscious mind, such as the "stop and contemplate" method of the Tian Tai teaching, involves the eighth consciousness. It does not address the nature which is neither produced nor extinguished. If one bases one's work on the nature which is neither produced nor extinguished, one can cultivate a samadhi which is neither produced nor extinguished. That is a genuine samadhi, one that cannot be moved by outside forces.

But Ananda used only his conscious mind in whatever he did. For instance, when he listened to sutras, he used his mind to remember the principles the Buddha spoke. But the conscious mind which remembered the principles cannot lead to the fundamental solution. So when Ananda encountered a demonic state, he failed to recognize it.

It is essential for people who cultivate the Way to be able to recognize their environment. If you can recognize states when they arise, you won't be influenced by them. They won't move you. Samadhi-power can be victorious over any state whether it be good, bad, agreeable, or disagreeable. In the midst of them all, you can remain "thus, thus, unmoving, completely and eternally bright." That is genuine samadhi-power.

If happy situations make you happy and sad events make you sad, you're being influenced by states. If you keep jumping from joy to anger, to sorrow, to happiness, you're being influenced by states. Not to be influenced by external states is to be like a mirror: when something appears it is reflected, when it passes there is stillness. The basic substance of the mirror is always bright. It cannot be defiled. To have samadhi-power and not to move is to have genuine wisdom, thorough understanding. It is very important to understand this.

"Shamatha" is a Sanskrit word which is interpreted to mean "still and pure." However, it is a stillness and purity which is forced. One attains a kind of samadhi by deliberately forcing the mind to have samadhi-power and not to strike up false thinking. It is not the ultimate samadhi. It is merely a kind of expedient device cultivated by those of the small vehicle. At the very beginning of his teaching, Shakyamuni Buddha taught this method to those of the two vehicles.

"Samapatti," also Sanskrit, is interpreted to mean "contemplation and illumination" of such principles as the twelve links of conditioned causation and the four truths.

"Dhyana," also Sanskrit, is interpreted to mean "thought-cultivation" or "still consideration." One uses the mind to trace the coming and going of thoughts, in much the same way as in the cultivation of "stopping and contemplating." The Tian Tai school lists three stoppings which relate to the three contemplations: empty, false, and the middle. That teaching is basically a good one, but it is nothing compared to the Shurangama Samadhi. Dhyana can be ultimate or non-ultimate. Those of the small vehicle cultivate using the conscious mind; they make discriminations using the conscious mind. Since the conscious mind is subject to production and extinction, its use will not lead to the genuine solid samadhi of the Buddha.

"What should we cultivate?" you wonder.

The Shurangama Samadhi.

"How do we cultivate the Shurangama Samadhi?"

The sutra text will gradually make that clear. If you attend to the explanation of the sutra and understand it, you will know how to achieve the Shurangama Samadhi. You won't be left in a daze[10]. At present you don't know where to begin and are like someone standing in a dense forest on the side of a mountain while trying to see what the face of the mountain looks like. As the poet Su Dong Po put it:

I can't tell what Lu mountain really looks like
Because I myself am standing on the mountain.

If he had walked away from it, though, he could have seen. Now we are within the Shurangama Samadhi; you are boring your way into the Shurangama Samadhi and if you continue to progress you will gradually come to see it clearly. Then you will know you have obtained a real gem. You'll be able to climb the jeweled mountain, grab two big fistfuls of gold, fill your arms with the gems and go back down the mountain. Even if you continually take from it, the supply will never be exhausted. It will be an endless supply, more than you could ever use in a lifetime. In the future you will be able to achieve the Shurangama enlightenment and then go on to teach and transform living beings.

Sutra:

At that time bodhisattvas as numerous as the sands of the Ganges, great arhats, pratyekas, and others from the ten directions, were also present. Pleased at the opportunity to listen, they withdrew silently to their seats to receive the sagely instruction.

Commentary:

That time is when Ananda asked Shakyamuni Buddha to explain how the Tathagatas of the ten directions had realized bodhi, that is, right enlightenment. It has already been mentioned that **bodhisattvas as numerous as the sands of the Ganges** were present, so this refers to yet more bodhisattvas. The Ganges River is miles wide and its sands are as fine as flour, like fine motes of dust. During a storm, the sands and stones fly about, as dangerous as desert dust-storms. Now, how many grains of such fine sand would you estimate there to be in a river some 15 miles wide?

---

10. The *leng* (楞) of *leng yan* (楞嚴), Shurangama, means "a daze" and is the state a Sangha-member is said to enter when he or she commits the Shurangama Mantra to memory; they are said to be *leng ban nian* (楞半年), "dazed for half a year."

Could you figure it? Probably even the best mathematician would be unable to come up with a number. Since the Ganges' sands are unreckonable, they are used to represent a non-existent number, a number beyond all calculations.

A bodhisattva, an "enlightened being," is also called "a living being with a great Way-mind." No matter how badly people may act towards him, he doesn't hold it against them. He absolutely never becomes irritated, never loses his temper. His Way-mind is firm and vast. A bodhisattva is also called a "dedicated lord," since he has already resolved to be a bodhisattva.

The ten directions. The *Amitabha Sutra* speaks of the Buddhas of the six directions, but it does not mention the ten directions. The six are north, east, south, and west, up, and down. The additional four are northeast, southeast, northwest, and southwest. I say, though, that basically there isn't even one direction. The earth is round, so what directions can there be? But the Buddhist sutras speak of ten directions, and besides, the "round" I speak of is not yet an established fact; so don't rely on what I say. As I see it, the world is transformed from a single source; everything is within the great light treasury, the Tathagata store, where there is no north, south, east, west, or the four intermediate points, or up or down. That is the way I see it, but perhaps it is not right.

There were, not little arhats, but **great arhats**, whose Way was great. It does not mean that they were physically big, that they were particularly tall. It means that their dharma-nature was great, the power of their teaching was great, their cultivation of virtue was great.

Arhat has three meanings:

1. Worthy of offerings.

They were worthy of the offerings of gods and people. In the causal ground a bhikshu "begs for his food" and as a result, as an arhat, he is "worthy of offerings."

2. Killer of thieves.

The Buddha taught people not to kill. Isn't killing a violation of precepts? No, not in this case, because the thieves referred to are not external thieves, but the thieves within you.

"What are the thieves within us?" you wonder.

There are the thieves of ignorance, the thieves of affliction, and the six thieves – the eyes, ears, nose, tongue, body, and mind. Unbeknownst to you, they rob you. You don't realize it, but when your eyes look at things, your essential energies were originally full, but once you start looking at a lot of things the thieves which are your eyes steal your valuable treasures. When you listen to things all the time, then your hearing-nature disperses and your vital energies are stolen away. You shouldn't say, "My eyes are my best friend and my ears always help me out, my nose smells things and my tongue distinguishes tastes – they are all very helpful."

No. These six thieves steal your unsurpassed true treasures. They plunder the wealth of your household without your even realizing it. You've got a thief for a neighbor but don't even realize it; you say, "Don't blame him for stealing my things!" This is a very, very important point I am making. Don't be mistaken and think I am just joking. If you hadn't lost these things, you would have realized Buddhahood long ago. Look into it, think it over. You feel you haven't lost anything? Well, I know that the things you have lost are priceless treasures no money could buy. You've lost them and you still think everything is just fine. "My eyes can see so far – clearer than anyone else's," you say and think that this is good. But the more clearly you see the more essential energy is lost.

At this point you say, "Dharma master, one of your lectures is more than enough. You haven't said anything that has the least bit of principle to it."

Since you haven't yet understood what I say, of course you are going to think it lacks principle. Wait until you understand and then you will know that what I say is genuine principle.

3. Not born.

Not born, arhats are also not extinguished; they are not subject to production and extinction. They have attained the patience of the non-production of phenomena. They do not have to undergo birth and death again. That is, they have "done what had to be done and do not undergo any further existence." They will not fall into the three realms, although they haven't attained *anuttarasamyaksambodhi*, the unsurpassed proper and equal right enlightenment.

In the *Sutra in Forty-two Sections* the Buddha said,

> "Be careful not to believe your own mind: your mind cannot be believed. Once you have attained arhatship, then you can believe your own mind."

"Why can't one believe one's own mind?" you ask.

Because your mind is false thinking, and if you believe false thinking you will do false things; if you do false things, you must undergo a false birth and death. If you don't believe the false thoughts, if you don't trust your own mind, then you can avoid the false birth and death.

"When can one believe one's own mind?"

When you attain the fourth stage of arhatship you can believe your own mind. Until then you shouldn't choose to listen to yourself instead of to the advice of a good and wise advisor. The right thing to do is to listen to the instructions of a good and wise one.

Pratyekas, pratyekabuddhas – those enlightened to conditions and solitarily enlightened ones – **and others** were also present. **Pleased at the opportunity to listen, they withdrew silently to their seats to receive the sagely instructions**. There were many, many more beings as well, not just one or two, who all wanted to hear the sound of the dharma the Buddha was speaking, the wonderful sagely instructions, the doctrines of the holy ones. They really liked to listen, and they sat silently to one side to hear the Buddha speak.

CHAPTER 5

The Way to Shamatha

D2 The Tathagata replies about Shamatha.
E1 He explains the wonderful samadhi from beginning to end.
F1 He explains the general name of the Buddha's samadhi causing Ananda to know the causes cultivated and the fruition obtained by all Buddhas.

Sutra:

In the midst of the great assembly, the World Honored One then extended his golden arm, rubbed Ananda's crown, and said to Ananda and the great assembly, "There is a samadhi called the King of the Foremost Shurangama at the Great Buddha's Summit Replete with the Myriad Practices; it is a path wonderfully adorned and the single door through which the Tathagatas of the ten directions gained transcendence. You should now listen attentively." Ananda bowed down to receive the compassionate instruction humbly.

Commentary:

Originally this section appeared later in the text, but the elder Dharma Master Yuan Ying saw that it did not fit well there and so he moved it to this place. I have also looked into this several times and I agree that this section of text should appear here. It does not seem appropriate in the other place; it does not tie with what proceeds and follows it there. Here it fits in sequence.

Then means when the great arhats and the great bodhisattvas as many as the sands in the Ganges River had all assembled from the ten directions, wishing to receive the sagely instruction, and when Ananda had implored the Buddha to explain the initial expedients of cultivation by which the Tathagatas of the ten directions had attained wonderful *shamatha*, wonderful *samapatti*, and wonderful *dhyana*: it was then that **the World Honored One extended his golden arm** and **rubbed Ananda's crown**.

The Buddha's arm was naturally golden; it isn't that he had gilded it. In Buddhism, rubbing the crown of the head represents compassionate loving protection for living beings. Now the Buddha, too, speaks of love, but this is not the ordinary love; rather it is a compassionate, universally pervasive love which protects all beings and causes all their demon-obstacles to disappear. It is not the selfish, emotional love which most people refer to. Take careful note of this point.

Of all the kinds of love in the world, the strongest is parents' love for their children. No matter how bad a child may act toward his parents, they'll still forgive him. "He's just a child," they'll say. "He doesn't understand things." Even when a small child strikes his father or scolds his mother, the parents simply regard it with amusement, and don't feel that he has done anything wrong.

"Why are parents like that?" you ask.

Because they love their children so much. The love of parents for their children is deeper and fiercer than the love between husband and wife.

I admire Americans in this respect. By the time their children are eighteen years old they are allowed to stand on their own. Sometimes parents don't pay any attention to them after that age. That is fine; it is very good to raise sons and daughters to be independent of their parents. The only problem is that the children are often not experienced enough at that age to exercise mature judgement and so they easily get off to a wrong start. They are easily blown over by the winds of current trends or are pulled into the water by friends who are not upright, and once they have landed in the water it is not easy for them to get back out by themselves. As a result, at the present time in America there are many young people who don't recognize their country, who don't know the meaning of a home, even to the point that they don't even know what they themselves are all about. From morning to night they take LSD, marijuana and other drugs until they lose all clarity and are totally confused from dawn to dusk. If you ask them what they do for their country they say, "What does it have to do with me?" If you inquire about their family they say, "I don't have any." You might say they have left home, and yet of course they haven't, although they claim to have no home. They're caught in a total vacuum and that to me is most pitiful.

The Buddha's loving protection for all living beings is like that of parents for their children yet stronger. Rubbing the crown is an expression of that loving protection. Just as an acupuncture needle revitalizes your blood and energy, so, as he rubs your crown, the Buddha's hand emits light which dispels all the darkness within you. In this way he relieves you of all evil and increases your good roots.

"I've missed the opportunity," you lament. "If only I had been born when the Buddha was in the world, I could have asked the Buddha to rub my crown so my evil would be eradicated and my good roots increased."

Who told you not to be born at the time when the Buddha was in the world? Who told you to be born now? You can't blame anyone but yourself. And regret is of no use. Don't be regretful. You can't blame other people. You can't blame heaven. And you can't blame the Buddha. We have been born now, so now we should study the Buddhadharma. If we are sincere enough the Buddha will be moved and will come and rub our crowns in expression of his loving protection. Although the Buddha has entered nirvana, his pure dharma body pervades all places. You should not think that the Buddha has left us. The Buddha is always with us; it's just that we cannot see him. All our daily activities – walking, standing, sitting, lying down, eating, getting dressed – take place within the Buddha's dharma body. So we are always with the Buddha. It is just that the eyes of ordinary people haven't the spiritual penetration to see the Buddha.

The Buddha rubbed Ananda's crown and said to Ananda and the great assembly, "There is a samadhi called the King of the Foremost Shurangama at the Great Buddha's Summit Replete with the Myriad Practices; it is a path wonderfully adorned and the single door through which the Tathagatas of the ten directions gained transcendence." Not only Ananda but everyone in the great assembly as well – the great bhikshus, great bodhisattvas, the king, elders, and laypeople – was instructed by the Buddha in the ultimately durable King of Samadhis, which includes within it all the samadhis of all the myriad methods of cultivation. All Buddhas of all places have reached Buddhahood along this wonderful, splendid path and through this one door.

You should now listen attentively. "Listen carefully. Pay attention," the Buddha told Ananda. "Don't be nonchalant when you listen to me speak sutras. Take all of your essential energy and pour it into your ears. Don't strike up false thoughts. Don't sit there during the sutra lecture and be thinking about running out on the streets to see what is happening."

Ananda bowed down to receive the compassionate instruction humbly. When Ananda heard the Buddha say that, he stood up and then bowed, and humbly awaited the holy teaching. He remained kneeling ready to listen to what the Buddha was about to say about the Shurangama, the King of Samadhis.

F2 He explains the path of Shamatha, causing Ananda to awaken to the secret cause and have a great blossoming forth of complete understanding.
G1 He destroys upside-down thinking by speaking of the empty Tathagata store.
H1 The Tathagata smashes the false and reveals the true.
I1 He casts out and destroys the false mind to which Ananda attaches by opening the way to Shamatha.
J1 He establishes that Ananda grasps at the mind.
K1 He asks him about his resolve based on grasping at the appearance he saw.

Sutra:

The Buddha said to Ananda, "You and I are of the same family and share the affection of a natural relationship. At the time of your initial resolve, what were the outstanding characteristics which you saw in my dharma that caused you to suddenly cast aside the deep kindness and love found in the world?"

Commentary:

Ananda waited humbly to receive the Buddha's compassionate instruction. But first the Buddha questioned him about his reasons for leaving the home-life.

The Buddha said to Ananda, "You and I are of the same family and share the affection of a natural relationship." Ananda and the Buddha were paternal first cousins. The Buddha was saying, "You and I are like brothers." One speaks of the "affection of a natural relationship" because in the world, natural relationships take precedent over everything else. Such relationships form a natural cycle. After being a son or daughter you become a father or mother and then you become a grandfather or grandmother, and if you are filial to your father and mother, your children will be filial to you. If you aren't filial to your parents, your sons and daughters won't be filial to you. It is said:

> Of all the kinds of good practices
> Filial piety is the first.
> Of all the myriad evils,
> Licentiousness is the worst.

In China, filial feeling is considered the root of goodness, its most fundamental form. There are twenty-four paragons of filial virtue in Chinese history, among whom some of the most notable were Tan Xiang, Meng Zhong, and Wang Xiang.

Tan Xiang's father and mother were sick and wanted some sweet melon to eat, of a kind grown in northern China. However, it was winter and the snow was heavy on the ground, so how could there be any melons? Tan Xiang planted a melon seed in the frozen earth, stretched out on top of it to warm the ground, and began to cry. "How can I get this melon to grow quickly so I can harvest it for my parents?" he lamented. He cried and cried until suddenly something very strange happened. It's not certain whether it was a response evoked from a bodhisattva or from a Buddha or from a ghost or spirit, but right then and there a melon grew, blossomed, and bore fruit for Tan Xiang to harvest and carry home to his parents, a miraculous response to his one true thought of sincere filial regard. So it's said, "Tan Xiang cried for melons."

Meng Zhong's parents wanted some bamboo shoots to eat, and unable to find any, he began to weep. He wept until he suddenly saw tender bamboo shoot sprouting in the spots where his tears had fallen. Such strange events are incomprehensible. Don't try to use your thinking mind to figure them out. "Meng Zhong's tears sprouted the bamboo."

In the dead of winter, Wang Xiang's parents both fell ill and wanted some carp to eat. Wang Xiang didn't have any money to buy fish, and all the waters were frozen over, so he opened his clothing and lay down on the ice. In northern China the ice gets very thick in the winter, but his warm skin melted the ice through. It was his plan to fish for a carp through the hole, but suddenly a carp jumped out of the hole all by itself. Wang Xiang hurried home with it and told his parents what had happened. "We won't eat the carp," his parents decided, "because it is probably the son or grandson of the Dragon King who sent it to us." Although they didn't eat the carp, their illness was cured nevertheless. "Wang Hsiang lay down to catch a carp."

True filial conduct can move heaven. Sons and daughters should pay particular attention to the practice of filial piety. The great Emperor Shun of China was so filial that elephants were moved to plow for him and birds did his weeding.

At the time of your initial resolve, what were the outstanding characteristics which you saw in my dharma that caused you to suddenly cast aside the deep kindness and love found in the world? The Buddha asked Ananda what first made him decide to renounce worldly love and leave the home-life; what good states of mind did he experience that led to his resolve.

In this world the kindness of parents is very great and the love between couples is particularly intense. If people could transform the love which exists between married couples into love for the study and practice of the Buddhadharma, then there wouldn't be anyone who didn't realize Buddhahood. Unfortunately, most people can't do that. If you can, that is inconceivably fine.

What made Ananda pay no further attention to his parent's deep kindness or his wife's emotional love? What made him totally disregard everything except following the Buddha and leaving the home-life?

Sutra:

Ananda said to the Buddha, "I saw the Tathagata's thirty-two characteristics, which were so supremely wonderful, so incomparable, that his entire body had a shimmering transparence just like that of crystal.

Commentary:

"Speak up! Quickly!" the Buddha said. "Don't think about it, just tell me straight out about what made you decide to leave home."

Since he was supposed to speak plainly, **Ananda said to the Buddha, "I saw the Tathagata's thirty-two characteristics."** From the invisible crown on the top of his head down to his level, well-proportioned feet, thirty-two major and eighty minor characteristics adorn the Buddha's body.

"These thirty-two characteristics were **so supremely wonderful, so incomparable**, finer than anything I'd ever seen," Ananda said. "Nothing in the world can compare to the wondrous adornment of your appearance, Buddha."

The Buddha's reward body, **his entire body had a shimmering transparence just like that of crystal**.

Sutra:

"**I often thought to myself that these characteristics cannot be born of desire and love. Why? The vapors of desire are coarse and murky. From foul and putrid intercourse comes a turbid mixture of pus and blood which cannot give off such a magnificent, pure, and brilliant concentration of purple-golden light. And so I thirstily gazed upward, followed the Buddha, and let the hair fall from my head.**"

Commentary:

When Ananda **often thought to** himself **that these characteristics cannot be born of desire and love,** he used his ordinary discriminating consciousness, his ordinary mind which is subject to production and extinction. How, he thought, could the thirty-two special characteristics of the Buddha be born from emotional, lustful, desire and thoughts of love? **The vapors of desire are coarse and murky. From foul and putrid intercourse comes a turbid mixture of pus and blood.** Men and women have intercourse and think it is good, but it actually gives off vapors which are extremely rancid. We can't rely on our bodies born from the desire of men and women to **give off such a magnificent, pure, and brilliant concentration of purple-golden light**, the color of distant mountains, which constantly illumines the Buddha's body.

Thinking this, Ananda **thirstily gazed upward, followed the Buddha, and let the hair fall from** his **head**. Ananda forsook one kind of love, his emotional love for his family, and took up another kind: he fell in love with the Buddha's appearance. And that is the reason Ananda left the home-life.

Right here is where Ananda made his mistake. He didn't leave home out of a genuine desire to cultivate the Way and after he left home he concentrated too heavily on studying the sutras. Earlier, I said that you should change the love which exists between married couples into a love for the Buddhadharma. But that doesn't mean that merely by love alone you can put an end to birth and death.

"What must be done?" you ask.

You need to genuinely cultivate the Way. You have to be mindful of what you are doing at all times and in all places. You must never forget for even a moment to practice and uphold the Buddhadharma. Early in the morning and late at night you should be studying the *Shurangama Sutra*, sitting in meditation, and listening to the sutra lectures. Don't have false thinking and don't talk so much, since neither can help you at all in your study of the sutra or your investigation of Chan. You should stake your very lives on the work and sacrifice everything else in order to study Buddhism. Then the understanding you gain will enable you to be genuinely wise and truly intelligent.

But since Ananda was solely concerned with loving the Buddha, he didn't cultivate samadhi. He thought (as he confesses in the text), "The Buddha is my older cousin. When the time comes the Buddha will give me samadhi power." He didn't realize that no one could stand in for him, in body or in mind. Ananda was very intelligent, probably more intelligent than any of us, but when he concentrated on studying the sutras at the expense of cultivating samadhi, he was too smart for his own good. He mastered the words but not the substance. He could remember all the dharma the Buddha had spoken and never got one word of it wrong, but without any samadhi-power, he fell under the spell of the Brahma Heaven mantra of Matangi's daughter.

Instead of imitating the Buddha's wisdom, his awakening, and his Way-virtue, Ananda just modeled himself on the Buddha's appearance. In past lives he was probably attached to appearances, and so he concentrated on the superficial aspect of things. Although he remembered the sutras the Buddha spoke, he didn't pay a lot of attention to what they said. He was more concerned with the Buddha's appearance to the point that if on any given day he just saw the Buddha, that was enough to make him happy.

Anyone who wants to obtain genuine samadhi power must first cast love aside. But to replace love with hate is another mistake. "I don't love anything," you say. "I despise whoever I see. Stay away from me! I want to be alone. I want to cultivate by myself." With this attitude, you'll never obtain samadhi. You must neither hate nor love. It should be as if there were no difference between you and other people. Everyone is equal. If you are one with and equal to other people, who is there to love? Who is there to hate? No one.

"I can't manage that," you say. "That's hard work."

If you can work hard, then you can obtain what is true. If you don't work hard, you won't obtain it. Follow the teachings, and don't listen to your own thoughts about it. The ordinary mind is the Way.

Because Ananda liked the Buddha's adorned appearance, he was able to reject the deep compulsion for worldly kindness and love and let the hair fall from his head. When the Buddha was in the world, those who left home under him did not have to shave their heads. The Buddha simply said, "Good man, you are now renouncing worldly life and leaving home. Let your beard and hair fall of itself and let you be robed in the kashaya." As soon as the Buddha said this the bhikshu's hair and beard would fall out, because the Buddha used his spiritual penetrations to cause it to fall. Now that the Buddha has entered nirvana we have to receive the precepts at a precept-platform, but when the Buddha was in the world one became possessed of the precept substance when he spoke those few words, and one was robed in the precept sash.

In China the precept-platform used to be three years long. But three years eventually proved too long, so a scientific method was adopted to speed up the process so that one could receive the precepts in fifty-three days. Now some places transmit the precepts in eighteen days, and there are even places that will do it in a week. Now from mechanization we've advanced to electronics, to the point that in Hong Kong on Ta Yu mountain there are places where the precepts are transmitted in three days' time. Actually, a three-day precept-platform is not in accord with dharma.

K2　He points out that all living beings have a misconception.

Sutra:

The Buddha said, "Very good, Ananda. You should all know that all living beings are continually born and continually die, simply because they do not know the everlasting true mind, the bright substance of the pure nature. Instead they engage in false thinking. It has been so since time without beginning. Their thoughts are not true, and so the wheel keeps turning.

Commentary:

The Buddha said, "Very good, Ananda." The Buddha encourages Ananda, telling him he has done a very good thing to resolve to become a bhikshu. Then he addresses the entire assembly, the great bhikshus, great arhats, great bodhisattvas, and all the people present, saying that they **should all know that all living beings are continually born and continually die** – birth and death are undergone in a continuous succession which never ceases, and we leave behind a pile of bones as large as a mountain. Birth and death; death and birth; birth and death. Where did you come from, and where are you going? You don't know. You are dragged about by your karmic conditions, your karmic obstacles. Where will you be born next? Where were you before? You don't even know how you got here and you don't know where you will go after you die.

"Why is there birth and death?" you ask.

Because you don't understand, **do not know the everlasting** true mind which does not move or waver, which is not produced or extinguished, which is not defiled or pure, and to which there is nothing added or taken away. Because this mind does not move or waver it is called "everlasting." Because there is nothing to be added or taken away from it, it is called "true."

Merely to know of the true mind is not enough; you must also recognize **the bright substance of the pure nature**. This is your own self-nature, your dharma-nature. It is clear and pure, and its brilliance pervades and illumines everything everywhere. But you aren't aware of it; you've forgotten it. It is like a bright pearl hidden in your clothing.

The *Dharma Flower Sutra* tells of a wealthy man whose son was unhappy at home and ran away. But just before he left, his parents, who feared their son would end up penniless and become a vagrant sleeping in the streets, secretly sewed a pearl that grants all wishes into the youth's clothing. The son left, and as predicted soon ended up a drifter. But he didn't realize that a priceless pearl was sewn in his clothing, so he couldn't take advantage of the benefit it would provide him. The bright substance of your everlasting pure nature, your true, unchanging mind, is like the youth's priceless pearl: since you are unaware of it, you can't use it to good advantage. **Instead** you **engage in false thinking. It has been so since time without beginning**. You use the conscious mind, which is subject to production and extinction. Its **thoughts are not true**, but it takes control of you and makes you murky and confused; it spins you around and pulls you into the mire. Since your actions are based on it, **the wheel keeps turning** in a perpetual cycle of birth and death. But if your false thinking is cast out and exhausted once and for all and no more is produced, and you recognize your true mind, your births and deaths will cease.

The False Consciousness is Without a Location

J2 He actually destroys the false mind.
K1 The Tathagata thoroughly refutes three points of confusion.
L1 His refutation that the false consciousness is without a location.
M1 He instructs that Ananda should reply to the teaching with a straightforward mind.

Sutra:

"Now you wish to investigate the unsurpassed bodhi and actually discover your nature. You should answer my questions with a straightforward mind, because that is exactly the way the Tathagatas of the ten directions escaped birth and death. Their minds were all straightforward, and since their minds and words were consistently that way, from the beginning, through the intermediate stages to the end, they were never in the least evasive.

Commentary:

The *Vimalakirti Sutra* says, "The straightforward mind is the field of enlightenment." And thus the Buddha instructs Ananda: **Now you wish to investigate the unsurpassed bodhi and actually discover your nature. You should answer my questions with a straightforward mind.** "Don't think about it," he says, "don't use false thinking to try to figure out how to answer me correctly. Don't approach it as if you were in combat with me and must figure out what maneuver you should make to defeat me, as if this were the martial arts where one must decide how to counter-attack." The

Buddha was concerned that if Ananda tried to answer in a roundabout manner, it would be impossible to arrive at true principle.

Why is the straightforward mind the field of enlightenment? At the point when you have not yet given rise to a first thought, that is your true mind, your Way-mind. This is the state of "primary thought," the primary truth that exists prior to the spoken word. As soon as you begin thinking, that is to say, as soon as you strike up false thinking, it is no longer your true mind at work. It is your conscious mind which is full of "second thoughts." Instead of speaking up directly, and using your straightforward mind to express yourself, you start thinking about it: "Ah, I shouldn't say that; if I say that I'll be wrong. I should say this." But then you think about it again and change your mind again.

When you speak, use your primary thought. Why? **Because that is exactly the way the Tathagatas of the ten directions escaped birth and death.** There is a verse about the Chinese character *xin* (心), "mind," which goes:

> Three small dots like a cluster of stars,
> And a hook shaped like a crescent moon.
> Beget animals with fur and horns,
> Yet perfection of Buddhahood comes from it too.

The ten dharma realms are not beyond a single thought of the mind. Your thoughts can send you not only into the animal realm, but into Buddhahood as well. Not only are Buddhas made from the mind, ghosts are creations of the mind, and so are gods, arhats, and bodhisattvas. For instance, you are now studying the Buddhadharma, investigating the *Shurangama Sutra* without fear of whatever difficulties may arise. This is because you repeatedly planted a single indestructible seed of thought into the field of your mind in countless former lives. A bodhi-seed has taken root so that now you are studying the Buddhadharma. Of course this single thought of the true mind has been helped along by the conscious mind, which thought over and over, "Should I study the Buddhadharma or not?"

You kept sawing the issue back and forth until finally you cut through it.

Their minds were all straightforward, and since their minds and words were consistently that way. The Chinese characters *ru shi* (如是) "that way" refer specifically to the straightforward mind and do not have the same meaning as when they occurred in the opening sentence of the sutra where *ru shi* means "thus" in "Thus I have heard."

From the beginning, through the intermediate stages to the end. "The end" refers to wonderful enlightenment, the achievement of Buddhahood. "The beginning" refers to the stage of dry wisdom, which precedes the ten faiths. These positions will be discussed later in the text. "The intermediate stages" are the long period of cultivation between the stage of dry wisdom and the achievement of Buddhahood, through the various stages of bodhisattvahood to equal enlightenment and then wonderful enlightenment. Through all that time the Buddhas of the past **were never in the least evasive** and used only their straightforward minds. And so they became Buddhas.

Ananda would not use his straight mind to answer the questions, but would answer in round-about ways, making it impossible to arrive at any true principles. So the Buddha first wanted to explain to him clearly that he should give straight answers and not be muddled about it. "Now I am describing essential methods for you," said the Buddha, "I'm explaining how to actually discover your nature, the initial doctrines concerning the realization of Buddhahood, so you can't be casual or do a lot of hedging when you answer me. You must use your straightforward mind to answer me."

M2 He asks Ananda about his ability to see and his ability to love.

Sutra:

"Ananda, I now ask you: at the time of your initial resolve, which arose in response to the Tathagata's thirty-two charac-

teristics, what was it that saw those characteristics and who delighted in them?"

Commentary:

The Buddha again questions Ananda: **Ananda, I now ask you: at the time of your initial resolve.** In making his decision to cultivate the Way, when Ananda used his conscious mind to think about the Buddha's appearance, **the Tathagata's thirty-two characteristics,** Ananda was taking advantage of the situation. This is the meaning of **in response to**. So the Buddha asks: **What was it that saw those characteristics and who delighted in them?**

Sutra:

Ananda said to the Buddha, "World Honored One, this is the way I experienced the delight: I used my mind and eyes. Because my eyes saw the Tathagata's outstanding characteristics, my mind gave rise to delight. That is why I became resolved and wished to removed myself from birth and death."

Commentary:

Ananda said to the Buddha, "World Honored One, this is the way I experienced the delight: I used my mind and eyes." Most people would say that this was correct, that he used his eyes and mind to see the Buddha. But as the sutra text continues you will come to find out this is a mistake.

"Because my eyes saw the Tathagata's outstanding characteristics, my mind gave rise to delight. I used my eyes to look at the Buddha's thirty-two major and eighty minor characteristics and in my mind love arose. What was it I loved? I saw the Buddha's characteristics and adornments were immaculately pure, not at all filthy like bodies born from love and desire. **That is why I became resolved and wished to removed myself from birth and death.** I wanted to follow the Buddha, leave the home-life, and cultivate the Way. The history of my leaving home is like that." That is how he answered Shakyamuni Buddha's question.

| M3 | He asks Ananda where his mind and eyes are. |

Sutra:

The Buddha said to Ananda, "It is as you say, that experience of delight actually occurs because of your mind and eyes. If you do not know where your mind and eyes are, you will not be able to conquer the wearisome dust.

Commentary:

Ananda told the Buddha that the reason he decided to leave the home-life was because he saw the Buddha's supreme characteristics and in his mind he loved them.

The Buddha said to Ananda, "It is as you say, that experience of delight actually occurs because of your mind and eyes." Nonetheless, do you know where your mind is? Do you know if your eyes have the ability to see? Do you know where your eyes are?

"Those kind of questions are totally senseless," you object. "His eyes were in his face and his mind in his body. Anybody knows that."

But that's not your true mind. Nor is that genuine seeing. Behind the Buddha's questions lies the wisdom of the Tathagata. **If you do not know where your mind and eyes are, you will not be able to conquer the wearisome dust.** The "dust" means defilement, and "wearisome" means disturbing. The dust disturbs your mind, and it troubles your nature, so that you can't change your false thinking into your true mind. It's just as when two armies clash, and one becomes the victor. You are the victor if you are able to conquer the dust, that is, if you are able to cut off the road to birth and death.

Sutra:

"For example, when a king's country is invaded by thieves and he sends out his troops to suppress and banish them, the troops must know where the thieves are.

Commentary:

The Buddha then presents an analogy: **For example, when a king's country is invaded by thieves** who wish to seize the land, **he sends out his troops to suppress and banish them,** to quell them and drive them out. But the troops he sends **must know where the thieves are.** In the same way, the reason you cannot put an end to the beginningless eons of birth and death is because you do not know where your mind and eyes are.

Sutra:

"It is the fault of your mind and eyes that you flow and turn. I am now asking you specifically about your mind and eyes: where are they now?"

Commentary:

The more the Buddha says the less principle there is in it! "I will tell you further that **it is the fault of your mind and eyes that you flow and turn.** Why do you get born and die? What causes you to flow and turn in birth and death, revolving endlessly on the turning wheel of the six paths? Your mind and eyes are to blame. Your mind and eyes are at fault for making you undergo birth and death and rendering you incapable of obtaining liberation. Since they are to blame, **I am now asking you specifically about your mind and eyes: where are they now?** Speak up quickly!" the Buddha exhorts Ananda.

M4 The seven places which are attached to are all non-existent.
N1 Ananda attaches to the mind as being in the body.
O1 Ananda brings up the ten kinds of beings as all alike reckoning the mind as inside.

Sutra:

Ananda said to the Buddha, "World Honored One, all the ten kinds of living beings in the world alike maintain that the conscious mind dwells within the body; and as I regard the Tathagata's blue lotus-flower eyes, they too are on the Buddha's face.

Commentary:

In this section of the text Ananda has not answered with a straightforward mind. He's being evasive. When Ananda was asked by the Buddha, "Where is your mind? Where are your eyes?" he was at a loss and didn't know what the best answer was. Still, he had to speak, so he sized up the situation and said: **World Honored One.** I believe at this point Ananda was speaking in a very soft voice. Why? Because he wasn't sure of himself. He didn't know if he was right or not. He just guessed based on what he knew; he was hesitant, on the verge of speaking and yet not daring to do so.

He brought up **all the ten kinds of living beings**. These will be discussed later so we will not explain them here. They include those born from wombs, those born from eggs, those born from moisture, those born by transformation, those with thought, and so forth as listed in the *Vajra Sutra*. Basically, there are twelve kinds of living beings, but here the kind without form and the kind without thought are omitted.

So Ananda said in a soft voice, "All of the ten kinds of living beings **in the world alike maintain that the conscious mind dwells within the body.**" The "conscious mind" is the mind subject to birth and death, the discriminating, calculating mind. Ananda doesn't mention himself. He talks about the ten kinds of living beings. He didn't talk about himself for fear he might somehow be different from other living beings. So he says, "All the ten kinds of living beings are like that, it's not just I, Ananda, alone, who am that way." There was a bit of condescension in his tone, implying, "After all, everyone knows that the mind is inside."

"And as I regard the Tathagata's blue lotus-flower eyes, they too are on the Buddha's face. As I lean forward and scrutinize the Thus Come One's eyes, so bright and wide that they resemble lotus flowers, they are on the Buddha's face," Ananda says. His remark was also subtly implying: "Plain as can be, your eyes are on your face; why do you still have to ask me?" But he didn't dare actually come out and say that.

Sutra:

"I now observe that these prominent organs, four kinds of defiling objects, are on my face, and so, too, my conscious mind actually is within my body."

Commentary:

Ananda said, "World Honored One, your blue lotus-flower eyes are on your face. **I now observe that these prominent organs, four kinds of defiling objects, are on my face.**" The "prominent organs" refer to the eyes, ears, nose, and tongue, all of which are located on the face. They are quite distinct and visible. "**And so, too, my conscious mind actually is within my body.** As I now think about it further, my discriminating conscious mind which can know pleasant and unpleasant, good and bad, is actually in my body." That is how Ananda answered the Buddha's question.

O2   The Tathagata uses not seeing inside the body to refute this.
P1   The Tathagata brings up an example.

Sutra:

The Buddha said to Ananda, "You are now sitting in the Tathagata's lecture hall looking at the Jeta Grove. Where is it at present?"

"World Honored One, this great many-storied pure lecture hall is in the Garden of the Benefactor of the Solitary. At present the Jeta Grove is in fact outside the hall."

Commentary:

Having heard Ananda's answer that his mind was in his body and his eyes were on his face, the Buddha initially did not make any direct reply. Instead, the Buddha asked Ananda another question.

The Buddha said to Ananda, "You are now sitting in the Tathagata's lecture hall looking at the Jeta Grove. As you gaze at Prince War Victor's grove, **where is it at present?"** The Buddha didn't give any indication whether the mind is indeed inside or outside. He just fired another question back at Ananda in order to combat Ananda's thought process.

Ananda answered the Buddha, "**World Honored One, this great many-storied pure lecture hall is in the Garden of the Benefactor of the Solitary.** The Buddha's large, pure and clean lecture hall is in the garden of the elder Anathapindaka. **At present the Jeta Grove is in fact outside the hall.** The pure lecture hall, the place where we all are, is in the garden. Prince Jeta's grove is actually outside the hall."

The Buddha then said to him:

Sutra:

"**Ananda, as you are now in the hall, what do you see first?**"

"**World Honored One, here in the hall I first see the Tathagata, next I see the great assembly, and from there, as I gaze outward, I see the grove and garden.**"

Commentary:

Shakyamuni Buddha heard Ananda say his external organs, his eyes, ears, nose, and tongue, the four defiling objects, forms, sounds, smells, and tastes are outside of him, while his conscious mind is in his body. The Buddha then asked him where the Jeta Grove was. Now the Buddha asked: **Ananda, as you are now in the hall, what do you see first?** Ananda has said his mind was in his body, and so the Buddha asked him what he saw first when he was in the hall.

Ananda answered, "**World Honored One, here in the hall I first see the Tathagata.** The first thing I see when I'm in the lecture hall is the Buddha," he replied, "You, World Honored One."

Next I see the great assembly. After that I see the great bodhisattvas, great arhats, and the sound-hearers. **And from there, as I gaze outward, I see the grove and garden.** I see the Jeta Grove and the Garden of the Benefactor of Orphans and the Solitary.

Sutra:

"**Ananda, why it is you are able to see the grove and the garden as you look at them?**"

"**World Honored One, since the doors and windows of this great lecture hall have been thrown open wide, I can be in the hall and see into the distance.**"

Commentary:

The Buddha continued: **Ananda, why it is you are able to see the grove and the garden as you look at them?** How can you see them? What's the reason you are able to see them?

"Each time the Buddha seems to speak with less and less principle," you say.

But within what he says is deep meaning. As we investigate more deeply, you will come to realize it.

Ananda answered: **World Honored One, since the doors and windows of this great lecture hall have been thrown open wide, I can be in the hall and see into the distance.** From inside I can see the Jeta Grove and the Garden of the Benefactor of Orphans and the Solitary.

P2 The place where the text originally was.
P3 The Tathagata questions him about the example.

Sutra:

The Buddha said to Ananda, "It is as you say. When one is in the lecture hall and the doors and windows are open wide, one can see far into the garden and grove. Could there be someone in the hall who does not see the Tathagata and yet sees outside the hall?"

Ananda answered: **"World Honored One, to be in the hall and not see the Tathagata, and yet see the grove and fountains is impossible."**

"Ananda, you are like that too.

Commentary:

In this section of text the Buddha sets up a question to come back on Ananda. **The Buddha said to Ananda, "It is as you say. When one is in the lecture hall and the doors and windows are**

open wide, one can see far into the garden and grove. You are absolutely right. You are inside now and yet you can see the Jeta Grove and the Garden of Anathapindaka. **Could there be someone in the hall who does not see the Tathagata and yet sees outside the hall?** Could there be a living being who doesn't see the Thus Come One, but sees only the grove and garden outside the hall? Is this possible?" the Buddha asked.

Ananda answered, "World Honored One, to be in the hall and not see the Tathagata, and yet see the grove and fountains is impossible. If someone were inside," Ananda says, "he certainly would be able to see the Buddha. There's no way he could see what's outside the hall and not see the Buddha, who's inside the hall."

Ananda's answer was very decisive.

"Ananda, you are like that too," the Buddha replied. Ananda said it was impossible to be inside and not see the Buddha inside, and the Buddha proceeds to tell Ananda that Ananda himself is just like someone inside the hall who can't see the Buddha, but can only see outside the hall.

P4   From that example comes the refutation.

Sutra:

"Your mind is capable of understanding everything thoroughly. Now if your present mind, which thoroughly understands everything, were in your body, then you should be aware first of what is inside your body. Can there be living beings who first see inside their bodies before they observe things outside?

Commentary:

It is said that people are the most capable among the myriad things, and that of all their attributes their minds are the most capable. However, **your mind** which **is capable of understanding everything thoroughly** refers only to the conscious mind. **Now if your present mind, which thoroughly understands everything,**

were in your body, then you should be aware first of what is inside your body. The Buddha argues that if Ananda's mind is really inside his body, as Ananda says, then he ought to be able to know first of all what the inside of his body is like, in the same way that someone inside the lecture hall is able to see the people inside. "But **can there be living beings who first see inside their bodies before they observe things outside?**" the Buddha asks. The Buddha knew that Ananda had not yet understood, and that he still did not know what the basic substance of the true mind is like. He was still adroitly making use of his false-thinking mind, his conscious mind. So the Buddha continues his explanation:

Sutra:

"Even if you cannot see your heart, liver, spleen, and stomach, still, the growing of your nails and hair, the twist of your sinews, and the throb of your pulse should be clearly understood. Why don't you perceive these things? If you cannot perceive what is inside at all, how can you perceive what is outside?

Commentary:

"You say your mind is in your body, and your power of seeing is in your eyes," the Buddha tells Ananda. But if your mind, with its power to know, is inside, you should know what your **heart, liver, spleen, and stomach** are like. **Even if you cannot see** them, you should be able to perceive things that are happening on the surface like **the growing of your nails and hair**. You should be able to know how many fractions of an inch they grow each second. In fact, **the twist of your sinews, and the throb of your pulse should be clearly understood.** You should know all about them. **Why don't you perceive these things?** Why don't you know?

If you cannot perceive what is inside at all, how can you perceive what is outside? Your mind is inside and you don't know what's going on inside you. So how could you know what is going on outside?

P5	The concluding refutation.

Sutra:

"Therefore you should know that you state the impossible when you say that the aware and knowing mind is in the body."

Commentary:

"Your argument won't stand," the Buddha tells Ananda. "Since you can't perceive what is inside you, **therefore you should know that you state the impossible when you say that the aware and knowing mind is in the body.**" After using various analogies and arguments, the Buddha tells Ananda directly that it is wrong to place the considering, thinking, knowing mind inside the body.

N2	Ananda attaches to the mind as being outside the body.
O1	Ananda presents the analogy of the lamp and determines it is the same as the Buddha's meaning.

Sutra:

Ananda bowed his head and said to the Buddha, "Upon hearing such expression of dharma as the Tathagata has proclaimed, I realize that my mind is actually outside my body.

Commentary:

Ananda's argument that the mind is inside the body did not hold up. Shakyamuni Buddha jolted him out of his folly and destroyed his position. And so **Ananda**, who was well versed in etiquette, **bowed his head**, which means he prostrated himself, **and said to the Buddha, "Upon hearing such expression of dharma as the Tathagata has proclaimed, I realize that my mind is actually outside my body."** "My mind is not in my body! It has run outside. I'm sure that's where it is!" exclaims Ananda. One doesn't know when his mind ran outside, but now he suddenly says that's where it is.

Sutra:

"Why? For example, a lamp alight in a room will certainly illumine the inside of the room first, and only then will it pour

through the doorway to reach the recesses of the hall. For all living beings who do not see within their bodies but only see outside them, it is as if the lighted lamp were placed outside the room, so that it cannot illumine the room.**

Commentary:

"**Why?** Why do I say my mind has run outside? **For example, a lamp alight in a room will certainly illumine the inside of the room first, and only then will it pour through the doorway to reach the recesses of the hall.** If my mind were inside," Ananda reasons, "I would certainly be able to see what is happening inside my body, in the same way that a lamp inside a room will certainly light up the room."

For all living beings who do not see within their bodies but only see outside them, it is as if the lighted lamp were placed outside the room, so that it cannot illumine the room. The Buddha pointed out that one cannot see one's heart, liver, spleen, and stomach, and so Ananda concludes that the mind is outside, just like the lighted lamp outside the room. It is outside so one cannot see things inside.

Sutra:

"**This principle is certainly clear: it is absolutely beyond all doubt and exactly the Buddha's entire meaning, and so it isn't wrong is it?**"

Commentary:

"**This principle is certainly clear.** This doctrine I have presented is certainly correct," Ananda states emphatically. **It is absolutely beyond all doubt.** Ananda passes judgement in advance. There's no question about it; it is **exactly the Buddha's entire meaning**. "My argument is the same as the Buddha's complete meaning. I couldn't make a mistake. It isn't just my idea. I believe the Buddha will agree, won't he? **It isn't wrong is it?**" In fact, Ananda is still not positive. "I'm pretty sure this is not wrong."

O2 The Tathagata refutes by using the mutual awareness of body and mind.
P1 The analogy makes clear there would be no connection.

Sutra:

The Buddha said to Ananda, "All these bhikshus who just followed me to the city of Shravasti to beg in sequence for food have returned to the Jeta Grove and are rolling their food into balls as they eat. I have already finished eating, but consider the bhikshus: when one person eats, does everyone get full?"

Ananda answered, "No, World Honored One. Why? These bhikshus are arhats, but their individual lives differ. How could one person's eating cause everyone to be full?"

Commentary:

Ananda felt certain that the Buddha would agree that the mind is outside. Who would have suspected that the Buddha wouldn't even consider the proposal? **The Buddha said to Ananda, "All these bhikshus who just followed me to the city of Shravasti to beg in sequence for food have returned to the Jeta Grove and are rolling their food into balls as they eat."** They begged from house to house and then returned to the grove of trees donated by Prince Jeta. In India they ate by picking up pieces of food in their hands and rolling them into balls, and so this is how the Buddha and his disciples ate. In present-day Burma, bowls are used, but those who have left the home-life still eat their vegetables and rice with their right hand, without using a spoon or chopsticks. They take a piece of food in their hand and roll it over and over. Then they eat it. Eating this way is very appetizing to them, though whether it is ultimately very appetizing I don't know, since I've never tried it.

I have already finished eating, but consider the bhikshus: when one person eats, does everyone get full? I have eaten my fill, but take a look at the assembly: some bhikshus have not finished eating. Now if just one person eats, can the rest get full?

If there is any doubt about this principle, we can try it out ourselves tomorrow. Just serve me food, and all of you can look on while I eat, and you can see if you get full. That will prove the principle found in the sutra.

Ananda answered, "No, World Honored One. Why?" Having answered in the negative, Ananda was afraid the Buddha might not understand, so he proceeded to give the Buddha a commentary. "Why do I say they can't get full? **These bhikshus are arhats, but their individual lives differ.** Although they have become enlightened and they all have spiritual penetrations, still their bodies are not the same. Their appearances, their faces, are all different. If they were all one, then when one ate, all would get full, but they are not one; each has his own individual life. So **how could one person's eating cause everyone to be full?** Therefore, I say there is no such principle."

Sutra:

The Buddha told Ananda, "If your mind which understands, knows, sees and is aware were actually outside your body, your body and mind would be mutually exclusive and would have no relationship to one another. The body would be unaware of what the mind perceives, and the mind would not perceive the awareness within the body.

Commentary:

The Buddha told Ananda, "If your mind which understands, knows, sees and is aware were actually outside your body, your body and mind would be mutually exclusive and would have no relationship to one another." If the mind which has awareness, which calculates, which discriminates, and which has knowledge and views were outside the body, then there would be no connection between the two. They would have parted ways; they wouldn't reside together. Your body would be your body; your mind would be your mind, and your mind would be apart from your body. "You pay no attention to my business," they'd say, "and I won't pay attention to yours." **The body would be unaware of what the mind perceives, and the mind would not perceive the awareness within the body.** The body would not be aware of the mind or influenced by it, and if your awareness was within the body, the mind wouldn't know about it.

P2　Investigation shows there is a connection.

Sutra:

"Now as I show you my tula-cotton hand, does your mind distinguish it when your eyes see it?"

Ananda answered, "So it is, World Honored One."

The Buddha told Ananda, "If the mind and eyes create a common perception, how then can the mind be outside?

Commentary:

The Buddha's hands are extremely soft and supple, like cotton. Now I will relate a point of physiognomy. If you rub someone's hand and find it to be as soft as cotton, that person has a promising future and will eventually be honorable. Ordinary people's hands are very stiff. I know my hands, for example, are as stiff as a board, not soft like cotton. However, soft hands do not necessarily indicate a great future. The countenance is equally important in this matter. Are the features heroic? Is the person's appearance powerful? In general, women's hands are far softer than men's. If you don't believe it, you can notice next time you have occasion to shake hands with a woman. As for men, I have met only two whose hands were extremely soft. However, during the time I knew them neither one of them displayed signs of greatness. Their appearances didn't match up. I have one disciple with extremely soft hands – he had never done any physical labor, but he is also very ordinary. A fellow student of mine, who was also a relative, also had extremely soft hands, but before I came to America he had not done anything of great importance, and I don't know if he has accomplished anything since then.

The Buddha told Ananda, **"Now as I show you my tula-cotton hand, does your mind distinguish it when your eyes see it?** When your eyes see it, does your mind make a distinction that my hand is a tula-cotton hand?"

Ananda answered, "So it is, World Honored One." Yes. My eyes see it and my mind distinguishes it. My mind makes a discrimination of fondness. "Ah," it says, "the Buddha's tula-cotton hand is the very finest. This is one of the thirty-two hallmarks of the Tathagata."

The Buddha told Ananda, "If the mind and eyes create a common perception, how then can the mind be outside?" If your mind knows what your eyes see, how can you say that your mind is outside your body? If it were outside, how could it perceive what the eyes see? Note, though, the Buddha does not say that the mind is inside. It has already been made clear that that too, is a mistake.

P3 Concluding refutation.

Sutra:

"Therefore you should know you state the impossible when you say that the mind which knows, understands, and is aware is outside the body."

Commentary:

Since Ananda's argument that the mind is inside the body did not hold up, he revised his contention to say that the mind is outside the body. The World Honored One has used all kinds of analogies to instruct him, but unfortunately Ananda only knows how to analyze the Buddhadharma by means of his conscious mind, which is subject to production and extinction. He does not perceive the pure nature and bright substance of the everlasting true mind. So the Buddha once again gives Ananda his critique: **"Therefore you should know you state the impossible when you say that the mind which knows, understands, and is aware is outside the body.** You were wrong," the Buddha says. The mind which calculates and understands is not outside your body. Do you understand? You have made a mistake.

N3	Ananda attaches to the mind's being hidden in the eyes.
O1	Ananda uses the analogy of crystals covering the eyes.

Sutra:

Ananda said to the Buddha, "World Honored One, it is as the Buddha has said, since I cannot see inside, my mind does not reside in the body. Since my body and mind have a common awareness, they are not separate and so my mind does not dwell outside my body. As I now consider it, I know it is in a certain place."

Commentary:

Ananda considered: here it is again. It is just because he keeps considering that he makes mistakes. **Ananda said to the Buddha, "World Honored One, it is as the Buddha has said."** Ananda says, "I followed the Buddha to leave the home-life and I listen to the Buddha's teaching, including the doctrine the Buddha has just spoken, those proclamations of the dharma. **Since I cannot see inside, my mind does not reside in the body.** If the mind were inside the body, I'd be able to see my heart, liver, spleen, lungs, and kidneys, the five viscera. **Since my body and mind have a common awareness, they are not separate and so my mind does not dwell outside my body.** The Buddha now says it is not outside. **As I now consider it, I know it is in a certain place.** Now I have another thought. Outside is not correct, inside is not correct, therefore it has to be in a certain particular place."

Sutra:

The Buddha said, "Now where is it?"

Ananda said, "Since the mind which knows and understands does not perceive what is inside but can see outside, upon reflection I believe it is concealed in the organ of vision.

Commentary:

The Buddha said, "Now where is it? Ah, you say it is in a certain place. What place? Where is your mind? Hurry up and tell me." That's how he questioned him.

Ananda said, "Since the mind which knows and understands does not perceive what is inside but can see outside, upon reflection I believe..." Before, he said, "As I now consider it," and here again he says, "Upon reflection." It's still his conscious mind at work. Consideration and reflection both make use of the conscious mind, the mind subject to production and extinction. What is his reflection? The mind **is concealed in the organ of vision.** The organ of vision refers to the eye. It is hidden away there, Ananda says. The mind was stashed there where no one could see it. That's what is meant by "concealed."

The Buddha doesn't reply to this right away. In fact the sutra text leaves you in suspense for a while. Today I heard someone say that he didn't understand the sutra. To say nothing of your not understanding, Ananda himself didn't understand at this point. You have to listen to the entire sutra; then you will come to understand. If you haven't heard it completely, how could you be expected to understand? Of course you don't understand. Why would you want to listen to sutras in the first place if you already understood them? You shouldn't say, "I don't understand what is being said so I'll stop listening." It's just because you don't understand that you should listen.

Sutra:

"For example, when someone places crystal bowls over his eyes, the bowls cover his eyes but do not obstruct his vision. The organ of vision is thus able to see, and discriminations are made accordingly.

Commentary:

Ananda gives the Buddha an **example** to explain his new contention. **When someone places crystal bowls over his eyes, the bowls cover his eyes but do not obstruct his vision.** Actually there is no such person, but Ananda invents someone who puts on eyeglasses – that is what is meant here. In the Buddha's day they were called crystal bowls. The glasses cover the eyes, but this does not stop the eyes from seeing out. In Ananda's analogy, the mind is represented by the eyes, and the eyes, where Ananda contends the mind is hidden, are represented by the glasses. Our mind, Ananda contends, is hidden in our eyes, but this does not stop our mind from seeing out.

The organ of vision is thus able to see, and discriminations are made accordingly. That is, as soon as you see, your mind knows it. Discrimination takes place in the organ of vision, where, Ananda says, the mind is hidden. "This time the doctrine I have expressed is the right one," Ananda says. He still considers himself to be very intelligent. "See how smart I am? I have an answer for everything the Buddha asks me." Why does Ananda keep making mistakes? It is because he uses the mind subject to production and extinction. No matter what the circumstance is, he always uses his thought-processes to consider it from each side. His considerations are grounded in the thoughts of his consciousness, and he recognizes the consciousness to be the true mind. He doesn't know that the "true mind" neither exists nor does not exist, and that the true mind is the nature. He is like one who gets off on the wrong road, and the farther he goes, the more he has lost his way, and the more he has lost his way the more he thinks he's on the right road. So now he brings up yet another analogy for the Buddha to pass judgement on.

Sutra:

"**And so my mind which knows, understands, and is aware does not see within because it resides in the organ. It can gaze outside clearly, without obstruction for the same reason: it is concealed in the organ.**"

Commentary:

"**And so** refers to the doctrine he was just explaining. **My mind which knows, understands, and is aware does not see within because it resides in the organ.** Why can't I see inside my body? It's because my mind is in my eyes. **It can gaze outside clearly, without obstruction for the same reason: it is concealed in the organ.** Why can I see outside but not inside? It is because my mind, which also refers to vision, the power of seeing, is concealed in the eye. So there is no obstruction when I look outside." Whether Ananda is right in his theory will become clear in the following passages.

O2 The Buddha uses a method show the analogy is not apt.
P1 He discusses its aptness.

Sutra:

The Buddha said to Ananda, "Assuming that it is concealed in the organ, as you assert in your analogy of the crystals: if someone were to cover his eyes with the crystals and look at the mountains and rivers, would he see the crystals as well?"

"Yes, World Honored One, if a person were to cover his eyes with the crystals, he would in fact see the crystals."

Commentary:

Having heard Ananda use the analogy of the crystals, **the Buddha said to Ananda, "Assuming that it is concealed in the organ, as you assert in your analogy of the crystals**: Suppose it is the way you explain it," the Buddha says, "and the mind is concealed in the organ. **If someone were to cover his eyes with the crystals and look at the mountains and rivers, would he see the crystals as well?** When the person in your analogy puts on his glasses in order to see, and he takes a look at the mountains, rivers, and the vast expanse of earth, does he see his glasses?"

"Yes, World Honored One, if a person were to cover his eyes with the crystals, he would in fact see the crystals. When someone wears glasses, he sees the mountains, rivers, the vast expanse of earth, and he also sees the glasses." That is what the Buddha asked Ananda and how Ananda answered him.

Sutra:

The Buddha said to Ananda, "If your mind is analogous to the eyes covered with crystals, then when you see the mountains and rivers, why don't you see your eyes?

Commentary:

The Buddha said to Ananda, "You put on glasses and can see the mountains, rivers, and the vast expanse of earth, and you can also see the glasses. **If your mind is analogous to the eyes covered with crystals**: if your mind dwells within your organ of vision, then your eyes are like the glasses in the analogy. So when your mind looks at the mountains, rivers, and the great expanse of earth, **then when you see the mountains and rivers, why don't you see your eyes?**"

Someone will say, "I see my eyes."

I also see my eyes – if I look in a mirror. If you could see your own eyes simply by turning your light back to reflect upon yourself, then the Buddha's argument here wouldn't work. But the flesh eyes of an ordinary person cannot see themselves. And although Ananda had attained the first stage of arhatship, his flesh eyes could not look into his own eyes either.

So the Buddha asks him, "You made up the analogy for the mind being hidden in the eyes, like eyes covered with glasses, didn't you? So your eyes would be like the crystals in the analogy and since you say you can see the crystals, then why can't you see your own eyes at this very moment?" That is what the Buddha asked him.

P2 Both possibilities explored and refuted.

Sutra:

"If you could see your eyes, your eyes would be part of the external environment. If you cannot see them, why did you say that the mind which understands, knows, and is aware is concealed in the organ of vision as eyes are covered by crystals?

Commentary:

Shakyamuni Buddha questioned him further: **If you could see your eyes, your eyes would be part of the external environment.** It has already been made clear that Ananda does not see his eyes, but the Buddha was concerned that Ananda would become so confused that he'd contend he could see his own eyes. So the Buddha points out that if Ananda could see his eyes, that would mean his eyes would be outside of him and not part of his body. And thus the organ of vision would not be able to see. You couldn't say, as you just did, that "the organ of vision is thus able to see, and discriminations are made accordingly."

If you cannot see them, why did you say that the mind which understands, knows, and is aware is concealed in the organ of vision as eyes are covered by crystals? If you cannot see your eyes, then how can you contend that your mind is hidden in your organ of vision the way eyes are covered by glasses? Your analogy of the crystals doesn't hold up. It too is incorrect.

P3 The concluding refutation.

Sutra:

"Therefore you should know that you state the impossible when you say that the mind which knows, understands, and is aware is concealed in the organ of vision in the way that the eyes are covered by crystals."

Commentary:

Therefore – because of the doctrine explained above – **you should know that you state the impossible when you say that the mind which knows, understands, and is aware is concealed in the organ of vision in the way that the eyes are covered by crystals**. To say that the aware and knowing mind is hidden in the eye is incorrect. Your doctrine is not right. You are wrong again.

N4 Ananda attaches to the mind as being divided between light and dark.
O1 Ananda takes seeing light and dark as divisions of inside and outside.

Sutra:

Ananda said to the Buddha, "World Honored One, I now offer this reconsideration: viscera and bowels lie inside the bodies of living beings, while the orifices are open to the exterior. There is darkness at the bowels and light at the orifices.

Commentary:

Ananda was criticized by the Buddha and so he came up with another theory to answer the Buddha's question. **Ananda said to the Buddha, "World Honored One, I now offer this reconsideration.** Now I think of it this way: **viscera and bowels lie inside the bodies of living beings, while the orifices are open to the exterior."** What is meant by living beings? This phrase has already appeared several times in the text but has not yet been explained. Living beings[11] are born from the mixing of a multitude of karmic conditions which result in birth. Each of you people are not engendered from one kind of karma but from many. Just as a field of crops requires many conditions beyond the simple planting of a seed – there must be earth, sunshine, and rain – we people are also born from a variety of causes and conditions. The "viscera and bowels": the heart, liver, spleen, lungs, and kidneys are said to be the five viscera, and the six bowels are the large intestine, the small intestine, the "triple warmer," the bladder, the gall bladder, and the stomach. The bowels can be said to be hidden because they are inside and they can also be called "filthy" because everything in them is either excrement or urine.

As to the apertures and openings, the eyes, ears, and nose are apertures, and the eye-socket, the entrance to the inner ear, and the nostrils are openings. Then, of course, there is the mouth-opening, an opening which you never manage to fill up. Today you eat your fill, but tomorrow you are hungry again. So you eat again and fill up the opening but by the following day you're hungry once more. Everything has moved out. Inside there is a constant assimilation of the new and elimination of the old. This process causes people a lot of trouble. Eating is a lot of trouble. Just think of it: if you didn't spend three hours a day eating three meals, we could use the extra time to lecture sutras or sit in Chan. But because you eat three times a day, you're kept extremely busy every day just filling up that mouth-opening. But in the end, you'll never fill it up.

[11.] Chinese 眾生 *zhong sheng*, literally "multitudes of births".

There is darkness at the bowels and light at the orifices. Since the bowels and viscera are hidden in the body, they are in darkness. How is it one knows external things? Because there are apertures, so there is light. Now Ananda isn't referring to them as eyes in his analogy, but as apertures. Ananda is really smart. He's decidedly intelligent.

Sutra:

"Now, as I face the Buddha and open my eyes, I see light: that is to see outside. When I close my eyes and see darkness, that is to see within. How does that principle sound?"

Commentary:

Ananda is more intelligent than we are. We couldn't think of so many ways to answer. How many methods has he come up with already? He has one opinion after another. Whatever the Buddha asks, he has an answer for it. He's always got something to say; he's full of theories and arguments and thoughts and considerations. He was, after all, foremost among the disciples in learning. Where there is no principle, he can expound a principle. He would have made a first-rate lawyer. **Now, as I face the Buddha and open my eyes, I see light: that is to see outside. When I close my eyes and see darkness, that is to see within.** When I see light, it is seeing outside; when I see darkness, it is seeing inside. **How does that principle sound?** What do you say to that?

O2 The Tathagata uses the fact that seeing inside is not possible as his refutation.
P1 His refutation: that which is seen is not inside.

Sutra:

The Buddha said to Ananda, "When you close your eyes and see darkness, does the darkness you experience lie before your eyes? If it does lie before your eyes, then the darkness is in front of your eyes. How can that be said to be 'within'?

Commentary:

Instead of telling Ananda whether his latest proposition is right or wrong, the Buddha asks Ananda another question. **The Buddha said** to Ananda, "**When you close your eyes and see darkness.** You say that when you close your eyes you see darkness, and that that is to see within. But **does the darkness you experience lie before your eyes?** Speak up. Tell me. **If it does lie before your eyes, then the darkness is in front of your eyes. How can that be said to be 'within'?** How can you say that to see darkness is to see inside?"

Sutra:

"**If it were within, then when you are in a dark room without the light of sun, moon, or lamps, the darkness in the room would constitute your 'warmers' and viscera. If it is not before you, how can it be seen?**

Commentary:

"**If it were within,**" the Buddha continues, "If you reason that the darkness before you is actually your insides, **then when you are in a dark room without the light of sun, moon, or lamps, the darkness in the room would constitute your 'warmers' and viscera.** That darkness would become your 'three warmers' and your viscera and bowels. The whole room would turn into your organs and intestines. Why? Because it is dark, and you've just said that the darkness you see is inside your body." The "three warmers" consist of the upper, the middle and the lower warmers. The function of these three is very important in the human body. If they become diseased, the resulting illness is not easy to cure.

If it is not before you, how can it be seen? If the darkness is not in front of your eyes, how can you see it? You can only see what is before your eyes. How can you see things that are behind your eyes. What about it? The Buddha is demolishing Ananda's latest proposition from every angle, and it's hard to say what line of reasoning Ananda might use to answer him next.

P2 His refutation: the ability to see is not actual.

Sutra:

"**If you assert that there is an inward seeing that is distinct from seeing outside. In that case, when you close your eyes and** see darkness, you would be seeing inside the body. Therefore, when you open your eyes and see light, why can't you see your own face?

Commentary:

The Buddha continues his questioning: **If you assert that there is an inward seeing that is distinct from seeing outside.** Suppose that there are two kinds of seeing and that you are able to face inward and see. **In that case, when you close your eyes and see darkness, you would be seeing inside the body. Therefore, when you open your eyes and see light, why can't you see your own face?** You argue that to see darkness is to see inside your body; then when you open your eyes to see outside, why can't you look at your own face and tell me what it's like? Note that Ananda doesn't protest that he can see his own face in a mirror, which is what someone else did upon hearing this argument. Maybe they didn't have mirrors then.

Sutra:

"**If you cannot see your face, then there can be no seeing within. If you can see your face, then your mind that knows and understands and your organ of vision as well must be suspended in space. How could they be part of your body?**

Commentary:

If you cannot see your face, then there can be no seeing within. I just asked you if you can see your face, and you didn't have anything to say. But if you can't see your own face with your eyes open, how can you close your eyes and see inside. This is what you have argued, but your contention has no basis in principle.

If you can see your face, then your mind that knows and understands and your organ of vision as well must be suspended in space. How could they be part of your body? If you say you actually can see your own face, though, then your discriminating mind and your eyes wouldn't be on your face; they'd be out in space. If they were on your face, then you couldn't see your face. But if you can see your face, then how can you say your mind and your seeing are inside?

Sutra:

"If they are in space, then they are not part of your body. Otherwise the Tathagata who now sees your face should be part of your body as well.

Commentary:

If they are in space, then they are not part of your body. Empty space is not your body, and if your mind and eyes were in space they wouldn't have any connection with you. **Otherwise** – if you say that they would have a connection with you – if you say that those separate entities in space would be part of your substance – **the Tathagata who now sees your face should be part of your body as well.** The Buddha told him, "If you want to say that your eyes and mind are in empty space, then they are not part of your body. If you say that this mind and these eyes of yours are hanging in space and yet are still part of your body, then it should be that the Tathagata, who sees your face from the vantage-point of space, is also part of your substance. In that case, I'd be you. I have become you. Is that possible?"

Sutra:

"In that case, when your eyes perceive something, your body would remain unaware of it. If you press the point and say that the body and eyes each have an awareness, then you should have two perceptions, and your one body should eventually become two Buddhas.

Commentary:

In that case, when your eyes perceive something, your body would remain unaware of it. Is that the way it is? **If you press the point and say that the body and eyes each have an awareness, then you should have two perceptions.** If you insist on this line of reasoning, then it follows that there are two kinds of awareness, that of the body and that of the mind. Each would have its own separate perception. **And your one body should eventually become two**

Buddhas. Why is that? It is a single perception which realizes Buddhahood. Now that you have dual perception, you should become two Buddhas. Can you become two Buddhas?

P3 Concluding refutation.

Sutra:

"Therefore you should know that you state the impossible when you say that to see darkness is to see within."

Commentary:

Therefore you should know: because of the various doctrines just discussed, you should know **that you state the impossible when you say that to see darkness is to see within**. Once again, your argument is incorrect.

N5 Ananda attaches to the mind as being that which exists in response.
O1 Ananda reckons the mind exists in response to whatever it joins with.

Sutra:

Ananda said to the Buddha, "I have heard the Buddha instruct the four assemblies that because the mind arises all kinds of phenomena arise, and that because phenomena arise, every kind of mind arises.

Commentary:

Now Ananda questions the Buddha again. **Ananda said to the Buddha, "I have heard the Buddha instruct the four assemblies."** Before, Ananda used his own ideas to think of places where the mind and seeing might be located, and each idea was refuted by the Buddha. So now he doesn't speak for himself; he quotes the Buddha. He said, "I have heard the Buddha instruct the four assemblies." The four assemblies are the bhikshus, bhikshunis, upasakas, and upasikas. Bhikshus and bhikshunis are men and women who have left the home-life. Upasakas and upasikas are men and women at home who have received the five precepts[12].

---
[12]. Not to kill, not to steal, not to commit sexual misconduct, not to lie, and not to take intoxicants

Upasakas and upasikas are also called laypeople. These four groups comprise the four assemblies.

Because the mind arises all kinds of phenomena arise. Because you have a mind – the Buddha is speaking of the conscious mind – all kinds of phenomena arise. This refers to the manifestation, within the consciousness, of various states of being. Phenomena have no self-nature, but only come into being because of conditions. **Because phenomena arise, every kind of mind arises.** Because causes and conditions produce phenomena, every kind of thought arises. That is what you said, Buddha; this is a doctrine which the World Honored One explained, and so no doubt it is right, Ananda says. Now, based on that doctrine of the World Honored One, I have an opinion. What is it?

Sutra:

"As I now consider it, the substance of that very consideration is truly the nature of the mind. Wherever it comes together with things, the mind exists in response. It does not exist in the three locations of inside, outside and in between."

Commentary:

As I now consider it. Ananda's thinking again. What is he thinking? **The substance of that very consideration is truly the nature of the mind.** The substance of my thought is the nature of my mind. My being aware, my understanding, my knowing, these are the nature of my mind[13].

Wherever it comes together with things: Wherever the mind encounters causes and conditions, it joins together with those causes and conditions, and **the mind** comes into being **in response.** Whenever there is a joining together, there is the mind. If there isn't any joining together, there isn't any mind. **It does not exist in the three locations of inside, outside and in between.** It isn't inside, it isn't outside, and it isn't in between; rather, anywhere that it meets with causes and conditions, the mind comes into being. If

---

13. The nature he refers to is not the self-nature but is still the conscious mind.

there are no conditions then probably there isn't any mind. Once again, what Ananda says seems to be right but isn't. He still has not recognized it clearly. So...

O2 The Tathagata uses the refutation that it lacks a substance or a fixed place.
P1 His refutation that it lacks a substance.

Sutra:

The Buddha said to Ananda, "Now you say that because phenomena arise, every kind of mind arises. Wherever it comes together with things, the mind exists in response. But if it has no substance, the mind cannot come together with anything. If, having no substance, it can yet come together with things, that would constitute a nineteenth realm brought about by a union with the seventh defiling object, and there is no such principle.

Commentary:

The Buddha fires Ananda's explanation back at him. **The Buddha said to Ananda, "Now you say that because phenomena arise, every kind of mind arises. Wherever it comes together with things, the mind exists in response.** You say that the mind comes into being wherever it comes together with things. If there is no coming together, then, of course, there is no mind. That's the way you explain it. **But if it has no substance, the mind cannot come together with anything.** But does this mind you speak of actually have any substance to it? If it has no substance or appearance it cannot unite with anything. If there were no form or appearance, what would join with what?"

If, having no substance, it can yet come together with things. It would be unreasonable to insist that it can unite with things even though it has no substance, but suppose you do insist. **That would constitute a nineteenth realm brought about by a union with the seventh defiling object, and there is no such principle.** The eighteen realms would turn into the nineteen realms: the additional realm would be the one where, as you explain it, your mind comes into being. What are the eighteen realms? Eyes, ears, nose, tongue, body, and mind are the six organs. Forms, sounds, smells, tastes, touches, and mental constructs are the six defiling objects. And between the six organs and the six defiling objects are produced discriminations, called the six consciousnesses. Altogether, these make up the eighteen realms. The six organs and six defiling objects which face them are called the twelve places or twelve entrances. The six consciousnesses of seeing, hearing, smelling, tasting, touching, and mind are added to make eighteen realms. The Buddha points out that the logical extension of Ananda's argument is that there is a nineteenth realm, the place in which a supposed substanceless mind comes into being when it "comes together with things." These things the mind joins with would be a seventh defiling object. But there is no such principle. Ananda is wrong again.

P2 His refutation that a substance exists.

Sutra:

"If it does have substance, when you pinch your body with your hand, does your mind which perceives it come out from the inside or in from the outside? If it comes out from the inside, then, once again, it should see within your body. If it comes in from outside, it should see your face first."

Commentary:

The Buddha now explains his reason for saying Ananda is wrong again. **If it does have substance**: the Buddha has just shown it is absurd to say the mind has no substance. But if it does have a substance, if your mind has a mind-substance, **when you pinch your body with your hand, does your mind which perceives it come out from the inside or in from the outside?** Does the mind come forth from within or does its substance enter in from outside? At first you maintained that your mind is inside, but now you have stated that it is not inside, outside, or in between. Where, then, does your mind come from when it comes together with things as you say it does? Now I tell you to pinch yourself, and your mind comes together with that. Does your mind which perceives the pinch come from outside or from inside? **If it comes out from the inside, then,**

once again, it should see within your body. It's already been proven that the mind cannot be inside, since otherwise it would see inside the body. **If it comes in from outside, it should see your face first.** If your mind is outside, it would be seeing your face before it perceives the pinch. Does your mind see your own face?

Ananda got irritated with the Buddha at this point.

Sutra:

Ananda said, "Seeing is done with the eyes. The mind's perception is not that of the eyes. To say it sees doesn't make sense."

Commentary:

Ananda decided that the Buddha's explanation was too illogical, so he thereupon disagreed and began to argue. **Ananda said, "Seeing is done with the eyes. The mind's perception is not that of the eyes.** It is the eyes which see things. The mind just knows things. **To say it sees doesn't make sense."** You said the mind sees, but that is certainly wrong. That also lacks principle. Before, the Buddha criticized Ananda's idea and said "there is no such principle." And now Ananda retorts with the same criticism. "You say that if the mind comes from outside, it should see the face. But the mind merely knows things; it doesn't see them. What sees are the eyes." The farther he runs, the farther away he gets.

Sutra:

The Buddha said, "To suppose that the eyes can see is like supposing that the doors of a room can see. Also, when someone has died but his eyes are still intact, his eyes should see things. How can it be death if one can still see?

Commentary:

The Buddha said, "To suppose that the eyes can see is like supposing that the doors of a room can see. Can doors of a room see things? **Also, when someone has died but his eyes are still intact, his eyes should see things. How can it be death if one can still see?"** In fact, of course, once you're dead your eyes cease to see, though they may still be physically intact. If it were the case that after death the eyes can still see, how can this be death?

But these days dead people's eyes are removed and put in eyebanks. They still can be used. What does this prove about the Buddha's contention in the sutra that eyes can't see after death? Although it may be that the eyes can see, they still need to borrow the efficacious quality of the self-nature in order to see. If there is just an eye all by itself, although it has the potential to see, it is devoid of awareness. So it cannot see. You must add the efficacious bright aware nature of a person in order to enable it to see. The eyes are like doors or windows. They do not see by themselves. They are transparent bodies which act as windows through which people can look at things. In the body of a dead man they have no power.

Sutra:

"Furthermore, Ananda, if your mind which is aware, understands, and knows in fact has substance, then is it a single substance or many substances? Does its substance perceive the body as it now resides in it or does it not perceive it?

Commentary:

The Buddha continues to address his disciple. **Furthermore, Ananda, if your mind which is aware, understands, and knows in fact has substance**: if you are determined upon saying that your mind which calculates and discerns all things has a substance, **then is it a single substance or many substances?** Does your mind have one substance or many? **Does its substance perceive the body as it now resides in it or does it not perceive it?** Where is this substance in your body? Does it spread throughout the body or not?

Sutra:

"Supposing that it were a single substance, then when you pinched one limb with your fingers, the four limbs would be aware of it. If they all were aware of it, the pinch could not be at any one place. If the pinch were confined to one place, then the single substance you propose would not be possible.

Commentary:

Supposing that it were a single substance, then when you pinched one limb with your fingers, the four limbs would be aware of it. Let us suppose the mind is composed of a single substance which resides within the body. Then if you pinch one of your legs or arms, both legs and both arms should all have an awareness of it. Why? Because you said the mind has a single substance. But in fact if you pinch one limb, only that one limb feels pain. The other three limbs are unaware of the pinch. **If they all were aware of it, the pinch could not be at any one place.** If you say that when you pinch one leg, the other leg and both arms feel it, then how could you be able to locate the pinch on your body? It would feel the same as if you had pinched all four limbs. **If the pinch were confined to one place, then the single substance you propose would not be possible.** If you can feel the pinch in a certain single place, then you can't contend the mind is a single substance which pervades the body.

Sutra:

"**Supposing that it were many substances: then you would be many people. Which substance would be you?**

Commentary:

Supposing that it were many substances. This would explain why the three limbs don't feel a pinch on the fourth limb. But **then you would be many people.** If your mind has many mind-substances, then you wouldn't be just one person. In that case, **which substance would be you?** Which mind-substance is your mind-substance?

Sutra:

"**Supposing it were a pervasive substance: the case would be the same as before in the instance of pinching. But supposing it were not pervasive; then when you touched your head and touched your foot simultaneously, the foot would not perceive it if the head does. But that is not how you are.**

Commentary:

Supposing it were a pervasive substance: the case is the same as before in the instance of pinching. The Buddha patiently repeats his earlier explanation. If you say that the mind is a single substance that pervades the body, then when you pinch one spot, your whole body should hurt. **But supposing it were not pervasive; then when you touched your head and touched your foot simultaneously, the foot would not perceive it if the head does. But that is not how you are.** But if you say the substance of the mind does not entirely pervade the body, then your foot would have no feeling when you bump your head. But, bump your head or not, your foot still feels things. So you can't say the mind does pervade the body, and you can't say it doesn't, either.

P3 Concluding refutation.

Sutra:

"**Therefore you should know that you state the impossible when you say that wherever it comes together with things, the mind exists in response.**"

Commentary:

This was Ananda's fifth attempt to locate his mind, and the Buddha again showed his learned disciple's arguments are groundless.

N6 Ananda attaches to the mind as being in the middle.
O10 Ananda attaches to the mind as being in the middle
    of the organ and the defiling object.
P1 Ananda brings up the teachings and recklessly reckons
    the mind is in the middle.

Sutra:

Ananda said to the Buddha, "World Honored One, I also have heard the Buddha discuss true appearance with Manjushri and the other disciples of the Dharma King. The World Honored One also said, 'The mind is not inside and it is not outside.'

Commentary:

Ananda again uses the Buddha's words as a basis for his argument, to prove that his own opinion is valid. **Ananda said to the Buddha, "World Honored One, I also have heard the Buddha discuss true appearance with Manjushri and the other disciples of the Dharma King.** This is how you explained it, Buddha; it's not something I made up. You said it that way." As soon as he opens his mouth, he tries to justify himself by turning the Buddha's words to his own use. Ananda has a lot of nerve.

Manjushri is Wonderfully Auspicious Bodhisattva, also called Wonderful Virtue Bodhisattva. The other disciples of the Dharma King include Guan Yin Bodhisattva, the bodhisattva who regards the sounds of the world; Mahasthamaprapta Bodhisattva, the bodhisattva of great strength, and other great bodhisattvas. The Buddha is the Dharma King, and bodhisattva are his disciples.

What is meant by "true appearance?" True appearance has no appearance. There isn't anything at all. That is true appearance. And yet there is nothing which has no appearance. You say there isn't anything at all, but at the same time there is everything. Everything is produced from within true appearance. There is nothing which does not come forth from within it. We speak of true emptiness, of wonderful existence, and of true suchness; these also refer to "true appearance." Within true appearance is wonderful existence. In wonderful existence is true emptiness. So it is said that true emptiness does not obstruct wonderful existence, and wonderful existence does not obstruct true emptiness. At the ultimate point of emptiness there is existence. At the ultimate point of existence there is nothing at all.

"The World Honored One also said, 'The mind is not inside and it is not outside.' Buddha, this is just what you've said. If I repeat it, how can you say it is wrong?" is what Ananda is implying.

Sutra:

"As I now consider it, if it were within, it would see things it does not see; if it were outside, there would be no common

perception. Since it cannot see inside, it cannot be inside; and since the body and mind have common perception, it does not make sense to say it is outside. Therefore, since there is a common perception and since there is no seeing within, it must be in the middle."

Commentary:

As I now consider it: I am thinking it over again. **If it were within, it would see things it does not see.** Saying the mind is within the body would imply that we could see within the body. **If it were outside, there would be no common perception.** The Buddha has just demonstrated that if the mind were outside the body, the mind and body could not have the kind of common perception that they do have. **Since it cannot see inside, it cannot be inside.** Since the mind does not know what is inside the body, it won't work to say that it is located inside. **And since the body and mind have common perception, it does not make sense to say it is outside.** Our bodies and minds share knowledge of one another, as the Buddha just explained when he pointed out that Ananda experiences a common perception when his eyes see the Buddha's hand and his mind distinguishes it. If the mind were outside the body, there would be no common perception. So it can't be outside.

Therefore, since there is a common perception and since there is no seeing within – now that I understand this, I realize that **it must be in the middle**. Ananda now decides that the mind is in the middle. Precisely where this middle is he doesn't say. Is it in the middle of the body, or in a middle outside the body? That is how the Buddha proceeds to question him.

P2   The Tathagata says the location of the middle must be fixed.

Sutra:

The Buddha said, "You say it is in the middle. That middle must not be haphazard or without a fixed location. Where is this middle that you propose? Is it in an external place, or is it in the body?

Commentary:

The Buddha said, "You say it is in the middle. That middle must not be haphazard or without a fixed location. This middle of yours has to be somewhere; there has to be some sense and certainty about it. Therefore, **where is this middle that you propose?**" Consider that question. The Buddha presses the point: **Is it in an external place, or is it in the body?** Is your middle someplace outside, or it is in your body?

Sutra:

"**If it were in the body, it could not be on the surface of the body since that is not the middle. But to be in the middle is no different than being inside. If it were in an external place, would there be some evidence of it, or not? If there were no evidence of it, that would be the same as if it did not exist. If there were evidence of it, then it would have no fixed location.**

Commentary:

If it were in the body, it could not be on the surface of the body since that is not the middle. But to be in the middle is no different than being inside. Supposing this middle you say the mind is located in is in the body: is it on the surface of the body? But then it isn't in the middle. Is it in the middle of the body? But that is to say the mind is inside the body, and we've already rejected that as impossible. **If it were in an external place, would there be some evidence of it, or not?** If you say that the middle is somewhere else, can you point out where it is? Is there something about it that allows us to discern it? **If there were no evidence of it, that would be the same as if it did not exist.** If there is nothing to indicate its presence, if you can't point to it as being in a certain place, then it does not exist. You still haven't shown me a middle. **If there were evidence of it, then it would have no fixed location.** Why does the Buddha say this?

Sutra:

"Why? Suppose that someone were to indicate the middle by a marker. When regarded from the east, it would be to the west, and when regarded from the south, it would be to the north. The marker is unclear, and the mind would be equally chaotic."

Commentary:

Why? **Suppose that someone were to indicate the middle by a marker.** Someone pounds a sign in the ground reading: "This place is the middle." **When regarded from the east, it would be to the west, and when regarded from the south, it would be to the north.** Your sign may say "middle" but if you stand to the east of it, the sign is west of you: how is this the middle? Then you might stand to the south of it: now it is to the north of you. This is also not the middle. Basically, as I said earlier, the ten directions do not exist. You might say that something is south of you, but if you go south of it, it becomes north. You could then say it is north, but if you go north of that north, it becomes south again. So which is it? There is nothing fixed about it. The principle is the same here. **The marker is unclear, and the mind would be equally chaotic.** The marker doesn't indicate anything at all; it cannot fix a middle. If the mind were in the middle, it would be as unfixed as your marker; it would be chaotic. Ultimately, which place is the middle? There isn't any place that is the middle. So the middle you speak of is probably also a mistake.

P3 Ananda brings up an alternative view.

Sutra:

Ananda said, "The middle I speak of is neither of those. As the World Honored One has said, the eyes and forms are the conditions which create the eye-consciousness. The eyes make discriminations; forms have no perception, but a consciousness is created between them. That is where my mind is."

Commentary:

Ananda said, "**The middle I speak of is neither of those.** The mind isn't located inside or outside; this isn't what I meant, World Honored One. **As the World Honored One has said, the eyes and** forms are the conditions which create the eye-consciousness. It's just as you explained before, World Honored One."

Ananda is still using statements the Buddha made in the past as evidence for his points of view. "World Honored One, you said that when the eye encounters forms, the eye-consciousness is created between them. **The eyes make discriminations.** Why are the conditions for the arisal of the eye-consciousness, of seeing, created when the eyes encounter form? Because the eyes make discriminations. **Forms have no perception, but a consciousness is created between them. That is where my mind is.** The defiling object of form has no awareness of its own, but when the eyes encounter it, a kind of discriminating mind arises in their midst, and this is where my mind is. The middle I'm talking about is the place where the eyes and forms meet to create the eye-consciousness. That is the mind."

O2 The Tathagata uses combining the two or not combining the two to refute his argument.
P1 He brings up two possibilities.

Sutra:

The Buddha said, "If your mind were between the eye and an object, does the mind's substance combine with the two or does it not?

Commentary:

The Buddha listened to Ananda dispute his explanation and replied, **"If your mind were between the eye and an object, does the mind's substance combine with the two or does it not?** Suppose it is as you say, and the mind is in the middle between the eye and the defiling object of form. Do they combine? Are they one or are they two?"

P2 He shows that both possibilities are impossible.

Sutra:

"If it did combine with the two, then objects and the mind-substance would form a chaotic mixture. Since objects have no

perception, while the substance has perception, the two would stand in opposition. Which is the middle?

"If it did not combine with the two, it would then be neither perceiver nor perceived and would have no substance or nature. Where would the characteristic of 'middle' be?

Commentary:

If it did combine with the two – if your mind, the mind you say is in the middle, includes the sense organs and their objects – **then objects and the mind-substance would form a chaotic mixture**. Which, then, is the substance of your mind, and which are the objects? Can you make a distinction? If you cannot, they are mixed chaotically together in a confusing disorder. **Since objects have no perception, while the substance has perception, the two would stand in opposition.** Things don't know anything, while your eye-organ has a mind-substance. They are opposites. **Which is the middle?** Where is the middle you speak of? Is your mind in the middle of your eye, or is it in the middle of the objects the eye sees?

If it did not combine with the two, it would then be neither perceiver nor perceived and would have no substance or nature. If your mind does not combine with the eye and the object the eye sees, it will not be perceiving anything; it will have no nature that is aware. **Where would the characteristic of 'middle' be?** In the final analysis, where is your mind?

P3 Concluding refutation.

Sutra:

"Therefore you should know that for the mind to be in the middle is impossible."

Commentary:

For these reasons, Ananda, you should understand that your argument that the mind is in the middle won't stand. There is no such principle.

N7　Ananda attaches to the mind as being non-attachment.
O1　Ananda presents the idea of non-attachment as being the mind.

Sutra:

Ananda said to the Buddha, "World Honored One, when I have seen the Buddha turn the dharma wheel in the past with great Maudgalyayana, Subhuti, Purna, and Shariputra, four of the great disciples, he often said that the nature of the mind which perceives, makes discriminations, and is aware is located neither within nor outside nor in the middle; it is not located anywhere at all. That very non-attachment to anything is what is called the mind. Therefore, is my non-attachment my mind?"

Commentary:

One suspects that Ananda began to get nervous after hearing the Buddha refute yet another of his arguments. He had exhausted his knowledge and reached the end of his wits. By this time, there was no way out for him; there was no escape. So once again he transferred some of the principles the Buddha had spoken previously to the present situation in an attempt to save himself from defeat.

Ananda said to the Buddha, "World Honored One, when I have seen the Buddha turn the dharma wheel in the past with great Maudgalyayana," whose name means "descendent of a family of bean gatherers"; **Subhuti,** whose name means "born into emptiness"; **Purna,** whose name means "son of completion and compassion"; and **Shariputra, four of the great disciples**. They turn the dharma wheel together. What does it mean to "turn the dharma wheel?" It means to use the words spoken by the Buddha to teach and transform living beings. They are spoken this way and that way and all around, just as the principles of the *Shurangama Sutra* are now being explained over and over. That's why it is called a "wheel." Turning the dharma wheel reveals the principles and it crushes the heavenly demons and followers of other religions. When those of other religions encounter this wheel they are smashed by it. Obliterated.

He often said, he repeated many times in the Agama sutras and the Vaipulya sutras, **that the nature of the mind which perceives, makes discriminations, and is aware is located neither within nor outside nor in the middle; it is not located anywhere at all.** If the nature of the mind which calculates, knows, and makes distinctions is located neither inside nor outside, it should be located between them, in the middle; but it isn't there either. It isn't anywhere. **That very non-attachment to anything is what is called the mind.** The aware, perceptive mind is not attached anywhere at all, and since it has no place of attachment, it is called the mind. **Therefore, is my non-attachment my mind?** "Now, I'm not attached. The mind I speak of is also not attached. But I don't know whether one can call it 'mind.'" Ananda thought that if he asked it this way, the Buddha would certainly agree that what he referred to was the mind. After all, the Buddha himself had said so.

But what the Buddha had said previously was said in accordance with the way those in the world view things. His explanation then was geared to the understanding of the people he was speaking to then. People of the small vehicle do not understand great vehicle dharma, and if one were to explain the true mind to them without any introduction, they would not believe it; so the Buddha spoke to them about the conscious mind. He was complying with worldly dharmas. Now Ananda wishes to take the conscious mind of ordinary people as his mind. Is he right? Basically, Ananda's view would be acceptable from the point of view of ordinary people. But the mind the Buddha is speaking of is not the conscious mind. It is the permanently dwelling true mind, not the mind which has false thinking. Yet Ananda still thinks his false-thinking mind is his true mind; he continues to mistake a thief for his son.

O2 The Tathagata uses the existence or non-existence of the
   appearance of the mind as refutation.
P1 He asks if it exists or not.

Sutra:

The Buddha said to Ananda, "You say that the nature of the mind which perceives, makes discriminations, and is aware is

not located anywhere at all. **The entirety of things existing in the world consists of space, the waters, the land, the creatures that fly and walk, and all external objects. Does your non-attachment also exist?**

Commentary:

The Buddha again replied to Ananda's explanation with a question: **You say that the nature of the mind which perceives, makes discriminations, and is aware is not located anywhere at all.** To have no attachment is to have no location. **The entirety of things existing in the world consists of space, the waters, the land, the creatures that fly and walk, and all external objects.** There are two kinds of worlds: the sentient world, composed of living beings, and the material world, which includes all the mountains, rivers, the great expanse of earth, and all the various buildings. These and empty space and the myriad external objects together make up the two kinds of retributions: dependent retribution, which includes the land, the waters, the buildings; and proper retribution, which refers to our bodies. The world consists of these two. **Does your non-attachment also exist?** Among all these things in the world, where are you? What place are you not attached to? Is there someplace where there is non-attachment or is there not? If your non-attachment is nowhere, then that's the same as saying it doesn't exist.

P2 He shows that neither are possible.

Sutra:

"**If it does not exist, it is the same as hairs on a tortoise or horns on a rabbit. How can you speak of non-attachment?**

Commentary:

If it does not exist, it is the same as hairs on a tortoise or horns on a rabbit. Have you ever seen a turtle with hair or a horned rabbit? In other words, there is no such thing. **How can you speak of non-attachment?** If it doesn't exist, what is it you are attached to? Why did you bring up the word "non-attachment?"

Sutra:

"If non-attachment existed, it could not be said to be non-existent. To be non-existent is to be without attributes. To be existent is to have attributes. Whatever has attributes has a location; how then can it be said to be unattached?

Commentary:

If non-attachment existed, it could not be said to be non-existent. You propose that at a certain place there is a certain non-attachment. But you cannot say there isn't anything there. You speak of non-attachment, but if there is a certain thing called non-attachment, then you still have something; and how can you call that non-attachment? But if in fact it doesn't exist – if there is nothing there – why do you want to assign the name "non-attachment" to it? That is really a case of putting a head on top of a head or riding a donkey in search of a donkey.

To be non-existent is to be without attributes. If you haven't any attachment, that is non-existence. **To be existent is to have attributes. Whatever has attributes has a location; how then can it be said to be unattached?** But if it is not non-existent, then it has characteristics, and if something has form and an appearance, it thereby must have a location. If it has a location, how can you say it is unattached?

P3 Concluding refutation.

Sutra:

"Therefore you should know, to call the aware, knowing mind non-attachment to anything is impossible."

Commentary:

Ananda's seventh attempt to locate his mind has failed, as well. The Buddha says, **"Therefore you should know,** Ananda, **to call the aware, knowing mind non-attachment to anything is impossible.** To say that your mind is non-attachment won't work either. Your argument won't stand. It is unreasonable."

The False Consciousness is Not the Mind

L2 The Tathagata admonishes that the false consciousness is not the mind.
M1 Ananda reproves himself and asks for instruction.

Sutra:

Then Ananda arose from his seat in the midst of the great assembly, uncovered his right shoulder, placed his right knee on the ground, respectfully put his palms together, and said to the Buddha:

Commentary:

During the dialogue with the World Honored One, Ananda had spun in circles and couldn't escape; he went around and around and still had not found the right road, because he was using his discriminating conscious mind and mistaking it for his true mind. And so from beginning to end he was unable to enter into the realm of the mysterious. He didn't measure up; he didn't pass the test.

Then Ananda arose from his seat in the midst of the great assembly; at that time there were great bhikshus, great arhats, and great bodhisattvas in the dharma assembly. He **uncovered his right shoulder**. This means he let the right side of his robe fall, the way the sash I am now wearing over my robe is designed to leave the right shoulder uncovered. In China customs are such that exposing one's shoulder would not be considered respectful, but by Indian custom, uncovering the right shoulder is a gesture of respect, especially in Buddhism. When he uncovered his right shoulder and **placed his right knee on the ground,** that represents the purity of body karma. The body cannot create evil karma in that position. He **respectfully put his palms together**: that represents the purity of mind karma. **And said to the Buddha**: that represents the purity of mouth karma. Thus the purity of the three karmas of body, mouth, and mind are represented as Ananda requests dharma of the Buddha.

Sutra:

"**I am the Tathagata's youngest cousin. I have received the Buddha's compassionate love and have left the home-life, but I have been dependent on his affection, and as a consequence have pursued erudition and am not yet without outflows.**

Commentary:

Now Ananda thinks over how he has spent his time since he has left the home-life. He says: **I am the Tathagata's youngest cousin.** In Shakyamuni Buddha's family there were four kings and eight sons. His father was one of the four brothers, each of whom had two sons. Ananda was the youngest of them. **I have received the Buddha's compassionate love and have left the home-life.** I followed the Buddha and left the home-life. In leaving home, one leaves the home of ignorance which could be said to be everyone's house; one leaves the home of the three realms, that is, the realm of desire, the realm of form, and the formless realm; one leaves the home of affliction; and one leaves the worldly home, that is the home of one's family. When you leave home, you leave these and many other kinds of homes. But though Ananda left his worldly home, he had not yet severed his emotional feelings. He still had not left the homes of ignorance and affliction or the home of the three realms.

But I have been dependent on his affection. Ananda confesses that he has relied too much on his family tie with the Tathagata. He allowed himself to be disobedient sometimes in order to get the Buddha's attention. He would sometimes act like a child and be deliberately rambunctious, or he would purposefully not abide by the rules, and he expected the Buddha to sympathize with him, to take care of him. **And as a consequence have pursued erudition and am not yet without outflows.** He concentrated on learning at the expense of samadhi. Ananda had reached the first stage of arhatship, but it is not until the fourth stage that one is without outflows. At the fourth stage one puts an end to birth and death does not have to flow back into the three realms. But in the first stage, outflows remain.

Sutra:

"**I could not overcome the Kapila mantra. I was spun around by it and sank in the house of prostitution, all because I did not know the location of the realm of reality.**

Commentary:

I could not overcome the Kapila mantra. I was incapable of opposing the mantra that came from the Brahma Heaven which the religion of the yellow-haired used – that deviant method of that externalist teaching. I did not have enough strength to counteract it and **was spun around by it and sank in the house of prostitution.** The deviant mantra plunged me into confusion and I sank as if drowning in the sea. There is another explanation, since the Chinese character for "stank" is also the word for urine: Ananda is indicating that he came in contact with something unclean. He went into the filthy brothel where women sold themselves. He found himself stuck there as if in a cesspool and could not extricate himself. If the Buddha had not used the Shurangama Mantra to rescue him, Ananda would not have had the opportunity to compile the sutras. If the sutra store had been compiled at all, it would have been done by someone else. Ananda would have had no part in it. Fortunately Shakyamuni Buddha used the Shurangama Mantra to rescue him, so he was able to compile the *Shurangama Sutra* and give us a record of these causes and conditions.

All because I did not know the location of the realm of reality. The realm of reality is another name for the true mind. Why did I sink in the house of prostitution? Because I did not know where the fundamental true mind is. To this very moment, Ananda is still trying to find a location for the mind. He's being boggled by his own intelligence. He keeps spinning around in it and doesn't know how to get out.

Sutra:

"I only hope that the World Honored One, out of great kindness and pity, will instruct us in the path of shamata to guide the icchantikas and overthrow the mlecchas."

Commentary:

I only hope that the World Honored One, out of great kindness and pity. Now I only have one wish, that the World Honored One will extend his great compassion, to rescue me from my suffering and bring me bliss. I hope the Buddha **will instruct us in the path of shamata to guide the icchantikas and overthrow the mlecchas.** World Honored One, teach not only myself but all those in the great assembly, who upon hearing the dharma have given rise to doubts. Instruct us in how to develop concentration; show us the path to the cultivation of the practice of stillness.

Icchantika is a Sanskrit word which is interpreted to mean "insufficient faith." Icchantikas are those whose faith is deficient, and a deficiency of faith is the same as no faith at all. Icchantikas are also said to be those who have "burned up their good roots." What is left once their good roots are burned up? Bad roots.

Dharma Master Dao Sheng once explained the *Nirvana Sutra* in China before the final volume had arrived from India. In the first half of the sutra, it says that icchantikas have no Buddha-nature. Most dharma masters then explained the line as meaning that icchantikas cannot become Buddhas. Actually, in the final volume of the sutra it says that icchantikas can also become Buddhas, but at that time the final volume of the sutra was not known in China. Nevertheless, when Dharma Master Dao Sheng came to that passage of text in the first part of the sutra, he did not follow its apparent meaning, but explained instead that icchantikas can become Buddhas. As a result, the other dharma masters opposed him, were jealous of him, and said that he had had the nerve to contradict the sutra's meaning and had done it just to be different. Actually, Dharma Master Dao Sheng wasn't saying the sutra was wrong or that the Buddha had spoken incorrectly. He understood the principle behind it, and although he had not seen the final volume of the sutra, he already realized that the Buddha could not have spoken the dharma this way. But because jealousies had been aroused, no one came to listen to him explain sutras any longer, so he went to Su Zhou, near Shanghai, to Hu Qiu mountain. There he lectured the *Nirvana Sutra* to the rocks. When he again reached the passage of text that said icchantikas do not have the Buddha-nature, he asked the rocks, "I say icchantikas also have the Buddha-nature. What do you say? Am I right, or not?" The rocks on the mountain bowed their heads in silent assent. So it is said:

> When Sheng the venerable
>   spoke the dharma,
> Even the rocks
>   bowed their heads.

Basically, of course, rocks are senseless things which cannot move, but even so they agreed with Dharma Master Dao Sheng's explanation and so bowed their assent. There are reasons for this. I believe there were ghosts and spirits sitting or sprawled out on the rocks. On second thought, they couldn't have been sprawled out, because you have to sit up when you listen to sutras. When the dharma master asked his question, the ghosts and spirits were so exuberant in their agreement that they made the rocks shake. Or, perhaps in past lives these rocks had spiritual natures which were now hidden away in a casing of rock, and this is why they could register their agreement. So,

> When Sheng the venerable
>   spoke the dharma,
> Even the rocks
>   bowed their heads.

Still, icchantikas are extremely difficult to save. When you elucidate principle for them, they never quite believe you. "Hey," they say, "Who ever heard of such a thing?" No matter how well you speak dharma for them, they don't believe you. They are like Kaushthila who took "non-acceptance" as his doctrine. No matter what you said to him, he wouldn't listen, he wouldn't accept it. That's an icchantika.

Mleccha is a Sanskrit word which is interpreted to mean "a fondness for defilement." Mlecchas like unclean places. Mleccha also means "evil knowledge and views." Most people's knowledge and points of view are good, but these people's are evil. They are solely intent upon doing wrong. They exude nothing but poisonous fluids, which are not only bad for them but also influence others to imitate them. So we people should clean up a bit and not take special pleasure in filth. Ananda asked the Buddha to overcome the mlecchas and prevent people from falling victim to a fondness for unwholesome places, from having such a problem.

Sutra:

After he had finished speaking, he placed his five limbs on the ground along with the entire great assembly. Then they stood on tiptoe waiting attentively and thirstily to respectfully hear the instructions.

Commentary:

After he had finished speaking, he placed his five limbs on the ground. "Five limbs" refer to his two hands, his two feet, and his head. In Buddhism this is the most respectful gesture of all. He bowed **along with the entire great assembly**. Not only did Ananda bow to the Buddha after he finished making his request, everyone in the great assembly followed suit. **Then they stood on tiptoe waiting attentively and thirstily to respectfully hear the instructions.** "Attentively" indicates that they listened carefully, intent upon what instructions the Buddha would give them, upon the doctrine of samadhi which Ananda had requested. They were inexpressibly thirsty for the dharma as if their mouths were parched and they were waiting for a drink of water. The wisdom-life of the dharma-bodies of these people had dried up and withered, and they were waiting for the Buddha to pour the water of dharma over them and nourish their dharma bodies' wisdom-life.

The phrase "on tip-toe" refers to how people stretch up in readiness to listen when they are in the back of the room and wish to hear better. Those who compiled the sutras used these descriptive terms to indicate how happy these people were to hear the dharma. They "stood waiting": this also indicates that those far from the Buddha stood on tip-toe in order to get a better view of him as they waited for him to speak. Why did they want to see the Buddha? Because everyone is fond of the Buddha's thirty-two adorning hallmarks and eighty subtle characteristics, and everyone likes to gaze at them, including the great bodhisattvas, great arhats, great bhikshus, and laypeople in the Shurangama dharma assembly. I believe they were of more or less the same mind as Ananda. It was because of the Buddha's thirty-two hallmarks that Ananda had left the home-life, and it was probably because of the Buddha's hallmarks that the others in the assembly had come to hear the dharma.

The word "respectfully" is used to indicate again how the kings, the great ministers, the elders, and laypeople all stood waiting with great reverence to hear the Buddha explain the doctrine of samadhi.

M2 The Tathagata reveals it is not the mind.
N1 The display of light destroys the manifestation of all appearances.

Sutra:

Then the World Honored One radiated forth from his face various kinds of light, dazzling light as brilliant as hundreds of thousands of suns.

Commentary:

Then was when Ananda placed his five limbs on the ground and the great assembly attentively, thirstily stood on tip-toe waiting respectfully to hear the instruction. **The World Honored One radiated forth from his face**: the Chinese is *mian men* (面門),

literally "face-door," but this just refers to the face. You should not go looking for a door on the Buddha's face. He hasn't any doors on his face, just windows. His eyes are windows and his nostrils are caves in which people can sit in meditation and cultivate. Not only is that possible in the Buddha's nostrils, it can be done in any one of ours as well. If you want to say there is a door, the mouth could be called a door, but there is no reason to stick to every word so closely.

The Buddha emitted from his face **various kinds of light, dazzling light as brilliant as hundreds of thousands of suns.** The Buddha emitted not just one kind, but many kinds of light from his face. In general there are five colors of light, but in the five colors many, many color-combinations can be distinguished. The Buddha's light was more powerful than a lightning flash, brighter than an electric light, as it radiated back and forth. The sunlight in the world we live in is very powerful, but the Buddha emitted light whose intensity was a thousand times greater than the light of hundreds of thousands of suns. How much light would you say that was? When Ananda compiled the sutras he described the Buddha's light this way because this was the way he himself had personally witnessed it.

Sutra:

The six kinds of quaking pervaded the Buddharealms, and thus lands as many as fine motes of dust throughout the ten directions appeared simultaneously.

Commentary:

The six kinds of quaking pervaded the Buddharealms. All the billions of worlds where there was a Buddha – not only our Saha world but all the others – experienced the six kinds of earthquakes. Three kinds involve movement: quaking, erupting, and heaving up. Quaking is the motion of the earth in an earthquake. Erupting refers to intermittent agitations which cause the earth to little by little gush forth like water from a fountain. Heaving up refers to continual, violent upward movements of the earth. Sometimes the earth can be heaped up to form high places and sometimes it can sink to form depressions. At present our planet earth is in the midst of changes brought about by the six kinds of earthquakes.

The other kinds of earthquakes – cracking, roaring, and striking – involve sound. Cracking is not the same as quaking, which is a simple movement of the earth. When there is cracking, whole sections of the earth are torn asunder. The earth splits apart and often rends whole buildings in the process. Roaring occurs when the earth emits sound unheard in the world. Striking occurs when the earth splits apart and the two faces of the crevasse strike against one another.

The six kinds of earthquakes occur for various reasons: when someone in the world become a Buddha; when someone becomes enlightened, but has not yet realized Buddhahood, that is, when he accomplished the result of arhatship; and when a demon king wishes to disturb the minds of people in the world. So there are good earthquakes and bad earthquakes. When they are good, that is, when a Buddha accomplishes the Way or someone achieves enlightenment, no matter how great a disturbance the six kinds of earthquakes cause, no one will be injured. When a demon king comes to display his demonic power and disturb the minds of people in the world, he can kill people and wreak destruction. When there is an earthquake in one country and many people perish, and then the same thing happens in another country, that is a demon king who has decided to flex his muscles, awe the people of the world, and extend the scope of his power. It is just like a political demonstration: the demon kings stage demonstrations for us people, in order to say: "Take a look at how great my demonic powers are. I can overturn heaven and upset earth." Therefore we should be careful to determine whether each experience we encounter is a good or bad situation, since there are many distinctions.

Speaking of earthquakes, I remember experiencing an earthquake one night after my mother died, when I was practicing filial piety beside her grave. I was sitting in dhyana, and everything was empty – there was no self and no others – when suddenly I felt a movement, an agitation. I thought to myself, "Ah, what is this demon that can shake my body this way? Its strength is certainly formidable." I didn't realize it was an earthquake. The next day someone came to tell me there had been an earthquake – a very strange earthquake. During it, the well near where I sat had spouted fire. This was a water-well, not a volcano, and yet fire had come forth from it. There are many strange things in this world.

I believe someone is thinking, "I'm sure that beneath the well there was a vein of sulfur which fed a volcano, and that is why the well spouted fire." Maybe that's the way it was.

And thus: Once the six kinds of earthquakes occurred, **lands as many as fine motes of dust throughout the ten directions appeared simultaneously.** How many fine motes of dust are there? They are uncountable. Yet the lands which appeared were as incalculably numerous as dust-motes. The great arhats, great bodhisattvas, great bhikshus, elders, laypeople, and the king and his ministers all saw these lands appear simultaneously. What kind of experience would you say that was?

Sutra:

The Buddha's awesome spirit caused all the realms to unite into a single realm.

Commentary:

The Buddha's awesome spirit: Shakyamuni Buddha used his awesome spiritual strength, the power of his spiritual penetrations, to cause **all the realms**, all the lands as many as the fine motes of dust, **to unite into a single realm.** Although the lands were innumerable, they all came together into one. For example, nowadays we can enlarge a very small photograph into a very large one and reduce a very large photograph into a very small one; wouldn't you say that is a spiritual penetration? In the same way, Shakyamuni Buddha, by means of his spiritual power, made distant places close, by reducing all the myriad lands throughout the great trichiliocosm into a single one, as if he were reducing a photograph. And yet, though the lands were united into one, each remained perfectly intact in their original order, each still located in its respective position without being mixed up. The reason the Buddha brought all the worlds together was so that everyone in all the worlds could see and listen to him as he explained the inexpressibly wonderful dharma.

Sutra:

And in these realms all the great bodhisattvas, each remaining in his own country, put their palms together and listened.

Commentary:

Shakyamuni Buddha brought all the lands and realms together into one because he wanted everyone to be able to listen to the explanation of the great Shurangama Samadhi, so that the bodhisattvas in every land could come to understand this doctrine. So he emitted a great light from his face, a blazing light as brilliant as hundreds of thousands of suns, until every land was illumined. **And in these realms all the great bodhisattvas, each remaining in his own country, put their palms together and listened** to Shakyamuni Buddha speak dharma and explain the *Shurangama Sutra*.

N2 The two roots of true and false are revealed.
O1 The Tathagata brings up former reasons and illustrates them with an analogy.

Sutra:

The Buddha said to Ananda, "All living beings, from beginningless time onward and in all kinds of upside-down ways, have created seeds of karma which naturally run their course, like the aksha cluster.

Commentary:

After the Buddha had reduced the worlds to the number of fine motes of dust to a single world, in which all the respective worlds remained in perfect order, the great bodhisattvas in each of these worlds thirstily gazed at the Buddha with uplifted faces. Like Ananda, they were inexpressibly thirsty, wanting to drink the dharma-water of Shakyamuni Buddha.

All of you have probably experienced a severe thirst. When you are hungry, after a while the hunger seems to subside a bit and is not so severe, but if you are thirsty, perhaps as a result of eating something salty, not having any water to drink is very difficult to bear.

Why were the bodhisattvas so inexpressibly thirsty? They had eaten too much of the salt of affliction. Ananda, who had concentrated exclusively on being greatly learned and had neglected his samadhi-power, had eaten too much of the salt of being greatly learned. They wanted the water of samadhi to quench their thirst, to irrigate them, so they thirstily gazed upward. In explaining this, my own throat feels dry. But my dryness comes from talking, whereas the great bodhisattva's dryness came from not having obtained the dharma.

Some of you aren't clear about this and say, "I don't understand what I'm reading." If you know that you don't understand, that itself is understanding. If you truly didn't understand, you wouldn't even be aware of your lack of understanding. You would sit there and not know whether you understood. Now you are aware that you do not understand very much of the sutra you are reading, and that means you have some understanding. If you have the hope of understanding, the day will come when you will understand and be clear about the sutra. If you understood thoroughly right now, that would be something else again. In that case, this dharma master would be left with nothing to eat. If you understood the sutra before I even finished explaining it, what use would there be for me in the future? I would be useless! However, to understand the sutra immediately isn't possible. It's also impossible to understand everything there is to know about the affairs of the world in a single day. Some time is required. As you read more, you will quite naturally come to understand. Why don't you understand? Because you haven't read much.

The Buddha said to Ananda. Just as I am now explaining to you who are reading this, the Buddha explained to Ananda. But I'm not the Buddha and you are not Ananda. I am just explaining this recorded history about Ananda for you.

All living beings, from beginningless time onward. All living beings include those born from eggs, from wombs, from moisture, or by transformation; those with form, without form, with thought, or without thought; those not entirely with thought, and those not entirely without thought. When the Buddha spoke sutras, he himself couldn't completely explain the doctrines. He said, "From beginningless time onward" – from time without any starting-point. When would you say that was? If you were trying to be logical, you would say this passage doesn't make sense. But in fact there is no way to state when people came into being.

What is the beginning? By way of explanation, just take a single family. You say, "I am my father's son." Whose son is your father? Your father is your grandfather's son. Whose son is your grandfather? You keep tracing your family tree until you can't trace it any further. "This man was my family's very first founding father," you say. But who was his founding father? Trace that. Find out. You cannot find out. It is said that people evolved from monkeys. What did monkeys evolve from? If monkeys can turn into people, how do you know that all people evolved from monkeys? Couldn't any have evolved from pigs? or from dogs? or from cows? If monkeys can evolve into people, then all other living beings can evolve in the same way. All can undergo mutual transference. So you trace back and forth and you find there isn't any beginning.

Now, with scientific and archaeological discoveries, people know how many thousands of years ago things occurred, how many tens of thousands of years ago things occurred. They know where the remains of human bones from ten thousand years ago or a million years ago are found. So what? Is that proof of something? You cannot say it is. It doesn't prove anything.

"If that's not evidence of anything, then why do societies invest so much money in research and experimentation?" you say. That's the foolishness of this world. Having nothing to do, people look for something to do. If they hadn't done these muddled things, how could this world's resources have become so depleted and wasted away? If you truly understand, what can you say is real in this world? Find something real and bring it here for me to look at. Everyone is born in a stupor and dies in a dream.

"But they benefit the country! etc…" you say.

They're muddled people doing muddled things. They think themselves intelligent, but actually they are just cheating themselves, because one cannot find the beginning. "From beginningless time onward." One need speak of nothing more than one person's life and his genealogy which has no beginning or end. As to our lives, when would you say they began?

"Mine began at my birth in this life," you say.

If it really did begin just that short time ago, then there's no problem. It is just to be feared that it did not begin such a short time ago. That is why there is a problem.

And in all kinds of upside-down ways. That foolishness I spoke of before is just to be upside-down, and to be born in a stupor and die in a dream. You say, "I've got to give this body some good things to eat and some nice clothes to wear." And then what? Ultimately, then what? As I said before, you're just putting finery on a toilet. What's so great about it? That's to be upside-down. To invent something to do when there is nothing to do is to act "in all kinds of upside-down ways." It's to fail to recognize one's pure basic substance and to apply one's effort to false thinking instead. "Ah," you say, "So-and-so is really fine." So what if he is really fine? Or you say, "So-and-so is really rotten." So what if he is really rotten? If you investigate a little more deeply you'll find that these kinds of things do not exist. What is fine and what is rotten? It is discrimination through the eyes of living beings that divides things into fine and rotten, good and bad, right and wrong. In the treasury of the Thus Come One there are no such questions. There isn't anything at all in the treasury of the Thus Come One. It is absolutely clean. Our eyes may see the mountains, the rivers, the earth, and vegetation – all the myriad things – but they are simply manifestations of consciousness. When you really understand the principle of no production and no extinction, then there basically isn't anything at all. But this doctrine is not easy to comprehend. We must come to understand its meaning gradually.

They have created seeds of karma which naturally run their course, like the aksha cluster. Living beings' ignorance leads them to act in upside-down ways, and their various upside-down acts create every kind of karma. According to their various karmas, they undergo various retributions. Why do people do evil things? It is because of their ignorance, their lack of understanding, their state of delusion. Their delusion leads to the creation of bad karma, and since they create bad karma they undergo the retribution of suffering. It is a three-part process: delusion, leading to the creation of bad karma, which leads to the retribution of suffering. The Buddha compares the process to the *aksha*, a shrub found in India which bears three fruits in a cluster on one stem. Though you may have never seen an aksha, the sutra makes the meaning clear, and one cannot fail to understand it. The aksha cluster represents the three fruits of delusion, karma, and retribution, which are interconnected as if they were joined on a single stem. You can't say which precedes the other; they follow after one another in a continuous revolution, life after life, aeon after aeon. Where would you say it all began? There is no beginning. It's an endless cycle on the spinning wheel of the six paths of rebirth.

Each of us people born here in the world is like a fine mote of dust which suddenly rises high, suddenly falls low, is suddenly up and suddenly down. When your actions are good and meritorious you are born higher. When you do things which create offenses, you fall. Therefore we people should do good things and accomplish meritorious deeds. Don't do things which create offenses because this world runs on the principle of cause and effect, the law of karma. And the seeds of karma naturally run their course: you undergo a retribution for whatever you do.

There is a distinction between "karma" and "cause." It is said that whenever you plant a cause, you reap its effect. A cause is a particular action which will lead in the future to a particular effect. Karma is the general process by which this inevitably happens. It's like planting a seed in the ground in the spring: this is the cause which, at the end of the growing season, brings about the effect of the harvest in the autumn. The entire process, from planting through months of growth to maturity and harvest, is karma. The causes you plant will determine what harvest you reap. If you plant good causes, you will reap good results. If you plant bad causes, you will reap bad results.

Your karma is made up of whatever you ordinarily do most. For example, when you run a business you engage in "commercial karma." Your occupational karma can be good karma or bad. If you are a butcher, for example, you have the occupational karma of killing; if you are a thief, your occupational karma is stealing; if you do nothing but engage in illicit sexual affairs, you have the occupational karma of lust. If you never tell the truth, your occupational karma is lying. In general, whatever you do continually is your karma, and your retribution will be in accordance with it.

Thus karma is created from the very first ignorant thought, and from karma born of ignorance comes retribution. The three together are like an aksha cluster. This is how the Buddha clearly explains the process of karma to Ananda in this passage.

Sutra:
"The reason those who cultivate cannot accomplish unsurpassed bodhi, but instead reach the level of a sound-hearer or of one enlightened to conditions, or become accomplished in outside ways as heaven-dwellers or as demon-kings or as members of the retinue of demons is that they do not know the two fundamental roots and are mistaken and confused in their cultivation. They are like one who cooks sand in the hope of creating savory delicacies. They may pass through as many aeons as there are motes of dust, but in the end they will not obtain what they want.

Commentary:

The reason those who cultivate cannot accomplish unsurpassed bodhi. This includes those of all the outside ways as well as all Buddhists. People cultivate the Way in the hope of obtaining something, and accomplishing something. What they wish to accomplish is the unsurpassed enlightened Way. They want to obtain the unsurpassed fruition of enlightenment. "Bodhi" is the accomplishment of Buddhahood. Bodhisattvas are called "surpassed lords" because above them is the Buddha, while Buddhas are the "unsurpassed lords," and "unsurpassed bodhi" is the state of having accomplished Buddhahood.

But instead reach the level of a sound-hearer or of one enlightened to conditions. Can cultivators reach positions other than Buddhahood? Sound-hearers are those who hear the Buddha's sound and awaken to the Way. They cultivate the dharma of the four truths. Those enlightened to conditions cultivate the dharma of the twelve links of conditioned causation.

Or become accomplished in outside ways as heaven-dwellers or as demon-kings or as members of the retinue of demons. What is meant by "outside ways?" The term has been mentioned often. Those who "seek the dharma outside the mind" are said to follow an outside way. In fact, everyone who has not reached enlightenment or realized Buddhahood can be said, in a sense, to be an externalist.

There are many heavens. The one closest to us is the Heaven of the Four Kings. It lies halfway up Mount Sumeru on the north, south, east, and west. The four heavenly kings are the Heavenly King of Increase and Growth, the Heavenly King of Learning, the Heavenly King of the Broad Eyes, and the Heavenly King Who Upholds His Country. The lifespan of the inhabitants of the Heaven of the Four Kings is 500 years. However, fifty years among us people is equivalent to only one day and night in that heaven.

Above the Heaven of the Four Kings is the Trayastrimsha Heaven where the lifespan of inhabitants is 1000 years. A hundred years among people is equivalent to one day and night in the Trayastrimsha Heaven. Trayastrimsha is Sanskrit for "thirty-three," since the Trayastrimsha Heaven is made up of thirty-three heavens, eight each on the north, south, east, and west sides of Mount Sumeru, making thirty-two, with the thirty-third, the Trayastrimsha Heaven located on Mount Sumeru's peak.

The lord of the Trayastrimsha Heaven was a woman in the past. Once she saw a Buddha-image in a temple which had a leak in its roof. She resolved to repair the leak so the rain would not ruin the Buddha-image. She was a poor peasant woman, but she had friends, and she convinced thirty-two of her friends to join in her resolve. It was the merit and virtue derived from cultivating this vow which enabled those thirty-three people to be born in the heavens and become rulers of the Heaven of the Thirty-three. In the Shurangama Mantra, it is the phrase *Na Mwo Yin Two La Ye*. *Na Mwo* means homage to and *Yin Two La Ye* is the heavenly lord of the Heaven of the Thirty-three (*Indra*).

The Heaven of the Four Kings and the Heaven of the Thirty-three are the first two desire-heavens. The rest of the heavens will be explained in detail later.

The demon-kings dwell in the sixth desire-heaven. Not only demon-kings, but an entire population of demons dwells there: demon women, demon-children, and demon-grandchildren. Demons, too, have retinues, or followings, and the demon-kings hold court in the sixth desire heaven, where they reign supreme. Most of the methods cultivated in outside ways lead the cultivators to end up as demon kings at best, and more commonly as ordinary demons. At worst they will end up as demon-women. Demon-women are particularly beautiful and quite seductive. It doesn't matter who you are. Ananda, for example, who had accomplished the first stage of arhatship, didn't have enough samadhi-power to keep control of himself when he saw a demon-woman. He was ready to try anything. Demon-women are very powerful. You people who cultivate the Way should be careful not to let a demon attract you.

What do I mean by that? If you don't have sufficient samadhi power, you won't be able to maintain your composure when you encounter this situation, and the demon will spin you around and you will find yourself trailing along after a demon-woman into a demon's hole.

If I say any more, the demons will complain, "You're saying so much and exposing all our faults," so I'll stop talking. In general, just be careful. Develop your samadhi-power thoroughly, and then there will be nothing to fear. This is a most wonderful test I'm giving you.

Why can't they become Buddhas or even become demon-kings? It is **that they do not know the two fundamental roots and are mistaken and confused in their cultivation.** These two roots are extremely important and will be explained in the following passages. And they misunderstand; they are mistaken about how to cultivate and as a result become confused. They don't know how to work properly. For example, there is an outside way in India which professes to cultivate asceticism by sleeping on beds of nails. They say that one derives merit and virtue from bearing that kind of pain. What merit and virtue is there in that? Even if you were to sleep on knives, it would be of no use. Other people in India emulate the morality of cows and dogs. They mimic the behavior of those animals. Why? It is also a case of being mistaken and confused in their cultivation. They consider themselves genuine cultivators of the Way, but they are practicing non-beneficial ascetic practices which reap no fruit, no matter how hard you cultivate them.

What are they like? Now the Buddha gives us an example. **They are like one who cooks sand in the hope of creating savory delicacies. They may pass through as many aeons as there are motes of dust, but in the end they will not obtain what they want.** The sand will remain nothing but sand. It cannot change into food. Those who do not understand the two fundamental roots and are mistaken and reckless in their cultivation are doing what amounts to the same thing.

O2 The Tathagata explains what the two roots are.

Sutra:

"What are the two? Ananda, the first is the root of beginningless birth and death, which is the mind that seizes upon conditions and that you and all living beings now make use of, taking it to be the self-nature.

Commentary:

What are the two? The Buddha will now explain the two fundamental roots to Ananda, and I think everyone would like to know what they are. However, I'm not going to discuss them just yet. I'm going to tell you first about Ananda's elder brother Sundarananda, since I haven't introduced him to you yet. Sundarananda got along very well with his wife Sundari; they stuck together like glue. All day long they stayed right beside one another, they were so compatible. In fact, to distinguish him from Ananda, Sundarananda was given the name Sundari's Nanada – Sundarananda.

The day came when the Buddha went to cross Sundarananda over. He took up his bowl and went to Sundarananda's home to beg for food. When Sundarananda saw the Buddha coming, he withdrew from his wife and said, "Wait a bit, I am going to make offerings to the Buddha."

His wife said, "You are going to make offerings to the Buddha? Well, come back immediately. Don't go and then not come back." "Of course, I'll come right back," Sundarananda said.

Sundari then spit on the dirt floor and said, "You'd better be back before that dries, or I won't let you in my bed."

Sundarananda heeded the command and said, "I'll be back right away, for sure." And he took vegetables and rice to fill the Buddha's bowl.

He went to fill the bowl, but how was he to know that the Buddha would act so strangely? The Buddha used his spiritual power. Every time Sundarananda took a step forward to place the food in the Buddha's bowl, the Buddha backed up, so that Sundarananda couldn't reach the bowl. Sundarananda kept advancing to keep up with the Buddha, and in just a few steps they arrived at the Jeta Grove, despite the fact that it was a long way from Sundarananda's house. Once they got there, Shakyamuni Buddha said, "Don't go back. You stay here with me and leave the home-life."

Sundarananda was shocked; he got goose-flesh. "Impossible," he said emphatically. "I can't stay. Sundari is waiting for me. I can't remain here and leave home."

The Buddha said, "You can't leave home? Let me show you some things and see what you think." He took Sundarananda to a place where there were hordes of monkeys. "Which is more beautiful," the Buddha asked him, "these monkeys or your wife Sundari?"

"Obviously Sundari is more beautiful," replied Sundarananda. "How could Sundari be compared to a monkey?"

"Quite right," the Buddha agreed, and took him to the heavens. As they strolled among they noticed one particular palace was bustling with activity as servants scrubbed and polished. There were also 500 heavenly maidens in that palace, each one exquisite beyond compare.

"Why are you doing all this cleaning?" Sundarananda asked one of the servants.

"We're getting this palace ready for the Buddha's cousin Sundarananda," they replied. "After he cultivates he'll come to heaven to enjoy his blessings. These 500 heavenly maidens will be his wives."

Sundarananda was ecstatic.

"Tell me, Nanada," the Buddha said to him, "which would you say is more beautiful, Sundari or these heavenly maidens?"

"These maidens, obviously," Sundarananda replied. "Why, compared to these maidens, Sundari is as ugly as a monkey."

"Fine," said the Buddha, "this place is being readied for you." After they finished touring the place the Buddha took his cousin down to the hells. There they saw two ghosts heating a cauldron of oil. One of the ghosts was sound asleep and although the other one was awake, he didn't have his eyes open. Nanda sized up the situation and thought to himself, "These ghosts are suppose to be tending the fire under that cauldron, but they're not doing their job at all. Boy, are ghosts lazy!" Then he meddled a bit and nudged one, saying, "What are you doing this for?"

The little one's droopy eyes popped open and glared at him. "What's it to you?" he snapped.

"I just wondered," said Sundarananda.

"You gotta know, huh? Okay, I'll tell you. The Buddha's got a cousin who's cultivating the blessings of people and gods. He's going to get born in the heavens and enjoy 500 years of heavenly blessings before he falls. Once he topples, however, he'll come all the way down to hell and when he gets here, we're supposed to have this pot hot. He's to be deep-fried alive."

Sundarananda was horrified and his hair stood on end. He suddenly understood the whole picture and thought, "Those heavenly maidens are ravishing, but 500 years of bliss with them isn't worth it if I'm eventually going to end up in a pot of boiling oil. I'd better follow the Buddha, leave home, and be a monk." So he forgot about Sundari and left home.

In order to rescue Sundarananda, the Buddha had to accompany him to the heavens and the hells. But saving Ananda, Sundarananda's younger brother, was proving even more difficult. The Buddha explains one principle and Ananda doesn't understand. The Buddha explains another principle and Ananda still doesn't understand. The Buddha keeps on explaining and Ananda continues to be confused. Now the Buddha reveals the two fundamental roots that cause people to be mistaken and confused in their cultivation. He wanted to lead Ananda to understand how to direct his cultivation so that he could become a Buddha in the future.

Ananda, the first is the root of beginningless birth and death. From beginningless time onward you have endured birth after birth, death after death, death after death, birth after birth. I have already explained the meaning to you: "Unaware of the pure nature and bright substance of the permanently dwelling true mind, they use false thinking. Such thoughts are not true, and so the wheel keeps turning." In this passage once again the fundamental root of continual birth and death is revealed. It **is the mind that seizes upon conditions and that you and all living beings** – not just you, but all living beings – **now make use of.** To "seize upon conditions" is to act exclusively on the basis of false thought. For example, say, you go to school and knock yourself out trying to get on the good side of your professor by buttering him up. You flatter him by using all his titles and saying things you hope will please him. Why? In the hope that he'll give you a high grade. You think, "It's clear he's going to give me an 80, but if I'm nice to him and maybe give him a gift or a little something, he might raise my grade a couple of points." You gain advantages in imperceptible ways. That is an example of seizing upon conditions.

Another example occurs during elections for president, mayor, or senator. The candidates go around drumming up votes, and soliciting support from their friends. That, too, is a case of the mind seizing upon conditions, instead of letting things naturally take their course. If it were to happen naturally that you were to become president, you wouldn't have to campaign to let everyone see that you were a worthy candidate. Your virtue would be obvious and people would look up to you. You wouldn't have to persuade people; they quite naturally would elect you president. That's the ideal way to do it. Anything else falls in the realm of seizing upon conditions.

An incident involving the Chinese Emperor Yao illustrates the point. When Emperor Yao got old, he wanted to relinquish his kingdom to a virtuous and worthy person. He had heard that Chao

Fu and Xu Yu had great virtue and he decided to offer the empire to Chao Fu.

Why was he called Chao Fu, "nest?" For one thing, he lived in a pretty strange place. He built a nest in a tree, just like a bird, and lived there. His manner of life was so simple that he drank by just scooping up water in his cupped hands. Once some people saw him do that and realized he didn't have anything to drink from, so they gave him a gourd. He hung the gourd from a branch of his tree but it made such a racket when the wind blew that he finally threw it away; deciding it was just too much trouble.

Emperor Yao had heard how pure and lofty Chao Fu was, and he was determined to yield the throne to him. So he went to announce his intent. "I'm old now," he said to Chao Fu. "You should come and be emperor. I'll give my position to you."

No sooner had he gotten the words out of his mouth then Chao Fu plugged up his ears and marched off. "I'm not the least bit interested in such talk," he retorted. "In fact you've dirtied my ears by saying such things to me." He headed for the river, where he proceeded to wash his ears.

Now it so happened that Xu Yu was at the river, too, watering his ox. "Why are you washing your ears?" he demanded.

"That Emperor Yao is really odious," replied Chao Fu as he scrubbed away. "He came here to tell me he wants to bestow the country on me, and he asked me to become the emperor. His proposal has made my ears dirty, so I'm washing them."

"How can my ox drink the water you're using to clean your ear?" exclaimed Xu Yu. "My ox can't drink such filthy stuff." And he led the ox upstream for a drink of clean water.

You see, in ancient times, a sage would not only refuse the imperial throne, he would even say the very request had sullied his ears. And yet today it's "Hey! Vote for me as president!" "Select me as your governor!" as candidates barnstorm across country making connections, wining and dining, wheeling and dealing, and even buying votes. But Chao Fu and Xu Yu would not seize upon conditions. They represent the ultimate in pure and lofty virtue.

Making use of the mind that seizes upon conditions, you take **it to be the self-nature.** You mistake your ordinary mind for your self-nature, and that is why you cannot end birth and death. You haven't recognized it for what it is; instead you take a thief for your son, who in the future will plunder all the gems in your household. It is nothing but a false thought to think you can have any accomplishment by using the mind that seizes upon conditions. This is the mistake Ananda made.

Sutra:

"The second is the primal pure substance of the beginningless bodhi nirvana. It is the primal bright essence of consciousness that can bring forth all conditions. Because of conditions, you consider it to be lost.

Commentary:

The second is the primal pure substance of the beginningless bodhi nirvana. There is no beginning; therefore the Buddha calls it "beginningless"; it was even before the beginning itself had occurred.

"Bodhi" is Sanskrit; it is interpreted to mean "awakening to the Way." There are three kinds of bodhi:

1. The bodhi of the true nature, which refers to your inherent Buddha-nature. Originally, everyone has the Buddha-nature;
2. The bodhi of actual wisdom, which refers to your genuine wisdom, not false wisdom;
3. Expedient bodhi, which refers to the state of people who have accomplished bodhi and who then use expedient and clever means to teach and transform living beings.

These three kinds of bodhi can be said to be one. Divided they are three; in combination they are one. Together they are the bodhi of the true nature, and from it comes the bodhi of actual wisdom and expedient bodhi.

Where does bodhi itself come from? Bodhi doesn't come from anywhere or go anywhere. Each of us is endowed with it. No one person has any more or less of it than anyone else. It neither increases nor decreases, is neither produced nor extinguished, is neither defiled nor pure.

Most people think that nirvana follows upon death, but actually it is not necessarily an after-death state. It is the certification to and attainment of a principle. "Nirvana" is a Sanskrit word which is interpreted to mean "neither produced nor destroyed." Since it is neither produced nor destroyed, birth and death are ended. One attains nirvana when one reaches the position of not being subject to birth and death. But nirvana is not the Buddha's dying. When the Buddha dies, he enters nirvana; he enters and certifies to the principle of nirvana with its four virtues of permanence, bliss, true self, and purity. Some people who haven't seen things clearly in their study of Buddhism think that nirvana is just death, but nirvana is emphatically not death. One who holds this view does not understand Buddhist principle.

It is the primal bright essence of consciousness. "Primal" means that it is originally a pure substance, that is, one which is neither defiled nor pure, neither increasing nor decreasing. Originally its light illuminates everywhere. "Consciousness" here does not refer to the eight consciousnesses, nor to the eye-consciousness, the ear-consciousness, the nose-consciousness, the tongue-consciousness, the body-consciousness, the mind-consciousness, nor the manas or the alaya consciousnesses. It is not any of the eight consciousnesses. It refers to the essence of consciousness, which is but another name for bodhi nirvana. The phrase is used here to avoid repetition for the sake of literary style. It refers to the most essential and wonderful aspect of consciousness, the inherent Buddha-nature, the bright substance of the permanently dwelling true mind **that can bring forth all conditions. Because of conditions, you consider it to be lost.**

Because these causal conditions arise, you keep getting farther and farther away from where you want to be, like someone running farther and farther down the road. Didn't I say before that the more Ananda answered the Buddha's questions the farther off the track he got? All conditions are transformed and appear from within the primal bright essential consciousness, but after a long time of clutching at these conditions, it seems that something has been lost. What is lost? Nothing, really. The primal bright essential consciousness seems to be lost, but it isn't. The primal pure substance of bodhi nirvana is the true jewel in your household. Basically, it is right there with you but you don't know how to use it to your advantage. Since you can't use it, it seems to be lost. It is as if you had a valuable gem which you have hidden away so well that after a long time you can no longer remember where you put it. Once you forget where it is, you can no longer make use of it. Although you may be destitute, you don't know how to get at it and derive benefit from it. It's the same as if it weren't there. What do you use instead? You use your false thinking, your mind that seizes upon conditions. In the process you forget the true mind, and once it is forgotten, it is as good as lost. And this is why you have not become Buddhas and are bound up by birth and death instead: you have not found your true mind.

Sutra:

"**Living beings lose sight of the original brightness: therefore, though they use it to the end of their days, they are unaware of it, and without intending to they enter the various destinies.**

Commentary:

Living beings lose sight of the original brightness. Living beings seem to lose their pure basic nature, the bright substance of the permanently dwelling true mind. In actual fact it is not lost. **Therefore, though they use it to the end of their days, they are unaware of it.** Living beings use the pure nature and bright substance of the permanently dwelling true mind every day, since it is primarily from the true mind that the false-thinking mind which seizes upon conditions springs forth in the first place. Absolutely everything is a manifestation of the true mind, and it helps you from morning till night. But you don't realize it. All you know how to use is your false-thinking mind.

The true mind is manifest in seeing, hearing, smelling, tasting, awareness, and knowing. "What is the Buddha-nature?" someone once asked. Shakyamuni Buddha replied,

> In the eyes it is called seeing,
> In the ears it is called hearing,
> In the nose it smells scents,
> In the tongue it tastes,
> In the hands it is dexterity,
> In the feet it is agility.

He said, "What is the Buddha-nature?" It is the seeing-nature and the hearing-nature. It is the natural way in which the hands hold things. All of these are imperceptible manifestations of the true mind; but people are unaware of it. Now Ananda is still confused and so the Buddha uses all manner of analogies to explain to him.

And without intending to they enter the various destinies. Because they cling to the mind that seizes upon conditions, living beings enter their various destinies and yet are unaware of what they are doing. Your destiny is the place you tend toward. You walk right into it. Where do you end up? In the various destinies; that is, on the turning wheel of the six paths. There are the three good destinies of the gods, the asuras, and people, and the three evil destinies of the animals, the hungry ghosts, and the hell-beings. Whatever karma you create, you undergo a retribution for it. Without realizing it, you end up by entering one of the six paths. It is not that you particularly want to, but fall you do, just the same.

The destiny of the asuras is sometimes listed as an evil destiny. Asuras are said to be "strong in fighting," since fighting is what they like to do best. They are always ready to pick a quarrel with people. Asura is a Sanskrit word which is interpreted to mean "without wine" and also as "deformed." Asuras like to drink wine, but when they are in the heavens, they don't get any wine to drink. "Deformed" refers to the male asuras, whose bodies and faces are misshapen and ugly. They have hairlips and buck teeth. But the asuras women are gorgeous. The Jade Emperor encountered one such particularly beautiful female asura and chose her for his wife.

Now the Jade Emperor, Shakra, that is, liked to go hear sutras. He would transform himself into a man and come to this world to listen to sutras. But his asura wife "drank vinegar," that is, she got jealous. "You go off to the world every single day. I wonder what weird essence or fox spirit has got you in her clutches. You're chasing after a fox spirit, aren't you?" She was accusing him of playing around with another woman. Worldly women are not the only ones who get jealous about their husbands.

Eventually Shakra's wife decided to make herself invisible and follow along to find out what he was up to. (In this day and age there are private detectives to handle such matters, but probably they didn't exist then so she had to run her own investigation and spy on him for herself.) So, when the Jade Emperor arrived at the dharma assembly, he bowed to the dharma master, paid his respects, and then took a seat in the assembly. It just so happen that on that particular day there were women sitting on either side of him. When the asura woman saw that, she was beside herself, and she made herself visible right there in the assembly to confront the emperor. "It's no wonder you come here every day with so many women to keep you company," she began.

The Jade Emperor was outraged. "I come here to listen to sutras and you've barged in and disturbed the bodhimanda. You're really creating heavy offenses." He boxed her ears and she burst into tears and ran off to find her father. She demanded a divorce and refused to go back to her husband. Her father came to her defense and promised to wage war on the Jade Emperor. "I'll defeat him and take the throne," he consoled her. "Don't fret."

The fight was on. Every day the asura king did battle with the Jade Emperor. The emperor called out his full regalia, but the asura king's ferocious battalions were in their element, and little by little the Jade Emperor was beaten back. He was losing ground fast. As a faithful follower of the Buddha, he went to the Buddha and asked him to devise some strategy. The Buddha gave him his *kashaya* – his robe – saying, "Take this back with you, tear it into strips and have each of your soldiers carry a piece of it. Then tell them all to recite 'Mahaprajnaparamita' (great wisdom which has reached the other shore)."

The Jade Emperor did as he was instructed. The entire army began reciting "Mahaprajnaparamita" and when the next attack came the asuras fell. They were totally unprepared for the unprecedented force of the heavenly troop's blows and admitted defeat once and for all.

Asuras are said to be "deformed." They have the blessings of the gods, but not the virtue. There are asuras not only in the heavens but also among people. Soldiers and thieves are examples of human asuras. But a distinction has to be made here. In this country, military service is mandatory and people are drafted. Some of them are not asuras. Some of these that go into battle are just kids. At eighteen they're drafted and at that age they haven't the least bit of samadhi-power. They get jittery at the mere mention of war.

Front line troops should be trained for five years. For instance, they'll be twenty-three if they enter the service at eighteen and train for five years, and by that time they have a little samadhi-power and some experience, so that if they are sent into battle, they have sufficient courage to cope with it. If they're too young, their samadhi isn't strong, they lack experience, and they haven't got any guts. So I think that in the present circumstances, not every soldier is an asura. In former times, people who actually wanted to be soldiers or robbers could be classed as asuras.

There are other asuras besides soldiers. For instance, someone who has a big temper and is always picking fights with others has the nature of an asura. In general, asuras have violent tempers.

Wild stallions are an example of asuras. There are also asuras among the hungry ghosts. For the most part, living beings enter the four evil destinies. This is the meaning of this passage of text. Some living beings don't lose their way and are born in the path of people or in the heavens, but that is still to "enter the various destinies without intending to." You take the wrong road.

N3 The Tathagata tells him directly that the false consciousness is not the mind.
O1 The Tathagata firmly admonishes him with a straight, "hey!"

Sutra:

"Ananda, since you now wish to know about the path of shamatha with the hope of getting out of birth and death, I will question you further."

Then the Tathagata raised his golden arm and bent his five wheeled fingers as he asked Ananda, "Do you see?"

Ananda said, "I see."

Commentary:

Then the Tathagata raised his golden arm. As he was about to question Ananda, the Tathagata stretched his gold-colored arm out in front of him **and bent his five wheeled fingers as he asked Ananda, "Do you see?"** You can see how the Buddha is treating Ananda like a child by asking him such a simple question as whether he sees the Buddha raise his arm and bend his fingers. The fingers are said to be "wheeled" because the Buddha has the mark of the thousand-spoked wheel on his hands and on his feet. You could also say that "wheeled" refers to his bending his fingers in sequence: one, two, three, four, five.

It was something everyone could see. Why did the Buddha ask about such a simple matter? You may see it as simple now, but actually it is not. The more the Buddha's question is delved into as the text continues, the deeper and more wonderful it becomes. It is just in the course of ordinary every day matters that you can totally comprehend your inherent Buddha-nature. The familiar places you come in contact with every day are the representations of the

Buddha-nature. But when you don't know that through your own experience, then what is wrong seems right, and what is right seems wrong, and what is not lost seems lost. Basically you haven't lost it, but it seems lost to you. Basically you haven't forgotten it, but you can't quite recall it. So your own family jewels, the scenery of your homeland, are not easy to understand. Why? Because from beginningless time the fundamental root of birth and death – the mind that seizes upon conditions – has been too strong. If the mind that seizes upon conditions would disappear, you would understand your inherent Buddha-nature in an instant.

Ananda said, "I see." Take a look at this point. Why did the Tathagata stretch out his golden arm and bend his five wheeled fingers? It was to let Ananda know that the pure nature and bright substance of the permanently dwelling mind can manifest in the eye, in the seeing-nature. And that is why he concentrates on discussing doctrines involving seeing in the following passages. He wanted to lead Ananda to become enlightened through the seeing-nature.

So the Chinese patriarchs, the great virtuous ones of the Chan meditation school would often just point a finger when asked for instruction. That is another way of telling you to become enlightened through the seeing-nature. Sometimes when you requested instruction from them they stared at you wide-eyed and speechless. They were indicating that you should break through at that point and comprehend the meaning totally. So in the meditation school they use ferocious stares. The meditation master may make some gesture in order to lead his disciples to become enlightened. If you understand, you become enlightened; if not, you miss the opportunity. A lot of Chinese patriarchs were that way. But they were enlightened, and so it was appropriate for them to use such methods to teach people. But you cannot say, "I heard that patriarchs merely point their finger, so when I meet up with someone I'll point my finger and bring about his enlightenment."

Have you become enlightened yourself? If you yourself haven't become enlightened, how can you teach others to do so? If you haven't become enlightened, you shouldn't decide to go help other people while disregarding the fact that you yourself have outflows. To try to rescue others while paying no attention to whether you yourself have accomplished the Way first is to be like a clay bodhisattva crossing a river; he has a hard time protecting himself. Until he tries to cross the river, the clay bodhisattva stays intact, but as soon as he hits the water, he disintegrates and disappears. If you haven't attained the state of no outflows, and you nevertheless go out to help people, you will be influenced by the social environment you find yourself immersed in. You'll be transformed and won't be able to transform others. You'll be turned around by the affairs of the world instead of being able to turn them around. So before you have attained enlightenment and the state of no outflows, you are always in danger.

Take this sutra, for example. If I didn't understand the doctrines in it myself, I wouldn't be able to explain it for you. I dare not say that I thoroughly understand it, but to be frank about it, I am clearer about it than you. Because I know more than you, I am explaining what I know so that you can also know it. But even at that, I'm just explaining a little. If I were to explain to you everything I know, there wouldn't be enough time. I'm just bringing up the important points.

Sutra:

The Buddha said, "What do you see?"

Ananda said, "I see the Tathagata raise his arm and bend his fingers into a fist of light which dazzles my mind and my eyes."

The Buddha said, "What do you see it with?"

Ananda said, "The members of the great assembly and I each see it with our eyes."

The Buddha said to Ananda, "You have answered me by saying that the Tathagata bends his fingers into a fist of light which dazzles your mind and eyes. Your eyes are able to see, but what is the mind that is dazzled by my fist?"

Commentary:

The Buddha said, "What do you see?" The Buddha is still talking. He hasn't entered samadhi.

Ananda said, "I see the Tathagata raise his arm and bend his fingers into a fist of light which dazzles my mind and my eyes. World Honored One, I see you stretch out your arm and bend your five wheeled fingers, and your fist emits light. That light shines brightly that I can hardly even open my eyes. My mind is illumed by it as well."

The Buddha said, "What do you see it with? What is it that see?"

Ananda said, "The members of the great assembly and I each see it with our eyes." Ananda didn't speak just for himself; he included everyone in the great assembly. He's got witnesses, the way the defense in court calls in witnesses to testify that the defendant is not a thief. He calls in friends and relatives to act as character witnesses. So if Ananda were to speak for himself, his statement that he saw with his own eyes might still be subject to question, so he drags in some support by including the great assembly. "Everyone in this assembly maintains that the eyes see. They all use their eyes to see it."

The Buddha said to Ananda, "You have answered me by saying that the Tathagata bends his fingers into a fist of light which dazzles your mind and eyes. Your eyes are able to see, but what is the mind that is dazzled by my fist?" That is correct. Your eyes are capable of seeing. But what do you conceive to be your mind which is being illumined by my fist? What do you take to be the mind? The Buddha is taking another step forward.

Sutra:

Ananda said, "The Tathagata is asking where the mind is located. Now that I use my mind to search for it thoroughly, I propose that precisely what is able to investigate is my mind."

The Buddha said, "Hey! Ananda, that is not your mind."

Commentary:
Ananda said, "The Tathagata is asking where the mind is located. World Honored One, you now ask me where my mind is. Now that I use my mind to search for it thoroughly." He looked for his mind. "I have searched every which way, absolutely everywhere, exhausting all possibilities, I have been chasing my mind. **I propose that precisely what is able to investigate is my mind.** I can investigate things, and that means there is a mind; so that which is capable of investigating things is probably my mind." He says "propose"; that means he's not absolutely sure. But he thought what he said had a lot of principle, and he was confident that he had succeeded in finding the mind. Little did he know the Buddha would scold him.

The Buddha said, "Hey!" This was the same word the Buddha used to reprimand Aniruddha. "Hey! Hey! How can you sleep?" he asked him, and as a result of that reprimand, Aniruddha didn't sleep for a week, went blind as a result and then with the aid of the Buddha opened his heavenly eye. Here, the Buddha uses the same word to answer Ananda. He didn't say whether Ananda was right or wrong, he just used an expletive to yell at him. Why did the Buddha yell at Ananda? Because Ananda's answer was a grave mistake; it was totally wrong. Earlier, he had persisted in taking the conscious mind as the true mind, and that was already a mistake. Now he still hasn't understood. Sometimes people can wake up when they see something while their mind is totally concentrated. Ananda was extremely intent on his dialogue with the Buddha, and at that point the Buddha showed him his dazzling hand in the hope that Ananda would realize that it is the seeing-nature that sees. But Ananda disappointed the Buddha again by saying instead that it is the eyes and the mind that see. The Buddha guided him along by saying, "Fine, it's the eyes that see; and what do you take to be the mind?" But once again Ananda said that his ability to investigate is his mind. Yet that is merely the conscious mind.

So the Buddha used sound to lead Ananda to awaken to the Way through his hearing-nature. He shouted, "Hey!" in a harsh and stern tone, using his awesome virtue to cause Ananda to be enlightened upon hearing the sound. But Ananda had been steeped in confusion too long; he knew only scholarship and had neglected samadhi power. The Buddha had worked long and hard to teach and transform him, and Ananda still didn't understand. When the Buddha saw this, he used his compassionate heart to draw him in by explaining more gently, **"Ananda, that is not your mind."**

O2   Ananda is alarmed and asks what it is called.

Sutra:

Startled, Ananda leapt from his seat, stood and put his palms together, and said to the Buddha, "If it's not my mind, what is it?"

Commentary:

Ananda was so taken aback that he jumped to his feet, looking stunned and alarmed. He stood to avoid being disrespectful when he addressed the Buddha. **Startled, Ananda leapt from his seat, stood and put his palms together, and said to the Buddha, "If it's not my mind, what is it?** If it's not my mind, what do you call it then?" Ananda didn't know what to do. Suddenly he was without a mind.

O3   The Tathagata reveals its name and clears up the mistake.

Sutra:

The Buddha said to Ananda, "It is your perception of false appearances based on external objects which deludes your true nature and has caused you from beginningless time to your present life to recognize a thief as your son, to lose your eternal source, and to undergo the wheel's turning."

Commentary:

This section of text explains not only Ananda's problem but the problem of you and me and everyone else. Everyone should know that from beginningless time we have all taken thieves to be our sons. We have covered over our basic nature so it cannot appear.

The Buddha said to Ananda, "Ananda, don't be nervous. Ananda, don't be upset. You're asking what it is that is able to investigate, aren't you? Now I will tell you in detail. **It is your perception of false appearances based on external objects.**" "False" means it is unreal. The mind that investigates is not your self nature; it is not your true mind. It is merely a more subtle form of false thinking which makes distinctions. The shadow of external objects **deludes your true nature and has caused you from beginningless time to your present life to recognize a thief as your son.** You have mistaken the false perception of externals for your son, and so you have lost **your eternal source.** You have lost all your gems, all your family heirlooms; your basic, permanently dwelling, unchanging true mind. The meaning here is the same as it was above: it's not that you have actually lost it; it just seems to be lost. This causes you **to undergo the wheel's turning.** Because you are unaware of your own family treasure, you do not know how to make use of it, and so you rise and sink on the turning wheel of birth and death. The wheel governs you and turns you, and you cannot transcend its cycle. That is why you are the way you are now. This life, next life, life after life will follow that same endless turning, suddenly high, suddenly low, suddenly above, suddenly below. Sometimes you are born in the heavens and sometimes you fall back to earth. There is a saying that goes:

> Out of a horse's belly
>   into the womb of a cow.
> How many times back and forth
>   have you passed by Yama's halls,
> As you go from Shakra's palaces
>   down into Yama's pot?

Sometimes you become a horse, at other times you are a cow. In front of Yama's halls you trudge back and forth one knows not how many times. You are like Sundarananda, whom the Buddha took to the heavens, saying that if he cultivated the Way he would be rewarded with rebirth there, with 500 goddesses serving him.

Sundarananda was beside himself with joy. But he forgot King Yama's pot, for once your heavenly blessings are used up you fall again, perhaps into the hells, where you are boiled in a pot of oil. The path of the turning wheel is dangerous. Once you start spinning on it, you end up going the wrong way and if you are in the least bit careless, once you get started in the wrong direction it is difficult to get back. So now that you have been born a human being, you should hurry up and wake up from this dream. Hurry up and get enlightened. Don't continue as Ananda did to recognize a thief as your son.

The False Consciousness is Without a Substance

L3 Determining that the false consciousness is without a substance.
M1 Ananda expresses his fear and asks for instruction.

Sutra:

Ananda said to the Buddha, "World Honored One, I am the Buddha's favorite cousin. It is because my mind loved the Buddha that I was led to leave the home-life. It is my mind that not only makes offerings to the Tathagata, but also, in passing through lands as many as the grains of sand in the Ganges River to serve all Buddhas and good, wise advisors, and in martialing great courage to practice every difficult aspect of the dharma, I always use this mind. Even if I am slandering the dharma and eternally withdrawing my good roots, it would also be because of this mind. If this is not my mind, then I have no mind, and I am the same as a clod of earth or a piece of wood. Without this awareness and knowing, nothing would exist.

"Why does the Tathagata say this is not my mind? I am startled and frightened and not one member of the great assembly is without doubt. I only hope that the World Honored One will regard us with great compassion and instruct those who have not yet awakened."

Commentary:

After listening to the Buddha's explanation, Ananda still didn't understand. He still wanted to debate the issue. **Ananda said to the Buddha, "World Honored One, I am the Buddha's favorite cousin."** He said, "I am the Buddha's youngest and most favored cousin, and the Buddha loves me dearly. As I stand before the Buddha I am like a child." The word "favorite" means that the Buddha let him have his own way. He didn't try to control him. Ananda could do whatever he pleased. **It is because my mind loved the Buddha that I was led to leave the home-life.** Ananda says that it was his mind that loved the Buddha's thirty-two hallmarks. The Buddha's face is like the clear full moon, and like a thousand suns emitting light. His hallmarks are exquisite. "So the Buddha told me to leave home, and as soon as he suggested it I agreed, because I loved his adorning hallmarks and characteristics." Ananda hadn't forgotten that the causes and conditions for his leaving home were his seeing the Buddha's thirty-two hallmarks.

It is my mind that not only makes offerings to the Tathagata – my mind makes offerings not only to you, World Honored One – **but also, in passing through lands as many as the grains of sand in the Ganges River to serve all Buddhas and good, wise advisors** – when Ananda says "serve," he means "I go to attend on all Buddhas, to make offerings to all Buddhas, to bow to all Buddhas, and I do the same for teachers of vast knowledge and experience. **And in martialing great courage to practice every difficult aspect of the dharma, I always use this mind.** I do all the things other people cannot do. People fear suffering, but I am not afraid to suffer. I look after Buddhas and tend to their every need. I bear what others cannot bear and practice what others cannot practice, and what I use in doing so is my mind. The reason I am able to develop merit and virtue by making offerings to the Triple Jewel is because I use this mind. **Even if I am slandering the dharma and eternally withdrawing my good roots, it would also be because of this mind.** Even if you say that I am slandering the dharma to speak this way – even if I were to retreat and cut off my good roots to the point that there were none left, I would still be using this mind." This sentence can alternately be said to mean that Ananda is supposing that if he ever were to slander the dharma, he still thinks it would be his mind that would be doing it. **If this is not my mind, then I have no mind, and I am the same as a clod of earth or a piece of wood. Without this awareness and knowing, nothing would exist.** Ananda is really flustered to be speaking in this way. "I've become someone without a mind. I'm no different from dirt or wood. I have no mind. If I am separate from this conscious mind that makes discriminations, then what else is there? There isn't anything at all. My present ability to hear the sutra and listen to dharma is a function solely of this mind. Beyond that I have nothing.

"**Why does the Tathagata say this is not my mind? I am startled and frightened and not one member of the great assembly is without doubt.** Now I am really alarmed. You've talked me right out of my mind. And not only myself: I believe everyone has doubts regarding this, and the pain of my fears and the assembly's doubts is unbearable." By "doubts" is meant that they had not understood the doctrine and had questions about it. Why did Ananda say that the great assembly had doubts, but that he himself was alarmed? It's that all the others in the assembly were onlookers and so they had not thought to take the situation personally and put themselves in his place. They simply took note of the principles. But Ananda was being addressed personally, so when Shakyamuni Buddha said he didn't have a mind he was shocked. "No mind? That's too much. Next thing you know I won't have a life either."

Ananda says that everyone else who was listening to his dialogue with the Buddha had doubts about what they heard, but in fact that too was a deduction Ananda made with his conscious mind. "Probably they haven't understood either," he thought. He didn't realize that the great bodhisattvas who were present, although they hadn't said anything, had long since understood. Within his small frame of reference Ananda was deducing things about those whose frame of reference was much greater. Actually, however, I believe that members of the assembly such as Manjushri Bodhisattva, Guan Yin Bodhisattva, and Great Strength Bodhisattva, couldn't have had any doubts.

I only hope that the World Honored One will regard us with great compassion and instruct those who have not yet awakened. Compassion can pull people out of suffering. "Please rescue each of us from our distress," Ananda says, "and teach those of us who have not understood this doctrine so that we can understand."

M2 Tathagata comforts him.
N1 He bestows the profound meaning of the teaching.

Sutra:

Then the World Honored One gave instruction to Ananda and the great assembly, wishing to cause their minds to enter the state of patience with the non-existence of beings and phenomena.

Commentary:

Then the World Honored One. At the time that Ananda asked the Buddha to instruct those who had not yet awakened, Shakyamuni Buddha pitied his young cousin and felt a loving protectiveness for him. So he **gave instruction to Ananda and the great assembly, wishing to cause their minds to enter the state of patience with the non-existence of beings and phenomena.** What is meant by the "patience with the non-existence of beings and phenomena?" There are three kinds of patience: patience with beings; patience with phenomena; and patience with the non-existence of beings and phenomena. No phenomena come into being and no phenomena cease to be. When you attain patience with the non-existence of beings and phenomena, you see that in each of the four sagely and six ordinary dharma realms not even the minutest phenomena arises and not even the minutest phenomena is destroyed. The four sagely dharma realms are beyond the realm of desire, the realm of form and the realm of formlessness, while the six ordinary realms are within the three realms but in none of them is there any production or extinction; and yet the fundamental substance of every phenomena is in a state of unmoving suchness. Because they are in a state of unmoving suchness, there is neither production nor extinction.

Before you understand you think: "Oh no, there is no production or extinction, and all the myriad phenomena vanish!" A fear arises in your heart; you can't bear the idea of it. But if you actually experience the state of non-production and non-extinction, in fact it will not seem at all unusual and you will be able to bear it, because you attain patience with the non-existence of beings and phenomena. Then you will have gained a mutual response with the Way.

A mutual response occurs when you are about to attain enlightenment but have not yet done so. When the mutual response occurs, the only thing you can do is cherish it in your heart. You yourself know, but you cannot go around telling people about it. It is inexpressible. That is what is called patience with the non-existence of beings and phenomena. When you can see that the mountains, the rivers, the earth, and all that grows forth from them are things within your self-nature; that the three realms are only the mind, and that the myriad phenomena are only consciousness; once you attain that state, then everything, every phenomenon, is devoid of production and extinction. Everything you see – the mountains, the rivers, the earth, the plants – are all one true appearance. That is patience with the non-existence of beings and phenomena. Before you have truly realized and truly obtained this state, you must be patient. You must be able to bear it. That too is patience with the non-existence of beings and phenomena.

Now the Buddha spoke to the assembly, wishing to cause everyone there and all living beings to attain the state of patience with the non-existence of beings and phenomena.

N2 He often speaks of the wonderful mind.

Sutra:

> From the lion's seat he rubbed Ananda's crown and said to him, "The Tathagata has often said that all phenomena that arise are only manifestations of the mind. All causes and effects, the worlds as many as fine motes of dust, come into being because of the mind.

Commentary:

From the lion's seat. This does not mean that the Buddha mounted a lion and sat on it, or that his seat was carved in the shape of a lion. The Buddha's speaking dharma is like the roar of a lion, and so the place where the Buddha sits is called the lion's seat. **He rubbed Ananda's crown.** The Buddha rubbed the top of Ananda's head with his hand. In Buddhism, rubbing the crown is a gesture which represents the power of the utmost compassionate love to attract living beings and draw them in. **And said to him, "The Tathagata has often said that all phenomena that arise are only manifestations of the mind.** I, the Tathagata, have often said in the past that every single phenomenon, whether worldly or transcendental, is manifested entirely from within our minds. **All causes and effects**: cause upon cause, effect after effect, all that occur in this world and throughout the **worlds as many as fine motes of dust, come into being because of the mind."** They are all brought about because of our minds. So the ancients of China had a saying:

> If a man recognizes his mind
> There's not an inch of dirt left on earth.

What is there? Where did it go? That's the Chan meditation school's way of expressing the irony of the ineffable. Unfortunately, we have not recognized our minds, and so the great earth is still a big mound of dirt.

N3　He confirms that the true mind has substance.

Sutra:

"Ananda, when all the things in the world, including blades of grass and strands of silk thread, are examined at their fundamental source, each is seen to have substance and a nature, even empty space has a name and an appearance.

Commentary:

The Buddha called Ananda's name again, **"Ananda, when all the things in the world, including blades of grass and strands of silk thread, are examined at their fundamental source, each is seen to have substance and a nature, even empty space has a name and an appearance."** Absolutely everything in the world, including the mountains, the rivers, the earth, vegetation, and all the myriad appearances, even down to blades of grass or fine strands of silk thread, and even empty space, which still has the name "empty space" and has the appearance of empty space, all have a substance and a nature.

Sutra:

"How much the less could the clear, wonderful, pure bright mind, the essence of all thoughts, itself be without a substance?

Commentary:

How much the less could the wonderful pure mind have no substance? It, too, certainly has substance.

N4　He shows that the false consciousness has no substance.

Sutra:

"If you insist that the nature which knows and observes and is aware of distinctions is the mind, then apart from all forms, smells, tastes, and touches – apart from the workings of all the defiling objects – that mind should have its own complete nature.

Commentary:

If you insist – if you are determined to hold to all of your own fixed ideas, opinions, and deductions, as a miser hoards gold, saying **that the nature which knows and observes and is aware of distinctions is the mind, then apart from all forms, smells, tastes, and touches – apart from the workings of all the defiling objects – that mind should have its own complete nature.** If the mind which makes distinctions is the true mind, then it should exist apart from any connection with forms, sounds, smells, tastes, touches, or mental constructs. Although only four of the six sense objects are mentioned, all six are meant. If the conscious mind is indeed the true mind, then it should continue to exist as yet another complete nature beyond the experiences involving the six sense objects. There should be another mind besides the one that goes out the entrances of the six organs, the eyes, ears, nose, tongue, body, and mind.

Is that the way it is? No, but the Buddha offers this hypothetical explanation in order to teach Ananda.

Sutra:

"**And yet now, as you listen to my dharma, it is because of sound that you are able to make distinctions.**

Commentary:

Now the Buddha begins to explain that Ananda does not have a conscious mind that exists apart from its perceptions. **And yet now, as you listen to my dharma, it is because of sound that you are able to make distinctions.** Ananda, you are here listening to me speak this teaching, and it is the sound that allows you to make distinctions. It is not the case that you can hear sounds when are no sounds.

Sutra:

"**Even if you could extinguish all seeing, hearing, awareness, and knowing, and maintain an inner composure, the shadows of your discrimination of mental constructs would remain.**

Commentary:

Even if you could extinguish all seeing, hearing, awareness, and knowing, and maintain an inner composure; even if you could temporarily stop seeing, hearing, being aware, and knowing, it would simply be a state of emptiness. To attain it is a kind of skill. Once you do away with seeing, hearing, awareness, and knowing, you can dwell in inner repose; it is very quiet, there isn't anything going on, you don't do anything. You are empty and free from care. Adherents of outside ways consider this experience the highest one possible. They sit there and feel there is no self and no others, that everything is empty, that even their own bodies have disappeared, and they consider that to be real skill. That is what is meant by "maintaining an inner composure." In fact there is a bit of attainment, some amount of *gong fu*, of spiritual skill, in keeping that composure. You experience light ease, a small amount of peace, and concentration. Since adherents of outside ways take this state to be the ultimate, they struggle to maintain it so it won't be lost. They don't want to lose their *gong fu*.

But actually, in that kind of state **the shadows of your discrimination of mental constructs would remain.** The state of inner composure is still just a function of the sixth consciousness, the mind-consciousness; "mental constructs" refers here to the objects of the mind. The first five consciousnesses vanish: those of the eyes, ears, nose, tongue, and body. Vision and hearing aren't directed outside; smells and tastes do not affect you, and the body is not influenced by an awareness of touch. But the sixth consciousness is called the solitary mind-consciousness because it functions even when the other consciousnesses are extinguished. Dreaming, for example, is a function of the mind-consciousness. The state of inner composure is another example. The five consciousnesses are extinguished, and you feel that seeing, hearing, awareness, and knowing are all gone, but you still have thought. There remain the subtle defiling objects of mental constructs which are extremely hard to detect. They are subtle distinctions of the mind: the shadows of discriminations that fall on the mind. It is not a real state. When you have attained it, you feel that what is going on is very fine; but from the point of view of Buddhism, you haven't even taken the first step. Don't feel satisfied and think to yourself, "Oh, this is the skill that comes from sitting in Chan meditation." Instead, you should continue to make progress. If you stop at that place, it is easy to fall into dull emptiness, where the seeing, hearing, awareness, and knowing are extinguished and there seems to be nothing at all; but dull emptiness is of no benefit in developing your Chan skill. The sixth consciousness, the solitary mind-consciousness, is a place where it is easy to take the wrong road and go astray.

There are four aspects of the solitary mind-consciousness:

1. The solitary mind-consciousness in dissipation. This refers to our everyday mind which is scattered and makes discriminations.

2. The solitary mind-consciousness in insanity and incoherence. When someone goes crazy and speaks incoherently, the sixth consciousness is in an insane state, and it has control of him.

3. The solitary mind-consciousness in dreams. When you dream you see all kinds of colors and strange unusual things. That is the solitary mind-consciousness playing tricks.

4. The solitary mind-consciousness in samadhi. That is the state of inner composure that we are talking about here. The seeing, hearing, awareness, and knowing are all totally extinguished, but the solitary mind-consciousness in samadhi is still alive.

Sutra:
"I do not insist that you grant that it is not the mind. But examine your mind in minute detail to see whether there is a discriminating nature apart from the objects of sense. That would truly be your mind.

Commentary:
The Buddha further said to Ananda, "**I do not insist that you grant that it is not the mind.** I am not ordering you to agree with what I say. **But examine your mind in minute detail** – think about

it carefully – **to see whether there is a discriminating nature apart from the objects of sense. That would truly be your mind.**" If when you are apart from the objects of sense you still have a discriminating nature, that would be your genuine mind.

Sutra:

"**If this discriminating nature has no substance apart from objects, then it is shadows of discriminations of objects of mind.**

Commentary:

If this discriminating nature has no substance apart from objects – if you cannot find the substance of your discriminating nature apart from the defiling objects of sense – **then it is shadows of discriminations of objects of mind.** It is not your true mind.

Sutra:

"**The objects are not permanent, and when they pass out of existence, such a mind would be like hair on a tortoise or horns on a rabbit. In that case your dharma body would be extinguished along with it. Then who cultivates and attains patience with the non-existence of phenomena?**"

Commentary:

This passage of text explains the matter a little more clearly. **The objects are not permanent, and when they pass out of existence, such a mind would be like hair on a tortoise or horns on a rabbit.** If when you have a thought when confronted with an object, you say there is a discrimination and that that is your mind. If when confronted with an object you have a thought, when you aren't confronted with an object there is no thought. Sometimes objects disappear; they change and cease to be. Then you are not confronted with an object, and there is no thought, no discrimination. Then where is this mind you speak of? It is like hair on a tortoise or horns on a rabbit. When do tortoises grow hair? Never. When do rabbits grow horns? It's as if you didn't have a mind at all. **In that case your dharma body would be extinguished along with it.** Since you haven't any mind, your dharma body doesn't exist either. How can you have a dharma body without a mind?

Then who cultivates and attains patience with the non-existence of phenomena? What do you use to cultivate the Way and achieve enlightenment? If you have neither mind nor body, who awakens to patience with the non-existence of phenomena?

Sutra:

At that point Ananda and everyone in the great assembly was speechless and at a total loss.

Commentary:

The Buddha explained that if the mind exists in the discriminations of external objects, then apart from objects there is no discrimination, so doesn't that mean there is no mind? If there is no mind there is no dharma body either. And with no mind and no dharma body, who is it that cultivates and attains the patience with the non-existence of phenomena? Ananda and the members of the great assembly thought about it and saw that he was right. **At that point Ananda and everyone in the great assembly was speechless and at a total loss.** No one had anything to say. They just stared, but this time they didn't enter samadhi.

J3 Conclusion: the Tathagata reiterates the reason.

Sutra:

The Buddha said to Ananda, "There are cultivators in the world who, although they realize the nine successive stages of samadhi, do not achieve the extinction of outflows or become arhats, all because they are attached to birth-and-death false thinking and mistake it for what is truly real. That is why now, although you are greatly learned, you have not realized the accomplishment of sagehood."

Commentary:

The Buddha said to Ananda. The Buddha saw that everyone was fidgeting and practically beside themselves, not knowing what to do. They had all lost their minds.

In *Mencius*, Confucius says of the mind:

> Its goings out and comings in have no fixed time
> And its location is unknown.
> Just that is called the mind.

You don't know what time it leaves, you don't know when it returns, and you don't know where it went. Probably that is the mind. However, the mind Confucius speaks of is also the false-thinking mind, not the true mind. How could the true mind go out and enter? It doesn't have any exits or entrances.

Mencius also said:

> When a person's chickens and dogs get loose
>   he knows he should go look for them,
> But when his mind escapes
>   he doesn't know that he should search for it.

Here, too, he is talking about the mind which strikes up false thoughts from morning to night, running east, running west, running back and forth. He doesn't know enough to watch over his own mind, to tell it not to run down so many roads in vain. I've said your false-thinking mind allows you to be in New York in the space of a thought with no need to spend money on an airplane or train ticket; and you can play on the Brooklyn Bridge without bothering to take a bus; it's really a cheap way to travel but it is a tremendous exertion for the mind. That is what it says in Mencius about the conscious mind, the mind that Ananda is familiar with. The conscious mind is impermanent. The true mind is permanent.

There are cultivators in the world who, although they realize the nine successive stages of samadhi. The nine successive stages of samadhi are the first, second, third, and fourth stages of dhyana; the four places of emptiness:

1. the place of the heaven of boundless emptiness;
2. the place of the heaven of boundless consciousness;
3. the place of the heaven of nothing whatsoever;
4. the place of the heaven of neither thought nor no thought

and the samadhi of the extinction of feeling and thought. **They do not achieve the extinction of outflows or become arhats, all because they are attached to birth-and-death false thinking.** Why do they cultivate and achieve the nine successive stages of samadhi and yet cannot obtain the penetration of the extinction of outflows and accomplish arhatship? It is because they are attached to false thinking of birth and death **and mistake it for what is truly real.** They make the mistake of taking that false thinking to be true.

That is why now, although you are greatly learned, you have not realized the accomplishment of sagehood. By this time Ananda had reached the first stage of arhatship, so why does the Buddha say nevertheless that, despite the advantages that come with erudition, Ananda hasn't realized the accomplishment of sagehood? The Buddha means Ananda has not obtained the penetration of the extinction of outflows. He is not devoid of outflows. In the small vehicle, the first stage of arhatship is considered to be a level of sagehood, but among bodhisattvas it is not.

CHAPTER 6

Ananda Repents and Seeks the Truth

I2   He reveals the true nature that is inherent and causes him to see the substance of the Tathagata's treasury.
J1   Ananda renounces the false and seeks the true.
K1   He is sorrowful and repentant.

Sutra:

When Ananda heard that, he again wept sorrowfully, placed his five limbs on the ground, knelt on both knees, put his palms together, and said to the Buddha, "Since I followed the Buddha and left home, what I have done is to rely on the Buddha's awesome spirit. I have often thought, 'There is no reason for me to toil at cultivation' expecting that the Tathagata would bestow samadhi upon me. I never realized that he could not stand in for me in body and mind. Thus, I lost my original mind and although my body has left the home-life, my mind has not entered the Way. I am like the poor son who renounced his father and roamed around.

Commentary:

The Buddha has said that because Ananda was obstructed by his learning he had not realized sagehood. He had neglected samadhi and concentrated on acquiring erudition. **When Ananda heard that, he again wept sorrowfully.** Why did he cry? He realized he had been wasting his time, and the fact that he had not attained sagehood was truly pitiful. So he burst into tears. Then, too, the Buddha had instructed him about his true mind, and feeling very grateful to the Buddha for that, he was moved to tears.

He **placed his five limbs on the ground**. Ananda then placed his hands, feet, and head on the ground. After he bowed deeply this way he did not rise but **knelt on both knees, put his palms together, and said to the Buddha**.

Ananda was crying and talking at the same time, like a child who goes out to play and gets beaten up, and runs crying home to his parents to tell how he's been bullied. Now it is as if Ananda had taken a beating. What kind of beating? He's lost his basic frame of reference. As he explains it: **Since I followed the Buddha and left home, what I have done is to rely on the Buddha's awesome spirit.** Ananda was the Buddha's attendant, doing such things as helping straighten the Buddha's robe when he ascends the high seat. He left home, but as I mentioned before, one can leave the worldly home, the home of the three realms, and the home of affliction, and Ananda had left only the worldly home. He still hadn't left the other two. Now Ananda confesses that, although he has left home and bowed to the Buddha as his teacher, he still hasn't changed his way of thinking. What was that? He relied on the Buddha's awesome virtue. He thought, "As, I have the Buddha for a cousin. Who else in the whole world has the Buddha for a cousin?" He was extremely arrogant. He thought he had something both powerful and influential to depend on. He relied on the Buddha's awesome virtue and spiritual penetrations.

"**I have often thought, 'There is no reason for me to toil at cultivation' expecting that the Tathagata would bestow samadhi upon me.**" He thought to himself, "I have the Buddha for a cousin, I don't have to cultivate. I don't have to go through the bitterness and suffering of cultivation. Why not? Because my cousin had become a Buddha, why should I have to cultivate? The Buddha can give me samadhi-power." Ananda thought it wasn't necessary for one to cultivate samadhi-power oneself. The Buddha could just give it to him. Think it over. Isn't that naive?

I never realized that he could not stand in for me in body and mind, Ananda says. I believe that none of us could think like that. We all know that one cannot stand in for another. But Ananda says that he really didn't know that the Buddha's body is the Buddha's and his body was his body, and that the Buddha's mind is the Buddha's mind and his mind was his mind. We cannot substitute for one another. The Buddha cannot represent Ananda in body and mind and he cannot represent the Buddha in body and mind. He didn't know that he himself had to cultivate samadhi-power.

Thus, I lost my original mind. Because of that I took a great loss, Ananda admits. **And although my body has left the home-life** – that is, he has become a monk – **my mind has not entered the Way** – that is, he has not obtained samadhi-power.

I am like the poor son who renounced his father and roamed around. Ananda is referring, by way of analogy, to the case of an extremely wealthy elder who enjoyed many blessings. He had a son who didn't make use of his father's assets, but went out into the world to suffer poverty. What Ananda means is, "I followed the Buddha to leave home but I didn't cultivate the Way. Because I lack samadhi-power, I'm a poor son. Actually, I could have taken on the Buddha's family business, but, without any samadhi-power, I still don't have the authority to receive the dharma riches amassed as a result of the Buddha's merit and virtue." So Ananda sobbed grievously, just like a child.

Sutra:

"Therefore, today I realize that although I am greatly learned, if I do not cultivate, it is the same as if I had not learned anything; just as someone who only speaks of food will never get full.

Commentary:

"**Therefore, today I realize**: I just now realize this. I did not know before. **Although I am greatly learned, if I do not cultivate, it is the same as if I had not learned anything.** If I simply know a lot of things but don't put them into practice I will be like a stone man who can talk but not act." In other words, Ananda could remember things, he was widely learned and had a good memory, but he had no skill, no *gong fu* when it came to actual practice. He had never actually done it. If he does not put his learning into practice, it is the same as if he didn't know anything at all.

Just as someone who only speaks of food will never get full. It's like someone who continually talks about things to eat. For instance people who like vegetarian food say, "Let's make vegetable dumplings, they're really good." Or "Let's make oil cakes as they do in Manchuria, they're even better."

Those who eat meat say, "Such and such a Chinese restaurant is the best in town, the food there is really good. Let's go have Chinese food." Americans like to eat Chinese food. So they discuss the various dishes by name, but just speaking about them and never getting around to eating them is no way to get full. There's another saying:

> Every day you count others money
> but not half a cent of it is yours.
> Not cultivating in accord with dharma
> amounts to the same thing.

It doesn't matter what things you know, if you don't cultivate the Way, that's being the same as someone who counts other people's money. You have no share in it. If you don't actually go and cultivate, there will be no result from your efforts.

K2   He reveals his confusion and seeks instruction.

Sutra:

"**World Honored One, now we all are bound by two obstructions and as a consequence do not perceive the still, eternal nature of the mind. I only hope the Tathagata will take pity on us poor and destitute ones and disclose the wonderful bright mind, and open my Way-eye.**"

Commentary:

Ananda again called: **World Honored One, now we all are bound by two obstructions.** Everyone of us in the great assembly is tied up by two obstructions. The first is the obstacle of affliction. The second is the obstacle of what is known. The obstacle of affliction arises with the attachment to self. The obstacle of what is known arises with the attachment to the dharma. As to the obstacle of what is known, if you think, "I know a lot," that is an obstruction. It is not that the more people study things the more their knowledge increases; rather, the more they study the more they are obstructed by what they know. How is knowledge an obstruction? It makes people arrogant. "Take a look at me. I know things that none of you know. I am way beyond you. I can't even be compared to you. All of you are ignorant. But as for me, why, my learning ability stands second to none in this world; it is rare even in the heavens, how much the less can it be found on earth." As soon as that arrogance arises, it is the obstruction of what is known.

With the attachment to self comes the obstruction of afflictions. No matter what comes up you cannot see through it, you cannot let it go, and so you become attached to it. And once the attachment arises, the affliction follows right along. That's the obstruction of affliction.

These are the two kinds of obstructions which Ananda says have bound up the members of the great assembly. "Bound" means that they have not obtained liberation. They cannot get free because they have these two kinds of obstructions.

"And as a consequence do not perceive the still, eternal nature of the mind. I don't know the tranquil, unmoving, permanently abiding nature of my mind. Now, because I do not understand this doctrine, **I only hope the Tathagata will take pity on us poor and destitute ones and disclose the wonderful bright mind, and open my Way-eye.** Pity me, pity me." He's still relying on the Buddha. He is still not standing on his own. "Poor and destitute" means they had not obtained the dharma-wealth of the Shurangama Samadhi.

Ananda wants the Buddha to take pity on him and show him the wonderful, bright true mind and cause him to soon open his Way-eye, so that his wisdom can increase and he can accomplish sagehood. The essential thing is to accomplish sagehood.

J2 The Tathagata manifests the ultimate true substance.
K1 He displays light and promises to explain.

Sutra:

Then from the character wan 卍 [signifying "myriad virtues"] on his chest, the Tathagata poured forth precious light. Radiant with hundreds of thousands of colors, the brilliant light simultaneously pervaded everywhere throughout the ten directions to Buddharealms as many as fine motes of dust, anointing the crowns of every Tathagata in all the jeweled Buddhalands of the ten directions. Then it swept back to Ananda and all in the great assembly.

Commentary:

Earlier in the sutra the Buddha emitted light from his face – a blazing light as brilliant as a hundred thousand suns. What did it represent? It represented the breaking up of the false: the false-thinking mind. Now he again emits light, this time from the insignia *wan* ("myriad") on his chest. It represents the disclosing of the true: the true mind.

Then from the character wan 卍 [signifying "myriad virtues"] on his chest, the Tathagata poured forth precious light. You can see the character *wan* on Buddha images. It represents the adornment of the myriad virtues, since the Buddha's virtuous practices have attained perfection. **Radiant with hundreds of thousands of colors, the brilliant light simultaneously pervaded everywhere throughout the ten directions to Buddharealms as many as fine motes of dust.** The character *wan* poured forth precious light which radiated back and forth. It was an iridescent, shimmering light, with hundreds of thousands of colors, and it shone back and forth, pervading not only the Saha world, but all the Buddhalands simultaneously. Then it anointed **the crowns of every Tathagata in all the jeweled Buddhalands of the ten directions.** It illumined the crowns of Buddhas in as many Buddha-countries as there are fine motes of dust; it was as if their crowns reflected one another's light. **Then it swept back to Ananda and all in the great assembly.** After it illumined the Tathagatas of the ten directions, the Buddha's light returned and illumined Ananda's crown, and the crowns of all the great bodhisattvas, great arhats, great bhikshus, the king, the officials, and the elder in the dharma assembly. The Buddha emitted this kind of light as a sign to make everyone understand the pure nature and bright substance of the permanently dwelling true mind.

Sutra:

And said to Ananda, "I will now erect the great dharma banner for you, to cause all living beings in the ten directions to obtain the wondrous subtle secret, the pure nature, the bright mind, and to attain the pure eye.

Commentary:

And said to Ananda, "I will now erect the great dharma banner for you, to cause all living beings in the ten directions to obtain the wondrous subtle secret." The Buddha said to Ananda – referring to himself as "I" – "I will hoist a great dharma banner, not only for your sake but for the sake of all living beings in the ten directions, so that they may obtain the most extremely wonderful and infinitely subtle cause, that is, the secret cause mentioned in the title of the sutra." It is secret because it is not known to most people before the Buddha has pointed it out to them, just like a vein of gold which has not been discovered by geologists: most people don't know it is there. Once the gold is discovered, once the geologists arrive at the spot, investigate it and realize there is a deposit of gold there, then it can be mined. The secret cause is the same way.

"I will cause you to obtain **the pure nature, the bright mind, and to attain the pure eye**." The nature is pure and clear, the mind is luminous. Because your nature is pure and your mind bright, you attain the pure eye, which is the Way-eye that Ananda has just asked the Buddha to open for him. It is also called the wisdom eye. "Pure" means to be free of even the slightest defilement; it indicates that the vision of the wisdom eye sees principles very clearly and truly. If you have the pure eye, you will be unobstructed and able to understand any principle.

General Index

A

abbot
   meaning of 101
acharya 126—127
   five kinds of 127
affinities
   with living beings 58
afflictions 31—32
Ajnatakaundinya 94
   and Shakyamuni Buddha in a former life 94—97
aksha cluster 225—226
American children 153—154
Amitabha Buddha 1
Amitabha Sutra 149
Ananda
   and his excellent memory 86—87
   and his neglect of samadhi 35—37
   and Matangi 133—135
   should be thanked 128
   was extremely handsome 133
   wept for Dharma 142, 263
   see Shurangama Sutra, causes and conditions for
Aniruddha 245
   and Ananda, his four questions 84—86
arhat 98—99, 101—106
   four admirable virtues 102
   progressing further 7
   three meanings 149—151
arrogance 19
Ashvajit
   and Mahamaudgalyayana 70

asuras 238—241
attachment 6

B

begging
   equality of 131—132
beginning teaching 54
bhikshu
   bad natured 86
   meaning of 93—94
birth and death 30—31, 247
   ending 162—163
   karmic conditions for 188
bodhi
   three kinds of 235—236
Bodhisattva 113—114, 149
   benefiting others 15, 33
   cultivation 13
   has no self 82—83
   perfection of practice 7
body
   is filthy 81—82
Brahma Net Sutra 76, 100
Buddha 5, 88
   and living beings 30, 32, 58—59
   and spiritual powers 125
   knowledge and vision 34—35
   nature of 40
   ten names of the 10—11
   the Great Buddha 8—10
Buddhist Canon
   Twelve Divisions 26—29
Buddhist canon

C

Cao Cao, general 38
Chan
    and the pointing finger 242
chandalas, butchers 129
Chao Fu
    see mind, seizing upon conditions
complete titles
    see sutras, seven classes of titles
conditions
    seizing upon 233
Confucius
    on the mind 260—261
connecting teaching 53
cultivation
    being mindful 160
    firmness, sincerity and constancy 25
    of cows and dogs 42—43, 46
    see also Bodhisattva, cultivation

D

danapati 129
Dao Sheng, Dharma Master 214—215
Dao Xuan, Vinaya Master 17
delusion 48, 225
demons 41, 228—229
    tests one's cultivation 46
    see sickness demon
deportment 102
desire
    two kinds of 99
dharma eye 108
Dharma Flower Sutra 30, 31, 57, 100
    story of the hidden pearl 163
dharma-doors
    actual and provisional 49—50
dhyana 147

three treasuries 51

cultivation 42
    see six paramitas, dhyana concentration
Dipankara Buddha
    and Shakyamuni Buddha 27—28
discrimination
    see Ten Doors of Discrimination

E

Earth Store Bodhisattva 113
earthquakes
    fire from a water-well 219
    six kinds 218—220
eating
    by rolling into balls 178
    is a lot of trouble 188
    to get full 266
eighteen realms 195—196
eighth consciousness 146
elder
    virtues of 123—124
emptiness
    four places of 261
enlightenment 5
    and Chan meditation 34
    and the clay Bodhisattva 242—243
    is not fixed 54—56
    is unbounded 89—90
    of arhats, pratyekabuddhas 7
    three kinds of 5, 88
    to non-attachment 33
existence
    true and non-existence 12
externalists
    are not ultimate 41—42
    see also demons
eyes, of dead people 198

F

faith 79
Fang Yong, Prime Minister 68, 76—77
filiality 156—158
final teaching 54
    instructs Bodhisattvas 56
five kinds of terms not translated 21—22
five precepts
    ensures a human rebirth 70
    keeping them 71—72
fivefold mysterious meanings 3
flying 105
Forty-two Sections, Sutra 151
four applications of mindfulness 85
four assemblies 193
four dhyanas 20—21
four kinds of greatness 24
four kinds of self 81

G

Ganges, river 148
ghosts
    listening to Dharma 115
    see hungry ghost
giving
    three kinds of 14
    see six paramitas, giving
God 82
good and evil 39
Guan Shi Yin, Bodhisattva 105
Gui Bi, Dhyana Master 139

H

hands, soft 180
hatred
    casting aside 161
heavens 227—228
Hsuan Hua, Tripitaka Master
    and the sickness demon 43—45
    and Zhang Xuan 45
    monk in the grave 80
Hu Qiu, mountain 215
Huai Di, shramana 76
Hui Neng, Great Master
    reply to Shen Xiu's verse 48
hungry ghost 121

I

icchantika 214—216
intelligence 37—38
intoxicants
    reason for its prohibition 70—71

J

Jade Emperor
    see Shakra
Jeta Grove 90—92
Jeta, Prince 91

K

kalavinka, bird 116
Kalinga, King
    see Ajnatakaundinya 95
Kapila, religion 36, 133, 134
karma 225, 226
karmadana 93
kshatriyas, royal class 129

L

leaving home
    of ignorance 212
living beings 188
    can become Buddhas 5
    have radio receivers 58—59
    see Buddha, and livings beings

Lotus Sutra 19
lotus-posture, the merit of 137—139
love
    casting aside 161
    of parents 153
Luo Fu, Mountain 76

M

mad mind 6
Mahakashyapa
    begging from the poor 130—131
Mahakaushthila 106—108
Mahamaudgalyayana 108
    and Ashvajit 70
    and his mother 120—121
    and the bees 57—58
    and the Buddha's voice 117
Mahayana 51
Manjushri, Bodhisattva 2, 118, 125
    saves Ananda and Matangi 140
Mara, king of the heavenly demons 93
Matangi 36, 133
Maudgalyayana 94
Medicine King, Bodhisattva
    burns his body as offering 19—20
Meghashika, shramana 75
Mencius
    on the mind 261
Meng Zhong, filiality 157
Middle Way 144
mind
    cannot be believed 151
    purity of 104
    seizing upon conditions 233—235
    straightforward mind 164—166
    see mad mind
    see true mind
mindfulness
    four applications of 85

mleccha 216
money 14—16
moral precepts
    see six paramitas, moral precepts

N

Nan Luo, Monastery 76
nirvana 236

O

obstruction
    two kinds of 267
offerings
    to the Triple Jewel 124, 130
outflows
    three kinds of 99—100

P

Paramiti, Dharma Master 74, 75, 83
    and the Shurangama Sutra 68, 69
patience
    three kinds 252—253
    see six paramitas, patience
patra 128
perfect teaching 53, 54, 56
physiognomy
    of soft hands 180
plum blossoms
    why they are so fragrant 23
prajna
    three kinds of 22—23
    see six paramitas, prajna
Prasenajit, King 66, 119
pratyekabuddhas 63, 111
pravarana 112, 119
precepts 73
    kinds of 16—17
    receiving 72, 161—162

transmitter 93
see six paramitas, moral precepts
Purnamaitreyaniputra 108

R

rebirth
   how to be human again 70
response-bodies 104
retribution 225
   two kinds 209
robe
   uncovering the right shoulder 211

S

samadhi
   for realizing Buddhahood 143
   genuine 146—147
   lack of 24—25
   nine successive stages of 261
   obtaining 72—73
   proper cultivation of 40
   see Ananda, and his neglect of samadhi 35
samapatti 147
separate teaching 53
sexual desire
   and polygamy 99—100
Shakra, God
   and his asura wife 239—240
Shakyamuni Buddha 45, 117
   and Ajnatakaundinya in a former life 94—97
   and Aniruddha 245
   and Dipankara Buddha 27—28
   and Mahakaushthila 106
   and Mahamaudgalyayana 57—58
   and pratyekabuddhas 111
   and Sundarananda 230—232
   being tested by demons 46

reason for appearing in the world 30
   saving a child 50
   see Aniruddha's four questions
shamatha 147
Sharika, sister of Shariputra 106
Shariputra 94, 106
shastra treasury 51
Shen Xiu, Dharma Master
   bright mirror verse 48
shramana 73
   four kinds of 73—74
   meaning of 69
Shravasti, city 89—90
Shun, Emperor 158
"Shurangama" 24
Shurangama Mantra 140
   importance of 137
Shurangama Sutra 6, 25, 51, 59, 63, 67, 74
   and the Prajna Period 66
   causes and conditions for 35—50
   complete name 4
   function of 47
   national treasure of India 68
   ultimate in literary texts 141
sickness demon 43—44
six causes and conditions for the speaking of the Shurangama Sutra
   see Shurangama Sutra
six fulfillments 78—80
six paramitas 13—14
   dhyana concentration 20—21
   giving 14—16
   moral precepts 16—19
   patience 19
   prajna 21—24
   vigor 19—20
six paths 238
six perfections
   see six paramitas
sixth desire heaven 93

Sixth Patriarch
   see Hui Neng
small teaching 54
solitary enlightened ones
   see pratyekabuddhas
solitary mind-consciousness 257—258
Song of Enlightenment
   see Yung Chia, Great Master
storehouse teaching 53
Su Dong Po, poet 147
Subhuti 109
   begging from the rich 130—131
Sudatta
   and the Jeta Grove 90—92
sudden teaching 54
summer retreat 111
Sundarananda 230—232
Sundari
   see Sundarananda
sutras
   definition 25—26
   listening to 32
   seven classes of titles 1—3
   see Buddhist Canon
   see six fulfillments

T

Ta Yu, Mountain 162
Tan Xiang, filiality 157
Tathagata 10
teaching-substance
   the Four Doors 61—62
ten doors of discrimination 3
ten virtues of an elder 123
Theravada 51
three kinds of double titles
   see sutras, seven classes of titles
three kinds of enlightenment
   see enlightenment

three kinds of prajna
   see prajna, three kinds of
three kinds of single titles
   see sutras, seven classes of titles
three poisons 73
"Thus I have heard"
   four meanings 84—87
Tian Tai, school 20
   Four Teachings 53
   "stop and contemplate" method 146
   three stoppings 147
   see fivefold mysterious meanings
time
   beginningless 223—224
transformation-bodies
   see response-bodies
tripitaka treasury 51
true appearance 201
true emptiness 201
true mind 208, 238
   is forgotten 237
   is not the flesh heart 39
twelve divisions of the canon
   see Buddhist canon
twelve links of conditioned causation 110—111
two vehicles 65

U

Ullambana, festival 120, 122
   see also Mahamaudgalyayana, and his mother
understanding
   is just not-understanding 222
   with practice, combining 18—19
Upanishad 109

V

Vajra Sutra 10, 22, 90

vegetarianism 122
vigor
    see six paramitas, vigor
Vimalakirti Sutra 164
vinaya treasury 51
vows
    keeping them 45
    the power of 97
    see Mahamaudgalyayana, and the bees

W

wan, character 268–269
Wang Xiang, filiality 157
Wei Tuo, Bodhisattva 144
wisdom
    insane 39
Wu Tai, mountain 118
Wu Zai Tian, Empress 69

X

Xian Shou, school
    Five Divisions 53
    see ten doors of discrimination
Xu Yu
    see mind, seizing upon conditions
Xuan Zang, Tripitaka Master 22, 94

Y

Yama, King 248
Yao, Emperor 38, 233
Yong Jia, Great Master 12
Yuan Ying, Dharma Master 152
Yung Chia, Great Master
    "Song of Enlightenment" 12

Z

Zhang Xuan 45
Zhi Yi, Great Master 20
    divides Sutras to three sections 67
Zhi Zhi, Monastery 74
Zhong Nan, Mountain 17

Frequently Asked Questions

What is the Buddhist Text Translation Society?

When Buddhism first came to China from India, one of the most important tasks required for its establishment was the translation of the Buddhist scriptures from Sanskrit into Chinese. This work involved a great many people, such as the renowned monk National Master Kumarajiva (fifth century), who led an assembly of over 800 people to work on the translation of the Tripitaka (Buddhist canon) for over a decade. Because of the work of individuals such as these, nearly the entire Buddhist Tripitaka of over a thousand texts exists to the present day in Chinese.

Now the banner of the Buddha's Teachings is being firmly planted in Western soil, and the same translation work is being done from Chinese into English. Since 1970, the Buddhist Text Translation Society (BTTS) has been making a paramount contribution toward this goal. Aware that the Buddhist Tripitaka is a work of such magnitude that its translation could never be entrusted to a single person, the BTTS, emulating the translation assemblies of ancient times, does not publish a work until it has passed through four committees for primary translation, revision, editing, and certification. The leaders of these committees are Bhikshus (monks) and Bhikshunis (nuns) who have devoted their lives to the study and practice of the Buddha's teachings. For this reason, all of the works of the BTTS put an emphasis on what the principles of the Buddha's teachings mean in terms of actual practice, not just theory.

The translations of canonical works by the Buddhist Text Translation Society are accompanied by extensive commentaries by the Venerable Tripitaka Master Hsüan Hua and are available in softcover only unless otherwise noted.

Eight Regulations of the BTTS

What makes BTTS translations special are the high standards that all translators, editors and staff aspire towards:

1. A translator must free himself or herself from the motives of personal fame and reputation.
2. A translator must cultivate an attitudefree from arrogance and conceit.
3. A translator must refrain from aggrandizing himself or herself and denigrating others.
4. A translator must not establish himself or herself as the standard of correctness and suppress the work of others with his or her faultfinding.
5. A translator must take the Buddha-mind as his or her own mind.
6. A translator must use the wisdom of the selective Dharma-eye to determine true principles.
7. A translator must request the elder virtuous ones of the ten directions to certify his or her translation.
8. A translator must endeavor to propagate the teachings by printing sutras, shastra texts, and vinaya texts when the translations are certified as being correct.

Who is the Dharma Realm Buddhist Association?

(formerly known as the Sino-American Buddhist Association)

The Dharma Realm Buddhist Association (DRBA) was formed in 1959 to bring the orthodox teachings of the Buddha to the entire world.

At all of its monasteries, DRBA offers a rigorous schedule of Buddhist practice seven days a week from 4:00 A.M. to 10:00 P.M. The schedule includes at least three hours of group meditation, two and a half hours of group recitation, and a one-and-a-half-hour-long lecture on the Buddhist scriptures each day.

There are also daily courses in Buddhist and canonical language studies, week-long intensive recitation and meditation sessions, and a three to ten week meditation session in the winter. Residents gain a thorough understanding of the main teachings of all the major schools of Buddhism, develop skill in scriptural languages, and become adept at a wide variety of spiritual practices. The foundation of the practice is a high standard of ethics: All residents hold the Five Buddhist Precepts which prohibit killing of any living being (includes vegetarianism), stealing, sexual misconduct, lying, and taking intoxicants (including alcohol, drugs, and tobacco). These activities are offered through a government-approved three-year Sangha (monastic) and two-year Laity Training Program. The Sangha Training Program provides partial fulfillment of requirements for receiving the 250 Precepts of a Bhikshu or the 348 Precepts of a Bhikshuni through traditional ordination procedures.

One of DRBA's major tasks is the translation of the main Buddhist scriptures into the world's languages, primarily English. To date, under the auspices of the Buddhist Text Translation Society, DRBA has published over one hundred texts in English, Chinese, and Spanish.

DRBA has established various educational and social service programs to promote peace, happiness, and a high standard of ethical conduct for the world. At its main branch, the City of 10,000 Buddhas, are housed Dharma Realm Buddhist University, Developing Virtue Secondary Schools, and Instilling Goodness Elementary Schools.

The spiritual guide of DRBA is its founder, the most Venerable Tripitaka Master Hsüan Hua.

How Do I Show Respect for Buddhist Texts?

All Buddhist Sutras and books that propagate and reveal the Buddhadharma exist for the purpose of causing people to encounter auspiciousness and avoid harm, to change their falseness and move toward wholesomeness, to understand the cause and effect of the three periods of time, to recognize the original Buddha-nature we are all replete with, to transcend the suffering of being in the sea of birth and death, and to gain rebirth in the Lotus Country of Ultimate Bliss. Therefore, anyone reading such texts should bring forth a mind of gratitude and reflect upon how hard it is to encounter them. One should wash one's hands before handling these texts and wipe clean the surface upon which one places them. By being as reverent and sincere toward Buddhist texts as one would be when encountering the Buddhas or gods or as when one is beside one's teacher, one can attain limitless benefits. But if one is shamelessly negligent, sloppy and disrespectful, headstrong and prejudiced, and from such falseness gives rise to slander, then one's offenses will fill up the skies and one will suffer endless retributions. So all people of the world, please heed this advice: Stay far away from creating offenses and seek always for what is beneficial in order to leave suffering and obtain bliss.

唵嘛呢叭彌吽
Om Mani Padme Hum
Lecture given by Tripitaka Master Hsuan Hua

These six characters together make up the *Six Character Great Bright Mantra*; each one individually is able to emit brilliant light.

The first character is *nan* (唵, Sanskrit *om*). When you recite "*nan*" once, all ghosts and spirits must place their palms together. Why do they put their palms together? To maintain the rules and regulations. Conforming to the regulations, they follow the correct way. Recite this one character and all ghosts and spirits do not dare rebel and create confusion; they do not dare disobey orders. This is the first sound in the Mantra.

"*Ma ni* (嘛呢, Sanskrit *mani*)" means "silent wisdom". Using wisdom one is able to understand all principles, and thus is able to be silently extinguished, without production. It is also defined as "separating from filth" which means leaving all dust and filth. It can be compared to the "precious as-you-will pearl" which is extremely pure, with no defilement. Whatever excellence you wish to bring forth, if you have the "precious as-you-wish pearl" it can be done. It can also fulfill your wishes in accord with your thoughts. Every vow you make will be fulfilled. These are its benefits.

"*Ba mi* (叭彌, Sanskrit *padme*)" actually should read "*ba te mi* 叭特彌". It means "light perfectly illuminating" and is also defined as "the opening of the lotus". It is analogous to the wonderful lotus flower which can complete, perfect and fulfill without obstruction. It is the wonderful mind of Avalokiteshvara Bodhisattva. This is "*ba mi*".

Next comes "*hung* (吽, Sanskrit: *hum*)" which means "put forth". Anything at all can be born from this character "hung". It also means "to protect and support". Recite this character and all Dharma protectors and good spirits come to support and protect you. It also means "eradicating disasters". Recite this character and whatever difficulties there are will be eradicated. It also means "success"; whatever you cultivate can be accomplished.

Recite the *Six Character Great Bright Mantra* once, and the immeasurable Buddhas, Bodhisattvas, and Vajra Dharma protectors constantly support and protect you. Therefore, when Avalokiteshvara Bodhisattva finished saying this *Six Character Great Bright Mantra*, there were seven million Buddhas who came to support, protect, and surround him. The strength and ability of the *Six Character Great Bright Mantra* are inconceivable, the intertwining of the response and way unimaginable, therefore it is called the Secret School. If one were to explain in detail, the meanings would be immeasurable and unlimited; they cannot be spoken completely.

Buddhist Text Translation Society Publication

Buddhist Text Translation Society
International Translation Institute

http://www.bttsonline.org

1777 Murchison Drive,
Burlingame, California 94010-4504 USA
Phone: (650) 692-5912 Fax: (650) 692-5056

When Buddhism first came to China from India, one of the most important tasks required for its establishment was the translation of the Buddhist scriptures from Sanskrit into Chinese. This work involved a great many people, such as the renowned monk National Master Kumarajiva (fifth century), who led an assembly of over 800 people to work on the translation of the Tripitaka (Buddhist canon) for over a decade. Because of the work of individuals such as these, nearly the entire Buddhist Tripitaka of over a thousand texts exists to the present day in Chinese.

Now the banner of the Buddha's teachings is being firmly planted in Western soil, and the same translation work is being done from Chinese into English. Since 1970, the Buddhist Text Translation Society (BTTS) has been making a paramount contribution toward this goal. Aware that the Buddhist Tripitaka is a work of such magnitude that its translation could never be entrusted to a single person, the BTTS, emulating the translation assemblies of ancient times, does not publish a work until it has passed through four committees for primary translation, revision, editing, and certification. The leaders of these committees are Bhikshus (monks) and Bhikshunis (nuns) who have devoted their lives to the study and practice of the Buddha's teachings. For this reason, all of the works of the BTTS put an emphasis on what the principles of the Buddha's teachings mean in terms of actual practice and not simply hypothetical conjecture.

The translations of canonical works by the Buddhist Text Translation Society are accompanied by extensive commentaries by the Venerable Tripitaka Master Hsuan Hua.

BTTS Publications

Buddhist Sutras. Amitabha Sutra, Dharma Flower (Lotus) Sutra, Flower Adornment (Avatamsaka) Sutra, Heart Sutra & Verses without a Stand, Shurangama Sutra, Sixth Patriarch Sutra, Sutra in Forty-two Sections, Sutra of the Past Vows of Earth Store Bodhisattva, Vajra Prajna Paramita (Diamond) Sutra.

Commentarial Literature. Buddha Root Farm, City of 10 000 Buddhas Recitation Handbook, Filiality: The Human Source, Herein Lies the Treasuretrove, Listen to Yourself Think Everything Over, Shastra on the Door to Understanding the Hundred Dharmas, Song of Enlightenment, The Ten Dharma Realms Are Not Beyond a Single Thought, Venerable Master Hua's Talks on Dharma, Venerable Master Hua's Talks on Dharma during the 1993 Trip to Taiwan, Water Mirror Reflecting Heaven.

Biographical. In Memory of the Venerable Master Hsuan Hua, Pictorial Biography of the Venerable Master Hsü Yün, Records of High Sanghans, Records of the Life of the Venerable Master Hsüan Hua, Three Steps One Bow, World Peace Gathering, News from True Cultivators, Open Your Eyes Take a Look at the World, With One Heart Bowing to the City of 10 000 Buddhas.

Children's Books. Cherishing Life, Human Roots: Buddhist Stories for Young Readers, Spider Web, Giant Turtle, Patriarch Bodhidharma.

Musics, Novels and Brochures. Songs for Awakening, Awakening, The Three Cart Patriarch, City of 10 000 Buddhas Color Brochure, Celebrisi's Journey, Lots of Time Left.

The Buddhist Monthly–Vajra Bodhi Sea is a monthly journal of orthodox Buddhism which has been published by the Dharma Realm Buddhist Association, formerly known as the Sino-American Buddhist Association, since 1970. Each issue contains the most recent translations of the Buddhist canon by the Buddhist Text Translation Society. Also included in each issue are a biography of a great Patriarch of Buddhism from the ancient past, sketches of the lives of contemporary monastics and lay-followers around the world, articles on practice, and other material. The journal is bilingual, Chinese and English.

Please visit our web-site at **www.bttsonline.org** for the latest publications and for ordering information.

The Dharma Realm Buddhist Association

Mission

The Dharma Realm Buddhist Association (formerly the Sino-American Buddhist Association) was founded by the Venerable Master Hsuan Hua in the United States of America in 1959. Taking the Dharma Realm as its scope, the Association aims to disseminate the genuine teachings of the Buddha throughout the world. The Association is dedicated to translating the Buddhist canon, propagating the Orthodox Dharma, promoting ethical education, and bringing benefit and happiness to all beings. Its hope is that individuals, families, the society, the nation, and the entire world will, under the transforming influence of the Buddhadharma, gradually reach the state of ultimate truth and goodness.

The Founder

The Venerable Master, whose names were An Tse and To Lun, received the Dharma name Hsuan Hua and the transmission of Dharma from Venerable Master Hsu Yun in the lineage of the Wei Yang Sect. He was born in Manchuria, China, at the beginning of the century. At nineteen, he entered the monastic order and dwelt in a hut by his mother's grave to practice filial piety. He meditated, studied the teachings, ate only one meal a day, and slept sitting up. In 1948 he went to Hong Kong, where he established the Buddhist Lecture Hall and other Way-places. In 1962 he brought the Proper Dharma to the West, lecturing on several dozen Mahayana Sutras in the United States. Over the years, the Master established more than twenty monasteries of Proper Dharma under the auspices of the Dharma Realm Buddhist Association and the City of Ten Thousand Buddhas. He also founded centers for the translation of the Buddhist canon and for education to spread the influence of the Dharma in the East and West. The Master manifested the stillness in the United States in 1995. Through his lifelong, selfless dedication to teaching living beings with wisdom and compassion, he influenced countless people to change their faults and to walk upon the pure, bright path to enlightenment.

Dharma Propagation, Buddhist Text Translation, and Education

The Venerable Master Hua's three great vows after leaving the home-life were (1) to propagate the Dharma, (2) to translate the Buddhist Canon, and (3) to promote education. In order to make these vows a reality, the Venerable Master based himself on the Three Principles and the Six Guidelines. Courageously facing every hardship, he founded monasteries, schools, and centers in the West, drawing in living beings and teaching them on a vast scale. Over the years, he founded the following institutions:

The City of Ten Thousand Buddhas and Its Branches

In propagating the Proper Dharma, the Venerable Master not only trained people but also founded Way-places where the Dharma wheel could turn and living beings could be saved. He wanted to provide cultivators with pure places to practice in accord with the Buddha's regulations. Over the years, he founded many Way-places of Proper Dharma. In the United States and Canada, these include the City of Ten Thousand Buddhas; Gold Mountain Monastery; Gold Sage Monastery; Gold Wheel Monastery; Gold Summit Monastery; Gold Buddha Monastery; Avatamsaka Monastery; Long Beach Monastery; the City of the Dharma Realm; Berkeley Buddhist Monastery; Avatamsaka Hermitage; and Blessings, Prosperity, and Longevity Monastery. In Taiwan, there are the Dharma Realm Buddhist Books Distribution Association, Dharma Realm Monastery, and Amitabha Monastery. In Malaysia, there are the Prajna Guanyin Sagely Monastery (formerly Tze Yun Tung Temple), Deng Bi An Monastery, and Lotus Vihara. In Hong Kong, there are the Buddhist Lecture Hall and Cixing Monastery.

Purchased in 1974, the City of Ten Thousand Buddhas is the hub of the Dharma Realm Buddhist Association. The City is located in Talmage, Mendocino County, California, 110 miles north of San Francisco. Eighty of the 488 acres of land are in active use. The remaining acreage consists of meadows, orchards, and woods. With over seventy large buildings containing over 2,000 rooms, blessed with serenity and fresh, clean air, it is the first large Buddhist monastic community in the United States. It is also an international center for the Proper Dharma.

Although the Venerable Master Hua was the Ninth Patriarch in the Wei Yang Sect of the Chan School, the monasteries he founded emphasize all of the five main practices of Mahayana Buddhism (Chan meditation, Pure Land, esoteric, Vinaya (moral discipline), and doctrinal studies). This accords with the Buddha's words: "The Dharma is level and equal, with no high or low." At the City of Ten Thousand Buddhas, the rules of purity are rigorously observed. Residents of the City strive to regulate their own conduct and to cultivate with vigor. Taking refuge in the Proper Dharma, they lead pure and selfless lives, and attain peace in body and mind. The Sutras are expounded and the Dharma wheel is turned daily. Residents dedicate themselves wholeheartedly to making Buddhism flourish. Monks and nuns in all the monasteries take one meal a day, always wear their precept sash, and follow the Three Principles:

> *Freezing, we do not scheme.*
> *Starving, we do not beg.*
> *Dying of poverty, we ask for nothing.*
> *According with conditions, we do not change.*
> *Not changing, we accord with conditions.*
> *We adhere firmly to our three great principles.*
> *We renounce our lives to do the Buddha's work.*
> *We take the responsibility to mold our own destinies.*
> *We rectify our lives to fulfill the Sanghan's role.*
> *Encountering specific matters,*
>   *we understand the principles.*
> *Understanding the principles,*
>   *we apply them in specific matters.*
> *We carry on the single pulse of*
>   *the Patriarchs' mind-transmission.*

The monasteries also follow the Six Guidelines: not contending, not being greedy, not seeking, not being selfish, not pursuing personal advantage, and not lying.

International Translation Institute

The Venerable Master vowed to translate the Buddhist Canon (Tripitaka) into Western languages so that it would be widely accessible throughout the world. In 1973, he founded the International Translation Institute on Washington Street in San Francisco for the purpose of translating Buddhist scriptures into English and other languages. In 1977, the Institute was merged into Dharma Realm Buddhist University as the Institute for the Translation of Buddhist Texts. In 1991, the Venerable Master purchased a large building in Burlingame (south of San Francisco) and established the International Translation Institute there for the purpose of translating and publishing Buddhist texts. To date, in addition to publishing over one hundred volumes of Buddhist texts in Chinese, the Association has published more than one hundred volumes of English, French, Spanish, Vietnamese, and Japanese translations of Buddhist texts, as well as bilingual (Chinese and English) editions. Audio and video tapes also continue to be produced. The monthly journal Vajra Bodhi Sea, which has been in circulation for nearly thirty years, has been published in bilingual (Chinese and English) format in recent years.

In the past, the difficult and vast mission of translating the Buddhist canon in China was sponsored and supported by the emperors and kings themselves. In our time, the Venerable Master encouraged his disciples to cooperatively shoulder this heavy responsibility, producing books and audio tapes and using the medium of language to turn the wheel of Proper Dharma and do the great work of the Buddha. All those who aspire to devote themselves to this work of sages should uphold the Eight Guidelines of the International Translation Institute:

1. One must free oneself from the motives of personal fame and profit.
2. One must cultivate a respectful and sincere attitude free from arrogance and conceit.
3. One must refrain from aggrandizing one's work and denigrating that of others.
4. One must not establish oneself as the standard of correctness and suppress the work of others with one's fault-finding.
5. One must take the Buddha-mind as one's own mind.
6. One must use the wisdom of Dharma-Selecting Vision to determine true principles.
7. One must request Virtuous Elders of the ten directions to certify one's translations.
8. One must endeavor to propagate the teachings by printing Sutras, Shastra texts, and Vinaya texts when the translations are certified as being correct.

These are the Venerable Master's vows, and participants in the work of translation should strive to realize them.

Instilling Goodness Elementary School, Developing Virtue Secondary School, Dharma Realm Buddhist University

"Education is the best national defense." The Venerable Master Hua saw clearly that in order to save the world, it is essential to promote good education. If we want to save the world, we have to bring about a complete change in people's minds and guide them to cast out unwholesomeness and to pursue goodness. To this end the Master founded Instilling Goodness Elementary School in 1974, and Developing Virtue Secondary School and Dharma Realm Buddhist University in 1976.

In an education embodying the spirit of Buddhism, the elementary school teaches students to be filial to parents, the secondary school teaches students to be good citizens, and the university teaches such virtues as humaneness and righteousness. Instilling Goodness Elementary School and Developing Virtue Secondary School combine the best of contemporary and traditional methods and of Western and Eastern cultures. They emphasize moral virtue and spiritual development, and aim to guide students to become good and capable citizens who will benefit humankind. The schools offer a bilingual (Chinese/English) program where boys and girls study separately. In addition to standard academic courses, the curriculum includes ethics, meditation, Buddhist studies, and so on, giving students a foundation in virtue and guiding them to understand themselves and explore the truths of the universe. Branches of the schools (Sunday schools) have been established at branch monasteries with the aim of propagating filial piety and ethical education.

Dharma Realm Buddhist University, whose curriculum focuses on the Proper Dharma, does not merely transmit academic knowledge. It emphasizes a foundation in virtue, which expands into the study of how to help all living beings discover their inherent nature. Thus, Dharma Realm Buddhist University advocates a spirit of shared inquiry and free exchange of ideas, encouraging students to study various canonical texts and use different experiences and learning styles to tap their inherent wisdom and fathom the meanings of those texts. Students are encouraged to practice the principles they have understood and apply the Buddhadharma in their lives, thereby nurturing their wisdom and virtue. The University aims to produce outstanding individuals of high moral character who will be able to bring benefit to all sentient beings.

Sangha and Laity Training Programs

In the Dharma-ending Age, in both Eastern and Western societies there are very few monasteries that actually practice the Buddha's regulations and strictly uphold the precepts. Teachers with genuine wisdom and understanding, capable of guiding those who aspire to pursue careers in Buddhism, are very rare. The Venerable Master founded the Sangha and Laity Training Programs in 1982 with the goals of raising the caliber of the Sangha, perpetuating the Proper Dharma, providing professional training for Buddhists around the world on both practical and theoretical levels, and transmitting the wisdom of the Buddha.

The Sangha Training Program gives monastics a solid foundation in Buddhist studies and practice, training them in the practical affairs of Buddhism and Sangha management. After graduation, students will be able to assume various responsibilities related to Buddhism in monasteries, institutions, and other settings. The program emphasizes a thorough knowledge of Buddhism, understanding of the scriptures, earnest cultivation, strict observance of precepts, and the development of a virtuous character, so that students will be able to propagate the Proper Dharma and perpetuate the Buddha's wisdom. The Laity Training Program offers courses to help laypeople develop correct views, study and practice the teachings, and understand monastic regulations and ceremonies, so that they will be able to contribute their abilities in Buddhist organizations.

Let Us Go Forward Together

In this Dharma-ending Age when the world is becoming increasingly dangerous and evil, the Dharma Realm Buddhist Association, in consonance with its guiding principles, opens the doors of its monasteries and centers to those of all religions and nationalities. Anyone who is devoted to humaneness, righteousness, virtue, and the pursuit of truth, and who wishes to understand him or herself and help humankind, is welcome to come study and practice with us. May we together bring benefit and happiness to all living beings.

Dharma Realm Buddhist Association Branches

The City of Ten Thousand Buddhas
P.O. Box 217, Talmage, CA 95481-0217 USA
Tel: (707) 462-0939   Fax: (707) 462-0949
Home Page: **http://www.drba.org**

Institute for World Religions (Berkeley Buddhist Monastery)
2304 McKinley Avenue, Berkeley, CA 94703 USA
Tel: (510) 848-3440

Dharma Realm Buddhist Books Distribution Society
11th Floor, 85 Chung-hsiao E. Road, Sec. 6, Taipei, Taiwan R.O.C.
Tel: (02) 2786-3022   Fax: (02) 2786-2674

The City of the Dharma Realm
1029 West Capitol Avenue, West Sacramento, CA 95691 USA
Tel: (916) 374-8268

Gold Mountain Monastery
800 Sacramento Street, San Francisco, CA 94108 USA
Tel: (415) 421-6117   Fax: (415) 788-6001

Gold Wheel Monastery
235 North Avenue 58, Los Angeles, CA 90042 USA
Tel: (323) 258-6668

Gold Buddha Monastery
248 East 11th Avenue, Vancouver, B.C. V5T 2C3 Canada
Tel: (604) 709-0248   Fax: (604) 684-3754

Gold Summit Monastery
233 1st Avenue, West Seattle, WA 98119 USA
Tel: (206) 284-6690   Fax: (206) 284-6918

Gold Sage Monastery
11455 Clayton Road, San Jose, CA 95127 USA
Tel: (408) 923-7243   Fax: (408) 923-1064

The International Translation Institute
1777 Murchison Drive, Burlingame, CA 94010-4504 USA
Tel: (650) 692-5912   Fax: (650) 692-5056

Long Beach Monastery
3361 East Ocean Boulevard, Long Beach, CA 90803 USA
Tel: (562) 438-8902

Blessings, Prosperity, & Longevity Monastery
4140 Long Beach Boulevard, Long Beach, CA 90807 USA
Tel: (562) 595-4966

Avatamsaka Hermitage
11721 Beall Mountain Road, Potomac, MD 20854-1128 USA
Tel: (301) 299-3693

Avatamsaka Monastery
1009 4th Avenue, S.W. Calgary, AB T2P OK8 Canada
Tel: (403) 234-0644

Kun Yam Thong Temple
161, Jalan Ampang, 50450 Kuala Lumpur, Malaysia
Tel: (03) 2164-8055 Fax: (03) 2163-7118

Prajna Guanyin Sagely Monastery (formerly Tze Yun Tung)
Batu 5½, Jalan Sungai Besi,
Salak Selatan, 57100 Kuala Lumpur, Malaysia
Tel: (03) 7982-6560 Fax: (03) 7980-1272

Lotus Vihara
136, Jalan Sekolah, 45600 Batang Berjuntai,
Selangor Darul Ehsan, Malaysia
Tel: (03) 3271-9439

Buddhist Lecture Hall
31 Wong Nei Chong Road, Top Floor, Happy Valley, Hong Kong, China
Tel: (02) 2572-7644

Dharma Realm Sagely Monastery
20, Tong-hsi Shan-chuang, Hsing-lung Village, Liu-kuei
Kaohsiung County, Taiwan, R.O.C.
Tel: (07) 689-3717 Fax: (07) 689-3870

Amitabha Monastery
7, Su-chien-hui, Chih-nan Village, Shou-feng,
Hualien County, Taiwan, R.O.C.
Tel: (07) 865-1956 Fax: (07) 865-3426

Verse of Transference

May the merit and virtue accrued from this work,
Adorn the Buddhas' Pure Lands,
Repaying four kinds of kindness above,
And aiding those suffering in the paths below.

May those who see and hear of this,
All bring forth the resolve for Bodhi,
And when this retribution body is over,
Be born together in the Land of Ultimate Bliss.

Dharma Protector Wei Tuo Bodhisattva